Comrade Jack

The political lectures and diary of Jack Simons,
Novo Catengue

**Edited by Marion Sparg,
Jenny Schreiner and Gwen Ansell**

publishers

First published in 2001 by STE Publishers
Apple Place, 110 Sivewright Ave, New Doornfontein
and
African National Congress
Albert Luthuli House
54 Sauer Street, Johannesburg

First printed 2001

Printed and bound in South Africa

ISBN 1-919855-02-3

The information in this book is furnished for informational use only, is subject to change without notice, and should not be construed as a commitment by STE Publishers and the African National Congress Department of Political Education. The ANC and STE Publishers assume no responsibility for any errors or inaccuracies that may appear in this book.

All political lectures and diary entries written by Jack Simons

Initially compiled and edited by Marion Sparg

Additional compilation of texts, conducting of all interviews, writing of narrative and editing by Jenny Schreiner

Final edit by Gwen Ansell

Book design by STE Publishers

Printed by Impress

Set in 9pt on 11.5pt point Sabon

For all the members of the June 16 Detachment, Novo Catengue
and for Marion

Contents

Foreword
By Dr OR Tambo
Former National President of
the African National Congress

This foreword by the late Oliver Tambo was written prior to the unbanning of the ANC and Umkhonto weSizwe, and the return to South Africa of many exiled ANC leaders.

I have much satisfaction in welcoming the publication of lectures and observations by Dr HJ Simons, formerly Professor of Social Sciences at the University of Zambia, and widely known in the South African liberation movement as "Comrade Jack".

The book includes a vivid account based on Jack's day-to-day diary of life in Novo Catengue, Angola, the military academy for recruits of Umkhonto weSizwe (MK), the armed wing of the ANC, together with the text of his lectures and comments by former students who recall the methods of instruction he employed whether in university classes, informal tutorials off the campus or in the camps.

I saw him in action in Novo Catengue at the passing-out parade and oath-taking ceremony of the June 16 Detachment on January 8-10 1979. He stayed on despite severe bouts of malaria until March 3, when he was evacuated against his will in anticipation of the SADF's bombing attack which razed the buildings in the camp to the ground.

Another reason for his return to base in Lusaka was a request by Mainza Chona, general-secretary of the United National Independence Party (UNIP), for him to take part in a lecturing programme at the President's Citizenship College in Kabwe. This he did as a matter of duty, though no longer a member of the University's teaching staff, from which he had resigned in March 1975. He made time at my request to attend a meeting in Mazimbu, Morogoro, Tanzania on 14-18 April 1979 to plan the building, staffing and teaching programme for the proposed Solomon Mahlangu Freedom College (Somafco) where he often taught during the next decade.

I recommend the book because it gives the reader a first-hand account of the stirring events that accompanied the systematic training of our cadres and is introduced to the general public at the time when MK's future is being debated in the ANC and government circles*. What emerges from the book is an impression of a specialist in the social sciences who did the jobs which he was called on to do in a wide variety of circumstances, and always with revolutionary dedication.

MK was demobilised on December 16, 1993 and integration into the SANDF began in April 1994

Foreword
By Kgalema Motlanthe
African National Congress
Secretary General

The African National Congress Political Education Department published this book in honour of the legacy of Jack Simons, who like many other commissars and political education officers contributed to the primacy of politics in our movement.

This approach over decades has enabled the ANC and the liberation forces to develop the capacity to manage ideological struggle within its ranks, to develop theoretical clarity on the National Democratic Revolution, and in the process ensure unity in action among all the motive forces involved in struggle. It enabled us to approach the country's problems with a view to find sustainable and lasting solutions, to identify and seize decisive moments.

Comrade Jack's lectures also provide a pointer to the universal character of the South African struggle — its capacity to learn from and act in solidarity with a wide variety of international forces in support of our struggle.

Political education has been a central and consistent feature of the work of the ANC. During the Nineties and into the 21st century we continued to face the challenge of reproducing the organisational culture of the movement, its history and politics, as we engaged with the complexities of the changing national and international situation. Comrade Jack's political methodology and the commissars, strategists and cadres trained by him played an invaluable role in this process.

The ANC faces an enormous challenge to lead the process of social transformation, to play its role in the renewal of the continent and fighting for a just and equitable world order. These lectures, and the rich legacy of Comrade Jack, will no doubt assist the movement to build and develop a cadreship that understands and is prepared to act on the challenges we face in transforming South Africa into a truly non-racial, non-sexist and democratic society.

Comrade Jack Simons was a teacher and an activist all of his life. We hope these political lectures will continue to activate and assist the learning process of ANC members in decades to come.

Introduction

This book is a tribute to Comrade Jack Simons' endeavours as a communist intellectual in the service of the liberation movement. At the same time, it is a record of aspects of the political instruction carried out in Umkhonto weSizwe (MK) in the post-Soweto period, which laid a foundation for political instruction in the African National Congress (ANC) and its Alliance partners.

"Comrade Jack made a profound contribution to this army and really laid the foundation [for] its future commissariat, the political instruction; the politics actually in the army." (Comrade Ché Ogara)

The book provides material that activists and intellectuals can use in teaching Marxism and a Marxist analysis of South Africa, but it also brings home some of the experiences of comrades in exile. In addition, the invaluable contribution that Comrade Jack made through his method of teaching has been highlighted. His approach to lecturing combined seminar-debate with structured input from the lecturer.

There was no time in Comrade Jack's working life when he was not involved in political education of one kind or another. This book selects two periods, Lusaka and Novo Catengue. The lectures on political sociology that he wrote at these times were typed up and copied and have survived the ordeals of exile and the return home. However, many of the lectures on South African and ANC history are lost to us. The problem of how Marxist theory relates to the South African experience is central to the analyses in these lectures.

The materials were developed at a time when membership of the ANC had been opened to all South Africans at the Morogoro Conference in 1969. Comrades who, before the banning of organisations, had been politically active in the Congress Alliance organisations, could now find their home in exile in the ANC itself. The ANC-South African Communist Party (SACP) Alliance*, (forged in struggle within the country before the SACP was outlawed and the ANC banned) remained firm in exile, as it has in the post-1990 period. The Alliance has always been based on independence and internal democracy, with members being accountable to each organisation for political actions carried out on that organisation's mandate. So when Comrade Jack was requested to teach in MK, he was approached as an ANC member, and was accountable to the ANC and MK leadership structures. While he drew on his experience within the Communist Party, his lectures were given to ANC and MK members as part of their army training.

At more or less the same time, there was discussion within the SACP about the need for a primer on historical and dialectical materialism for internal study

*The Alliance also included MK, SACTU and later COSATU. Originally the Revolutionary Committee (RC) was the highest structure of the Alliance.

programmes. The SACP constitution acknowledged the importance of both individual and collective study of theory, and analysis of South African conditions. The Central Committee realised it needed to provide suitable material to facilitate this process.

Comrade Ronnie Kasrils tells how he spent some time in 1979 with Comrade Jack trying to put together a manual. They were using Comrade Jack's Novo Catengue lectures, lectures given by Kasrils when he was based in Quibaxe, and lectures prepared by ANC members in London to assist cadres being sent to the German Democratic Republic for training. However, Kasrils ("ANC Khumalo", as he was then known) was transferred to Mozambique. He shifted his focus to underground work inside the country and the manual project was set aside.

When the idea of a primer first came up in 1979, a copy of the lectures was sent to Comrade Brian Bunting, editor of *The African Communist*. He in turn sent them to an academic, John Hoffmann, based at Leicester University in the United Kingdom. In· October 1979, Hoffmann returned them with extensive comments, acknowledging that the task was a "big job".

"It would require more than just editing each of the lectures as they stand and it needs to be done by someone with experience of teaching in the camps so that they can get the level and the subject matter just right." (*Letter to Brian Bunting from Hoffmann, 1/10/79.*) He provided lecture-by-lecture comments on his points of difference and on presentation and editing needs. Hoffmann's comments at the end of the letter — that it could not be done adequately by a relative outsider, that he was already committed to publishing another book and that he was keen to concentrate his theoretical energies on the struggle in his homeland, Zimbabwe — suggest that he had in fact been approached to transform the lectures into a primer.

In May 1981, Moses Mabhida, General Secretary of the SACP, wrote to Comrade Jack about decisions made by the Central Committee in November 1979. It had "decided that the lectures you had given to cadres in Angola should be compiled and made available for assisting our Party cadres" (*Letter from MM Mabhida to Comrade Jack, dated May 13 1981*) The decision was renewed at a Political Bureau meeting in early 1981, and Comrade Jack was asked to continue with the preparation of these lectures for publication. He was also requested to prepare an accompanying reading list.

In 1984, Marion Sparg was approached to undertake the task of editing the primer. Cadres working in the Party, both inside and outside the country, were demanding the published lectures. Over an extensive period, Sparg and Comrade Jack discussed the material and how it should be re-worked. In September 1984, she presented an incomplete set of chapters and a full chapter outline. She had worked on these draft chapters in a hurry, prior to leaving Lusaka to enter the country on a mission. She and Comrade Jack had no time to discuss the various marginal comments she had made as she went along. Sparg had been working from the original lectures given in Novo Catengue in 1977/8 and 1978/9.

Although the chapter order of her draft differs from that of the 14 lectures, the content is substantially the same. For this reason, the lectures have been allowed to stand on their own, and the primer's draft chapters have not been included.

Sparg was arrested, charged and sentenced to 20 years, and was only released from Pretoria Prison in late April 1991. She provided some of the information for this chapter in an interview from prison, and she had also written a letter to Comrade Jack which accompanied the draft chapters when she "went home". This was her plan for the primer:

"The chapters we have done so far then are:
Foreword and Introduction
Chapter 1 — A scientific approach
Chapter 2 — Change and Development
Chapter 3 — Historical Materialism
Chapter 4 — Productive Forces
Chapter 5 — Classes (the rewrite you want to do)
Chapter 6 — Social Formations
Chapter 7 — African perspectives
Part II Revolution
Chapter 8 — The Manifesto: A call to revolution.
Chapter 9 — Theory and Organisation
Chapter 10 — Bourgeois Revolution
Chapter 11 — Proletarian Revolution
Chapter 12 — Imperialism and Colonialism
Chapter 13 — National Liberation (not done yet)
Chapter 14 — One Society, One Nation
The chapters still to be done, are then:
13. National Liberation
Part III Socialism
14. Elements of Socialist Construction
15. Socialism and Nationalism
16. World Socialism: National Sovereignty
Part IV Our Strategy
17. Communist and National Liberation Movements
18. Politics and Economics of Inequality in SA
19. Strategy of the Liberation Struggle
20. The SACP and the ANC"

Sparg intended including a brief biography of Comrade Jack, but this had not yet been written. In addition, she had various proposals on the re-drafting of various chapters.

> *"... You will notice in the section on Revolution that I have drafted a chapter on imperialism and colonialism to precede the account of national liberation. I thought this was necessary to put national liberation in its proper context. In the chapter on national liberation, I thought we should give an*

*account of a few of the struggles (as we did in Proletarian and Bourgeois
Revolutions), and then I thought perhaps the place to include something of
'African' socialism etc, would be in the third part, on socialism. In the chapter
on Politics and Economics of Inequality in SA, I think it is necessary not only
to give some factual data, but also to specifically re-examine the whole question
of 'internal colonialism' and colonialism as it applies to SA. In the chapter on
Strategy of the Liberation Struggle, it is important to make the point that the
creation of MK was not by the ANC alone — but also by the party. There is
still the incorrect belief at home that the ANC created MK as its military wing
in 1960. We should put the position straight, that it was only much later that
MK came under the ANC — when the ANC was to lead the liberation
movement as a whole. I thought it also important to explore the point (which I
once discussed with Comrade Thabo) that the ANC on its own cannot be
described as 'the national liberation movement'. The SACP is as much a part of
the 'national liberation movement' as the ANC, and SACTU: 'South African
Trade Unions, forerunner of Cosatu' for that matter. And of course, we will
need to examine who, or what, is the vanguard in the SA context. Anyway, I
am now beginning to waffle. I'm really sorry that I didn't have a chance to see
this thing through to the end. I was really enjoying it. For the first time, I had a
chance to do a lot of reading (and thinking) and I think in the process I have
cleared up a lot of things for myself. I hope to see the booklet (book?) printed
very soon. Am I being too optimistic?.But, as once said, optimism is a necessary
ingredient of a revolutionary situation, isn't it?*

*I've told Ray already that I certainly will try to keep in touch as far as
possible. Thanks for all the discussion and help, and time. Look after yourself.
All my love, Marion"*

In 1987, the primer had still not seen the light of day, and Comrade Jack sent the
13 drafted chapters to the Central Committee to get some feedback on the project.
From an extract of a letter, apparently to the ANC Department of Political Education
(DPE) some time later, it appears that the Central Committee had not yet replied and
that Comrade Jack turned to the DPE to get some response and involvement in the
project. In the letter, he acknowledged the work done by Sparg and wrote:

*"I'd like to dedicate the book to her [Comrade Marion Sparg — editor] and
members of the June 16th Brigade in Novo Catengue."*

In February 1990, the events of the South African struggle overtook the
publication of the primer. Ray Alexander and Comrade Jack returned home to Cape
Town amidst jubilant celebrations. In discussion with him in 1991, it was debated
whether, given the changed circumstances nationally and internationally, the format
of a primer was still appropriate. It was agreed to add some historical material about
the camps and cadres trained. On this basis 18 interviews were conducted with
comrades trained by Comrade Jack or comrades involved in the political education

structures of MK. These interviews took place in August 1991.

It was felt, however, that the lectures still offered cadres in South Africa a basic text on historical and dialectical materialism as it applied to South Africa, and would also serve an important function in beginning to document the political education work done in exile. The developments in Eastern Europe and the Soviet Union confront all communists with serious challenges, and in reading these lectures we need to embark on a critical reassessment of the use of examples from the countries that made up the Soviet Union as explanations of solutions to such problems as the national question.

Comrade Jack instilled in his students the basic Marxist ability to think critically, historically, dialectically and materially. His approach was always described as anti-dogmatic, creative, reflecting constantly on the appropriateness of one's analysis — an approach that has done much to develop the theory of the South African revolution. These were qualities he passed on to many of his students, whether in the Modern Youth Society at the University of Cape Town or in Novo Catengue. A quote used in one lecture throws out a challenge to readers to assess their views constantly against the march of history:

"History has proved us, and all who thought like us, wrong." (Engels, 1895)

So it is wholly consistent with the spirit of Comrade Jack's teaching for historical materialists to use these lectures as a springboard to answer some key questions. In what way has socialist theory been wrong? Has it been the application of the theory in socialist countries, rather than the method of analysis, that has been at fault? What are the root causes of the economic, political and social crises of Eastern Europe and the Soviet Union?

This book aims to provide a tool for developing a critical approach to materialist analysis and socialist theory, as well as beginning to document the work of political education conducted by Comrade Jack in universities, private homes, camps and schools. The political instruction work in MK equipped the ANC with cadres of outstanding ability. The historical and dialectical materialism that Comrade Jack so skillfully transferred to the June 16 Detachment remains the guiding theory of the SACP.

The project has been expanded to begin the recording of the history of our comrades and organisations in exile, by including extracts from interviews with people who worked with, or were taught by, Comrade Jack. Reflections on the teaching methods Comrade Jack employed have also been included, since it became obvious from the interviews that the trainees had received far more than a set of lecture notes. Communist teaching as personified by him involved equipping comrades with the skills to analyse, research, present, argue and — above all — to learn from every contribution. He instilled in the generations of people he taught the belief that "The philosophers have interpreted the work in various ways: the point, however, is to change it." (Karl Marx, *Theses on Feuerbach*)

Editors' introduction

In 1991 the Education Resource and Information Project (Erip) at the University of the Western Cape undertook to get the lectures edited and published. Garth Strachan and Murray Michel oversaw the project and Jenny Schreiner was employed to get the material ready for publication.

It was agreed that the lectures themselves should be contextualised with an understanding of the teaching methods of Comrade Jack, the experiences of the MK soldiers in the camps and as learners guided by Comrade Jack. Accordingly Jenny Schreiner set up interviews with comrades who had been in the political education structures of MK or had been trained in the camps by Comrade Jack.

By April 1992 a vast manuscript had been prepared on the basis of the interviews, Comrade Jack's diary and his lectures. It was agreed that substantial editing was necessary to produce a reader-friendly book. Comrade Jack undertook to co-edit the manuscript with the then editor — a reflection of his desire to see the project finished.

Later in 1992 Comrade Jack raised concerns about the appropriateness of the timing of the publication given the sensitive stage of negotiations in the Transitional Executive Council concerning the integration of MK and the South African National Defence Force. This was discussed between the editor at the time and the team facilitating the publication. The concern was accepted and the project put on hold. It was suggested that if one of the publishing agencies went ahead with a general anthology of Comrade Jack's writings, the lectures could be included in that volume.

By March 1993, it was felt that the concern about timing was not a major issue. It was argued that the publication of a book that told part of the story of MK soldiers, their dedication to training and experiences in the camps would be an appropriate salute to the MK soldiers as they went into the integration processes. The publication of the material that had been collected through the interviews, the stages of work on the primer and the lectures themselves was strongly motivated for. Another editor was brought into the process.

After the first democratic election of 1994, many of the ANC cadres who had contributed to compiling the book found themselves redeployed to the far more urgent tasks of reconstructing and governing a liberated South Africa. Comrade Jack died in July 1995. But it was still felt that publishing his lectures, and the reminiscences of those who had worked and been taught by him, was an important task. As well as contributing to a larger and more long-term biographical project, it reclaims a little of the undocumented history of the ANC struggle and illuminates one part of the intellectual inspiration for that struggle.

The approach applied in the book was to collect together within an analytical framework all the material on Comrade Jack's educational approach. Understanding this approach will help future generations of political educators update the lectures (now more than two decades old) by drawing on the insights and experiences of their students. The lectures themselves have been kept intact, with the addition of some teaching suggestions and brief bibliographical notes. Alas, neither the timeframe nor the format envisaged for this publication allowed for the very extensive annotated academic bibliography Comrade Jack wished for — but some starting points for such a project are provided.

Publisher's Note

When I was asked two years ago to look at a manuscript with a view to preparing it for publication, I did not know that it would lead to a fascinating journey of discovery of the life and times, and more importantly, the work of a brilliant teacher. I did not know Jack Simons, and I feel that I am all the poorer for it. But through his writing, and my research for this book, I have come to know the essence of the man and the teacher as well as any. For that I am all the richer.

The many papers, manuscripts, lectures and teachings are the legacy of Comrade Jack and Comrade Ray Alexander. A rich heritage. We would do well to gather and share the heritage of Comrade Jack with the generations to come. As a nation we can be proud to have had a person like Comrade Jack touch our lives.

I would like to thank the Simons family, and particularly Comrade Ray Alexander, Mary Simons, Tanya Barben and family for their support and assistance. Thanks also to Kgalema Motlanthe, Febé Potgieter, Spunjy Moodley and Naph Manana of the ANC for their patience; Jenny Schreiner and Marion Sparg for the initial work, putting it all together; Gwen Ansell for a professional edit and Muff Andersson for proofreading the final text. Dr Anne Seidman, Professor Robert Seidman and Professor QN Parsons provided illuminating reminiscences of Comrade Jack the teacher. And the bibliographical research was done by Dr JC Myers of UCT and Comrade Dumisani Mphalala of the ANC Research Department. To all of these, warm thanks.

The making of a revolutionary teacher

"I came back from studying in London in 1937 with a PhD, an appointment at the university as lecturer in African Studies and my party card. Those were the three decisive factors that determined the pattern of my life."
(Interview with Comrade Jack Simons, September 3 1991)

That was Comrade Jack Simons' comment about his return to South Africa after studying in London. And no matter where he went subsequently — the University of Cape Town (UCT), the Umkhonto weSizwe (MK) camp at Novo Catengue, or Lusaka — his work, teaching skills and political commitment were the factors that shaped his life.

Jack Simons was born to an Anglo-Afrikaner mother (née Morkel) and an English father on February 1 1907 in Riversdale, in the Cape. Comrade Jack describes his hometown as "not poor, not prosperous" and talks about how he socialised with coloured, African and poor white children. But although the local population was small (only about 3 000, of whom 500 were white), he managed to avoid mixing with the petty bourgeoisie who ran the place.

"I was radical in outlook at an early age, that's all I can say. I didn't like the set-up, and it took me some time to find my way to an alternative. Because there was no suitable contact in the village itself, I had to go outside into the wider society, and I there encountered people, came across movements."
(Interview with Jack Simons by Julie Frederickse, January 1987)

His father ran a printing plant, edited a paper and was town clerk. His mother stopped teaching to raise Jack and his five siblings. After he matriculated in 1924, he was articled to a local firm of attorneys, completed the first part of the Law Certificate, and joined the civil service in 1926. He was stationed in Pretoria as a clerk in the Auditor-General's office, with responsibility for auditing the accounts of the police and prisons. Seeing how black prisoners were treated when he went into prisons to audit the books appalled him and motivated him further to seek alternatives.

But clerking was poorly paid, and to increase his income he registered in 1926 as an external student for the BA Law of the Transvaal University College. He graduated in 1929 and was awarded a scholarship for his MA, still as an external student. He graduated with an MA in political philosophy and was then awarded the Porter Scholarship. He resigned from the civil service and enrolled for a PhD at the London School of Economics in October 1932.

There he studied in the Department of Social Anthropology, headed by Professor Bruno Malinowski, the "father of modern social anthropology". Comrade Jack, however, saw himself as a political sociologist rather than an anthropologist. Working under Malinowski equipped him with a "method of studying traditional communities in a process of social change".

His thesis, *A Comparative Study of Crime and Punishment in Southern and Eastern Africa*, secured his PhD from the London School of Economics (LSE) in 1937.

In England his political views were influenced by the political upheavals of the Great Depression and the "Hungry Thirties": unemployed miners, mass marches, demonstrations and the threat of war. His involvement in political activities got him suspended from the LSE for six months — which he used to finish his thesis.

It was the combination of Malinowski's active research methods, Lenin's outstanding ability as a communist intellectual and strategist, and Comrade Jack's own creative mind and undogmatic approach to life that shaped him intellectually.

> *"I've always felt that the combination of LSE and Lenin was a very powerful one — it's a dialectical combination. In some respects they were at war with each other but it's a kind of a creative war between two methodologies. The Leninist is the activist methodology in which people take responsibility for their lives and try and chart out a way for themselves through a scientific analysis. The LSE methodology is going out into the field and discovering reality through direct contact with it — it's not simply data collection but it is imbuing all our thought with information. With Jack, the scientific methodology of the LSE, I think, played a very big role."* (Albie Sachs)

Comrade Jack's return to South Africa coincided with a crucial period of reassessment within the African National Congress, which had been dominated by cautious, reformist politics during the 1930s. He was approached to speak at an ANC conference in Bloemfontein in 1937, but initially felt that it was inappropriate for a white South African to do so. But when he arrived at the meeting he was appalled by the self-deprecating attitude of some leaders and decided he would, after all, speak. Although the ANC Constitution of the time excluded white members, Comrade Jack worked closely with ANC groups in Cape Town. But it was in the Communist Party of South Africa that he found his home.

He had returned to South Africa, Party card in pocket, to lecture on customary law to first-year social anthropology students at the UCT School of African Studies. For some years he lectured in Public Administration in the commerce faculty, but his real interest was in teaching students of Native Law and Administration, subsequently renamed Comparative African Government and Law. Ironically, this was a course designed to train colonial administrators. But Comrade Jack had no intention of turning out people who would operate the colonial system.

"I didn't set out to make them 'anti' anything, but analysed the social structure in which they would operate if they were administrators." (Interview with Comrade Jack by Julie Frederickse, January 1987)

He used a class analysis to unpack racial tensions and conflicts, telling his students that underneath the "race" factor they had to look for interest groups — capital and labour. That established a radical approach in the classes, and led ultimately to a number of people taking part in revolutionary activity and going to prison, and to Comrade Jack himself being expelled.

Professor Albie Sachs sets this pathbreaking role within the context of South African academic life:
"The basic text and sub-text of our intellectual life was that ideas came with the whites, and Africans just existed. What he introduced was the concept of African personality, customary law of highly sophisticated societies. Today it mightn't seem all that special. In those days you had the idea of the civilised and uncivilised, he was destroying that whole distinction. He was saying that in fact there was a level of civilisation in African society that in many respects was far in advance of the white society in terms of courtesy, culture, refinement, respect for people, for individuals and the courtesies of speech, of social organisation, of family life. That was quite remarkable for generations of people — black and white. It was a scientific and a dignified approach at the same time."

Comrade Jack challenged the colonial wisdom of South African academics by highlighting the traditional customs and values of African communities. His contribution to intellectual theory also included seminal research on the legal position of African women within South Africa, original work which established gender-sensitive studies as academically legitimate and indeed crucial to social analysis.

Jack Simons and Ray Alexander (still alive today and a veteran of the Communist Party, the trade union movement and the women's movement) married in 1941. All who spent time with the family remember the equality, love and respect within their marriage and their ability to combine family life, intellectual life and activism. From the start, they rejected stereotypes and tried to make their partnership embody the communist values of equality, communalism, humanity and discipline. Various comrades have described how Comrade Jack took on the responsibilities of parenthood in a way that was far ahead of its time; bathing the children and acting as both father and mother when Ray was away from home on union or political work, and sharing the household responsibilities when she was at home.

In 1946 Comrade Jack was arrested along with the rest of the CPSA Central Committee and charged with sedition. The trial — where Comrade Jack gave expert evidence on the political scene and the prosecution's documents — dragged on for more than two years, but eventually the charges were withdrawn. The 1950s were a period of repression against communism and the CPSA disbanded in the face of the Suppression of Communism Act in 1950. Comrade Jack himself was placed under successive bans from 1952. Although the initial banning orders did not prevent him from lecturing, in 1964 the then justice minister BJ Vorster banned him from teaching, writing for publications and attending gatherings.

Ray Alexander and Comrade Jack left the country to take up a fellowship at Manchester University in 1965. There, Comrade Jack completed the writing of *African Women: Their Status in South Africa* in 1968, and collaborated with Ray on their masterwork, *Class and Colour in South Africa 1850-1950*. Then they settled in Lusaka, which was to be their home until 1990. Comrade Jack was appointed Professor and Head of the Department of Social Science and Social Welfare at the University of Zambia. Later he also became co-editor of the prestigious university journal *African Social Research*.

The ANC entered into a "period of regrouping and recovery" from 1969 to 1974 (OR Tambo in *Report to ANC National Executive Committee, 1995*). On 25 April 1969, the ANC held the Morogoro Conference, aimed at bringing about organisational changes to address the new demands. The conference was preceded by widespread discussion within all ANC structures about how to lay a solid basis for future operations. The need for a new structure was balanced against the realisation that the ANC needed cadres who were better trained, both politically and militarily.

"The outcome of the discussion at the Morogoro Conference on the nature and character of the movement was the (now famous) 'Strategy and Tactics of the ANC'. The machinery was created to deal professionally and adequately with internal reconstruction and propaganda, planning of the commencement of sustained guerrilla operations and the injection back home of our trained personnel to form the core of the armed force.

"This was also needed to correct the imbalance between the work of the movement externally and internally; to correct our priorities and to bring home the idea of the primacy of internal needs; and the fact that the only possible justification for the existence and activity of the ANC outside the country was as an adjunct of the needs of the situation at home. The body responsible was later called the Revolutionary Council, the majority of whose members were relieved of all external work and administration except in so far as this had ...

bearing on the military side." (Francis Meli, *A History of the ANC: South Africa Belongs To Us,* 1988, London, James Currey)

It was in the aftermath of this conference that a self-selected group of ANC members approached Comrade Jack for study classes. From June 1969, a group of 20-30 people gathered once a week in the house of Comrade Jack and Ray in Lusaka to equip themselves for the new tasks ahead.

At the time the SACP was underground, even in Lusaka. Although the Zambian authorities were prepared to house the ANC, the one-party state system of government prevented the party from functioning openly. Thus the students did not know each other as communists. Among this group was the late Chris Hani, subsequently Chief of Staff of MK, member of the ANC NEC and of the Central Committee of the SACP.

This is how he remembers that time:

"This was a period after we'd become involved in Zimbabwe, together with ZAPU. We had just come back from the Botswana prison in Gaborone and we found a situation where there was some demoralisation and frustration. Because, despite the publicity around our participation in Zimbabwe, it had not led to a sustained presence there. We had not been able to root ourselves. Many of our comrades had been killed in action, and several captured, who were serving long prison sentences in Zimbabwe. More than a dozen had been sentenced to death. Those of us who managed to escape the dragnet of the Rhodesian-cum-South African security had been in prison in Botswana. So I would say this virtually marked an end to our participation in Zimbabwe, in terms of opening up a road to South Africa.

"Now, it was a period where comrades were beginning to question what they saw as an emphasis on solidarity work as opposed to a drive to build a movement inside the country. A few of us were sharply critical of the fact that the greatest part of the leadership's energy was spent on moving around the globe. Not that this work was not essential. It has always been felt that the mobilisation of the international forces in support of our struggle does form an essential part of our strategy. But we were questioning the imbalance between external work and internal work.

"It was at this stage that Comrade Jack Simons began to organise study groups intended to improve the quality of political understanding of the South African situation. The lectures were very different from the lectures some of us had seen before. They were applying political theory to South African conditions.

"Now, who were involved in these study groups? It was officials of the ANC, members of the National Executive Committee and members of Umkhonto weSizwe, members of the Women's Section and the Youth Section. The basic purpose of the lectures was to politically sharpen comrades who were involved in all the activities of the movement."

There had been a large-scale exodus of comrades from South Africa after the decision to take up armed struggle in December 1961. They had received military training at Morogoro, but it appears that there was little organised political education. Comrade Jack describes how many of the comrades who went into exile at this time remained uneducated and illiterate, unable to rise in the leadership because of these limitations. Even the classes run in the house were spontaneously organised rather than the result of a policy decision. As the lecture notes show, the series was never completed. It is not clear precisely why it stopped. Comrade Jack and Ray felt there had been intervention to stop them.

Hani understood it more as a result of redeployment of comrades in shifting times:
"Well, I think round about 1970/71, there was a move to send comrades to refresher courses in the Soviet Union. Others now went out of Lusaka, to some camps near the Zambezi River. So it was very difficult to have a sizeable number of people around Lusaka, that's what I think ... I don't think they were instructed to stop the lectures. I think what happened is that those who were active in terms of attending and participating left Zambia or were deployed in camps around the Zambezi River."

For a while after that, political instruction continued only through ANC branch discussions of current affairs.

Although Comrade Jack resigned from the university in 1975, (the last year in which he was ever paid a salary), his role as teacher was far from over. He continued to lecture to members of the Zambian ruling party, UNIP, to students at the Zambian President's Citizenship College, to cabinet ministers and the Party's Central Executive. He also continued to edit *African Social Research*, the journal of the Institute of African Social Research. He was then asked to teach politics to ANC students and MK cadres, and played an ongoing role in ANC structures, serving in the Department of Manpower Development and playing a crucial role in developing political education within the liberation movement. He developed courses of instruction for cadres in Lusaka and, most famously, for MK soldiers at Novo Catengue camp in Angola.

In 1977, the ANC faced a flood of young people who had left South Africa for training after the June 16 Soweto uprising. The need for larger-scale and more systematic training of both a political and military nature became apparent. Comrade Mzwai Piliso, of the MK Department of Personnel, and Commander Joe Modise asked Comrade Jack to undertake this task of political instruction and, true to form, he accepted without hesitation.

Aged 70, he went to join the youth in the camp. In the next three years, he spent two periods in Novo Catengue assisting in laying the basis for political instruction of MK recruits — from August or September 1977 until early 1978, and then from December 1978 until March 1979. In 1977 he concentrated on teaching the platoons and developing a core of instructors. In 1978/9 he spent more energy on re-orienting the cadres who had returned from further political study in Moscow, so that they could fulfil the political tasks allocated to them by the ANC and MK. Many of the trainees were from the black consciousness movement. Only about 10% had been regular wage-earners, the majority belonging to the "lumpen proletariat". But all the trainees developed a deep and lasting respect for Comrade Jack. Through the process of living, socialising with, and learning from Comrade Jack, many of this generation realised for the first time that there were indeed white South Africans in the ranks of the freedom fighters.

"Our composition was the basic composition of the South African youth. We had from a lumpen element to the most educated person as part of one detachment, and this had its own problems. Our interests were not necessarily the same, nor our appreciation. Also, for most people who had grown up in the urban areas that experience of country life was new, although very useful. People learning the basic things: to go and hunt, to be able to ensure there's meat in the camp. All that military training and interaction with local peasants in a way helped to harden some comrades. For some of us who had been at boarding school, it was an easier adaptation (than for) those who had always been around their families." (Comrade Reggie Mpongo)

The MK trainees went through a period of six months basic training consisting of military as well as political instruction.

Military training was:
*"Training in the use of **explosives** — that's basically what quantity destroys what, what type of bomb would be effective for what types of structures. And then you have **firearms** instructors who teach the actual use of the guns, the pistol, the rocket launcher — that small category of arms. **Artillery** instructor — he goes from cannon and anti-aircraft, anti-personnel guns, big target type of firearms. Then you had an instructor who taught **topography**: orientation — if you are in the middle of nowhere, how to know this is south, north, east, west or where you are heading. Then you also had instructions on **infantry**, fighting as a barefoot soldier, moving next to the tank and so on, being in a trench or manning a post as a guard ... also the science of **guerrilla warfare**."* (Comrade Thami Ngwevela)

When Comrade Jack arrived in Angola in September 1977 he worked under the Political Commissar, Mark Shope. Their task was to carry out both the actual teaching of the platoons and companies, and to develop a core of instructors who could carry on this work in their absence. The June 16 Detachment, the first of the Soweto generation of trainees, came to Angola at a time when ANC bases were practically non-existent. Comrades have described how they were first accommodated in an Angolan camp in Luanda, moving after a couple of months to the Engineering Camp in Benguela, and then after another couple of months arriving at Novo Catengue. It was only when they arrived there, in May 1977, that their training really began.

This situation also meant there were few comrades in the camp who had any training for the tasks they were given. There was a core of about 20-30 camp staff, some of them comrades who had left South Africa after the June 16 uprising, but who had been sent immediately to be trained as military instructors. Others were more experienced, such as Julius Mokoena, Camp Commander, and Mark Shope, Camp Commissar. Those who had to take on the tasks of company, platoon and section commanders and commissars were not trained in these tasks. They were deployed because they were better organisers and more educationally advanced than others in the detachment. Part of Comrade Jack's task was to transform trainees into a core of instructors and to build the commissariat.

> "We faced this really monumental task of organising the commissariat, organising the political instructors and at the same time imparting instruction to the detachment. At the time we had about four companies which constituted the detachment. Comrade Jack's task was to prepare lectures; lecture the companies during the day; in the afternoon assemble those who were already commissars and also deliver lectures to them; also circulate with the instructors; and he also had a set of lectures for the administration." (Comrade Ché Ogara)

Comrade Jack took on additional responsibilities as time proceeded. He described how after Black September (a crisis period when an enemy agent attempted to poison the entire camp) he ran a special class for the comrades who were working in the kitchens, since they could not attend the platoon lectures.

> "It was one of the moments one would never forget. But it helped in a way for us to appreciate some of the things the Cubans had been saying to us over a long period of time. We used to cook in tents, in the kitchen. If this week it's our company, then the four platoons would alternate the cooking and then the overall duty. But the Cubans always insisted that you can't have everyone in the kitchen; you just have to sacrifice; get some people whom you trust to stop their training, to act as cooks throughout the training and then thereafter others do it. You can't have everyone coming and going. We thought they were crazy. When the poisoning came, it dawned on us what they meant, because they were the only people who were safe — because they had their own kitchen and their own cooking. As a result they were the ones who were able to take care of the camp at the time when everyone was down. Afterwards, we started having teams of cooks. It was fortunate that no one died in that incident. The manner in which the Cubans reacted to the situation was quite an experience for us."
> (Comrade Reggie Mpongo)

Comrade Jack also ran special classes for the women comrades in an attempt to assist them to overcome their reluctance to speak out in the platoon classes. He said the women did as well as the men in military exercises, but commented that they were not utilised in the armed struggle, except as couriers and for non-combat tasks.

During this period Comrade Jack also ran a course for the military instructors in order to upgrade their political understanding.

"There was a contingent, 25–30 instructors faced with the task of organising this detachment and organising all its departments so that training takes place and comrades are able to go back home and fight and pursue their various tasks in the struggle. Although all of us (who) were the instructorate were trained militarily, unfortunately we had never had experience of instruction, especially from a military point of view. We were faced with a detachment of 500, with education levels that varied from comrades who had never seen the inside of the classroom to comrades who had been university graduates. Organising the military was the biggest task; also we faced the political task. None of us who were trained at the time were ever trained specifically to specialise in political work. That came much later." (Comrade Ché Ogara)

Comrade Jack had gone to the camp as a dedicated ANC member. At the time, membership of the outlawed SACP was secret. MK drew on him as an experienced educator, specialising in political sociology. He would not wear a uniform until his own clothes disintegrated and he was obliged to replace them with the only garments available in a military camp — uniform.

He was not formally a part of the army machinery and saw himself as a political instructor. Yet he is recognised as having given far more to camp life than his official duties ever required. Finally, in 1978, Comrade Jack took the oath of allegiance to MK. That was the year in which he began the re-orientation of comrades who had returned from specialised instruction in the Soviet Union.

Ronnie Kasrils came down to see him on that occasion:
"He was back in Novo Catengue and he was now handling the first group of comrades, who had been to the Lenin School; there must have been about 20 of them. They'd been there for a year, I suppose, it must have been the end of '78. He was in session with them every day. These were trained comrades who'd come back. They were being re-orientated for various tasks, to become instructors in the training camps in Angola, or to go and work in Lusaka, or in the forward areas. People like Mavis Nhlapo from Lusaka ... She was the commander of that group and Jack's kind of pet student, an incredibly impressive woman. Andrew Mkhize was another one, Klaus Maphepha. Really, they were a very interesting bunch."

Novo Catengue was a far cry from the lounge in the Simons' house in Lusaka and from the universities of Zambia and Cape Town, not only in terms of teaching facilities, but also in the harshness of everyday life. Comrade Mzwai Piliso recounts how, when the trainees were still in the camp in Luanda, he could tell just by driving up to the gate of the camp and assessing the level of activity, whether the comrades had eaten that day or not.

Those initial days of very meagre provisions did not last, although food remained one of the hardships facing the trainees. The Logistics Department organised food from various supportive countries to ensure a basic diet.

One of the comrades interviewed said that he had eaten enough tinned food in the camps to last him a lifetime! The basic camp rations were supplemented in whatever way possible.

"Where there was a forest we used to go game hunting, killing the zebras and so on, subsidising our food in the camps. Ayi, the food! It improved later. At the beginning it was very difficult. We had mainly rice; we had plenty of rice — well, the Cubans' stock. And fish, canned fish, and beans. That was basically the diet. Of course we had tea and occasionally we had flour and we had the kitchen staff baking." (Comrade Ché Ogara)

The words of the comrades who lived and trained in Novo Catengue describe the place eloquently. Despite the fact that it is many years since any of them have been in Novo Catengue, their memories of the hardships, and of the comradeship and vitality of camp life, are vivid.

"When we got to Novo Catengue we found there was a camp for people who had been building the railway. They had left, run away from that place during the Angolan war. So there were some structures, some buildings. One section held the Cuban instructors; another section was just for us. We had very few tents there. These structures could not accommodate all the people when you had to give a talk. True, we did have a small hall where we used to meet when we had domestic problems to be sorted out. We'd call the comrades into that hall, company by company, to discuss those problems." (Comrade Mark Shope)

"Our camp was situated within mountains. The railway line passed by it. Although it was a security risk for the camp itself, it sort of broke the monotony of life. When the train passed with people and all that, despite being told never to go there, we'd all go and peep and wave at the people. We regretted it two years later when they bombed the camp, because we realised we made it easier for whoever was reconnoitring." (Comrade Reggie Mpongo)

"The terrain was very mountainous, among a lot of shrubs; tall isolated trees, (one isolated tree among them was the baobab that Comrade Jack taught under) and the camp was completely surrounded by mountains. We were right down at the foot of the mountain. In the south of the camp, there was a stream of water. All the activities were within range of the camp. Within 5-10km, we had all these fields: engineering fields, tactics field, topography. Most of the practical things took place around that mountainous bush, rivers, which made it realistic to assimilate the type of training we were doing."
(Comrade Ché Ogara)

Despite the hardships, volunteers found life in Novo Catengue full and enriching. Not only were comrades developing the expertise to pursue the struggle, they were also living a broader life.

"The cultural life? Well, we used to organise indoor games. Maybe if you can sing, if you can do traditional dances and so forth, you call others, you teach them. They used to perform for us. We organised a stage and we had some days when we could perform these different things for entertainment. And football clubs and then sometimes we organised athletics for ourselves." (Comrade Precious)

"We had a six-day week. Saturday was a half-day. But the real free day was a Sunday and a lot of cultural activities and sporting activities would be organised in the camp. Cubans are generally a jolly lot and very informal outside work. They would organise a lot of activities. On Tuesdays or Wednesdays, at the camp level, we had the singing of revolutionary songs. Most weekends they had cultural evenings. We had four companies then, competing with each other. And this sort of broke the monotony of life." (Comrade Reggie Mpongo)

Life in Novo Catengue was organised according to strict military discipline, with a camp administration, trainees, medical staff, all with clearly defined responsibilities and hierarchy. However, the camp structures were not those of a bourgeois army, since the political life and welfare of the trainees was accorded deep significance.

Ché Ogara explains the structure of the June 16 Detachment:
"I was a Company Commissar, Second Company Commissar, responsible for 128 comrades. We had four companies, so there were four company commissars. Each company had four platoons, then we had under-platoon sections. Four sections made one platoon. There were commissars at all those levels, from the section of 10, platoon of 32, to the company of 128. That was the commissariat in the camp, all those commissars. And then we had instructors, political instructors. Each company had about two or three instructors just dealing, with lectures."

These political instructors fell under the political department, one of the many departments in the camp.

"The political department was the comrades responsible for the political education of the camp; political instructors were trained in the camp under those difficult conditions by Jack Simons himself, and among them he chose the head of the political department. I happened to be head of the political department and we also had a secretary. We divided up tasks: each of us dealt with so many platoons (a platoon is 30 to 32 comrades) and gave them political instruction. It was easier because with smaller numbers we had access to individual comrades. You know exactly whether they understand, you go at

their pace and you arrange studies for those comrades who don't comprehend the subject matter, and then they arrange additional classes for themselves. In the political department at that time were myself, Ché Ogara, Vuyisile Mati, Raymond Nkuku, Dan Cingi ... and others."(Comrade Ntokozo)

One of the most important differences between the structure in MK and a conventional army was the existence of the commissars.

A regional commissar himself in the 1980s, Ntokozo comments:
"Commissars, what are they? Their task is to look into the general life of people in the army, political life, morale, spirit, to develop their commitment, pride and love for their people, hatred of the enemy and brotherhood amongst comrades. Commissars are also responsible for the culture and welfare of comrades. We also had cultural evenings where comrades prepared plays, sang, danced. We arranged days to have presentations and of course we were also responsible for commemorative days, January 8, June 16, June 26, August 9, December 16*."

Ronnie Kasrils explains the historical roots of the idea of a commissariat and the role of such a structure within MK:
"The commissar's task was to attend to the political aspects of life in the very broad sense, not simply studying as a political subject but understanding and upholding the policy of the ANC. The political commissar's role was to ensure that his or her commander, whether of the camp or platoon or company, understood the politics as well. This stems from the Bolshevik tradition in the Civil War. All the liberation movements of the Sixties had utilised the concept of the commissar to ensure that the guerrilla force followed the political line. Obviously a key way of doing this was to ensure that proper political instruction was given — through the process of classes in the first place, but also through seminars and conferences and night study courses; also through the process of cultural activity in all its forms. And a commissar actually also had to be quite a psychologist, a kind of marriage counsellor, dealing with all the social problems too."

The composition of the trainees in the June 16 Detachment was skewed, racially, gender-wise and geographically, providing a complex set of factors for these "marriage counsellors" to balance.

"Almost all were African, about 5% or so Indian and coloured, but there were no white trainees in that group in the two years I spent there. We never at any time had many coloured people. It seemed to me we had a more significant

---

* *January 8: Founding of the ANC; June 16: Commemoration of June 16 uprising; June 26: Commemoration of Freedom Charter; August 9: Women's Day; December 16: Founding of MK*

number of Indians. I might be wrong. Also the great majority came from the Reef and then later with the Moncada Detachment, (which followed the June 16 Detachment), quite a sizeable number were from the Eastern Cape, the Cape areas in general and a few from Natal, but the balance was 60% from the Reef. In that earlier period, most of our instructors were comrades who had left in the Sixties, who mostly came from the Northern Transvaal, Eastern Transvaal, of rural origin. Some of them had a problem in dealing with a lot of urban youngsters with cocky attitudes like: 'This one can't tell me anything.' I mean, these were problems which we had to face. We started stabilising when some people who had left earlier, '74, '75, came in as instructors. But I think the comrades had patience with us. They had seen worse things, and to them our coming was a sign of hope that their sacrifice had not really been in vain."
(Comrade Reggie Mpongo)

The presence of women trainees in the camp raised both positive and negative aspects, and made Simons' teaching commitment to gender equity particularly important.

"We had some problems there, a serious imbalance. Out of that detachment of 500 there were less than 20 women. Maybe in some platoons no women at all. That tended to create some problems in the social life of the camp, in relationships. At a certain time, the administration took a decision that instructors were not allowed to have relationships with the women, although ordinary soldiers were.

"We found the women very inspiring. Those who were there, braving all the same tasks we were faced with. The women were in the forefront. We had women platoon commissars and commanders doing those duties whilst still undergoing training. They really made life pleasant and interesting in the camp — and they were also a challenge.

"Of course the commissariat had to give special emphasis to this question of educating our comrades about women's emancipation, so that they were treated like any of us, any soldier on an equal basis, but of course bearing in mind that they still remain women. There were extreme views from time to time, comrades would say: 'No, if we can do this, let them also do it.' But I can remember very few things the men were doing in the army which women were not also doing.

"I can't imagine how life would have been without those women in all spheres of activities, in our cultural activities, political, social; they were really part of us and inspiring us. I can't imagine how dull the camp would have been without those women." (Comrade Ché Ogara)

Some of the women did develop menstrual irregularities due to strenuous exercise and stress and were sent to Luanda for medical treatment. On medical advice, women trainees were put on a less strenuous physical training programme.

Women trainees' experience of the camps differed from that of the men, both in terms of accommodation, social life and how they experienced instruction. The women were accommodated in a separate barracks, but integrated into the sections, platoons and companies alongside the male cadres.

"As women we used to have our own woman commander. We used to organise ourselves as sort of a women's section, having our own political discussions because we discovered the men were ahead of us. So during our spare time we used to upgrade one another. We would organise some classes, then we would discuss issues which we didn't understand in class.

"Since we have August 9 [Women's Day], so we used to organise that ourselves. That day you find that men are going to cook and prepare tables for us. We would have new uniforms; we would have our one march as women that day.

"But otherwise we were just doing everything like them, there was no difference that this is a woman, this is a man.

"Sometimes it used to be tough: there's no water in the camps and then you are menstruating. We have to share a cup of water, it's just the way it used to be. And, I mean, our menfolk used to sacrifice some water for us, they'd say: 'No, at least women should try to bath. We are better off, we are men.'

"In the camp we used to have meetings to address problems. Some were within the camp as a whole, everybody could participate. But certain problems we used to discuss as women and then if we had reached a certain conclusion, we used to go to the camp commander, or maybe our commander would go and talk to the camp commander, then he would see what to do with the problem." (Comrade Precious)

The process of being in the ANC and in the camp challenged aspects of the Soweto generation's cultural background.

"Even for our group there were a lot of things we had to learn. We were a completely new group. So it was a whole process of reconstruction. Jack Simons himself was one of the people who were campaigning for women's rights in the camps. For me it was a relief that it was a male — and, for that matter, a very old person who might have been considered a traditionalist perhaps, at his age — to take such a position.

But it embarrassed a lot of young people — even young girls — to understand that they don't necessarily have to stay as they are and it was a man who was telling them. Mark Shope also —he is a man and he was one of our political instructors and he was always on the side of making sure that women in the camps were not unfairly treated." (Comrade Thami Ngwevela)

Piliso was approached by the ANC Women's Section who wanted to send a representative of the Women's Section to the camp to look after the women's interests. He refused, feeling that the camp structures and the Women's Commander were adequate to see to women's needs, and reluctant to have a representative who was not part of the army overseeing camp structures. The balance of educational levels among the women was different from that of the camp as a whole. Overall, it appears that more educated women chose to go into exile for training at that stage. From what comrades can remember, many of the women comrades had some level of university education, although there were at least two of the 20 women who were basically illiterate. As Peter Mayibuye explains, these divergent educational levels created a social dynamic within the camp that posed another task for the commissariat.

"There were some who were quite advanced among the women themselves. Some kind of programme was introduced by the women for discussion among themselves in the evening to try and uplift each other. But again some of the things would not work because you could find tension between individuals, a small group among them. And the tendency then developed that the few who were advanced would tend to group together and then the others who were less advanced would also tend to group together creating a problem.

"As for people's understanding of the gender question, I think it was the very first time that it was being addressed in the ANC. It always formed the basis for very interesting debates, some of them quite serious, some of them — of course — with the element of teasing and whatnot. I remember one particular discussion in a platoon, because I was presenting it, about Engels' 'The Origins of the Family, Private Property and the State', which always formed the basis for very interesting discussion. It was a bit high-flown, people would always come to easy solutions to the problems; easy, in the sense that ultimately everybody would agree: all you needed to do was create the objective conditions for the liberation of women. Before that, things would not be possible. That's my own experience, looking back and comparing it to the manner in which these things are discussed today. The challenge of actually liberating both men and women, psychologically and so on, as part of this whole process, was never addressed adequately. We'd always end up with the conclusion that when future societies and conditions had been created, it (gender) would be resolved ultimately."
(Comrade Peter Mayibuye)

All instruction was disrupted by an alert in February 1979 and the defensive strategy adopted in Novo Catengue. Some attempts were made to continue teaching, at least partially, in the areas surrounding the camp where comrades had retreated to defensive positions, but in fact instruction had to stop.

"They had already completed the training course. The bombing happened during the training of the Moncada Detachment, which had come after the June 16 Detachment, and I think they had already completed their training. Some had left the camp for advanced training abroad; some to be sent inside the

country. So most of those there had already completed their training. I think that was how we were able to form defence units, because already some people had completed their training. Around that time there was some training programme which was continuing to keep the comrades busy. You know soldiers should not be left idle, it becomes a danger. So it involved some specialised training. I was training a unit in artillery, to specialise in anti-tank guns. This was the unit that later on came to be deployed in the sector I was assigned to. And even, yes, in anti-aircraft guns, some comrades from the June 16 Detachment were taken to be given a crash course on how to use SAM-7 missiles." (Comrade Mshengu: one of the military instructors of the June 16 Detachment)

Ronnie Kasrils describes the lead-up to the bombing of the camp:
"*Arthur Sidweshu was the Commissar for Novo Catengue. I was sitting with Arthur tuned in to the Radio South Africa external broadcasting station. They referred to a report in a Portuguese newspaper, which said that SWAPO had a camp near Novo Catengue. We just looked at each other and he said: 'Jesus, this has slipped out somehow; they're making preparation for something and there's only us at Novo Catengue.' And on that we began to develop a plan and managed to obtain further information from home through our intelligence network.*

"*We came to realise that they were planning a big attack on Novo Catengue by air. So we actually began the process of withdrawing from the camp. We realised that it was just not possible to remain in that camp. The bombing took place in March. The camp was very heavily bombed. I would say about three weeks before the bombing took place we had basically evacuated the camp and we were living in the bush around Novo Catengue, including making use of the tunnels under the Benguela railway line.*"

Meshengu was in Novo Catengue when it was bombed. He was in charge of a unit that was guarding the approaches of the camp because it was expected that the SADF would also come with ground forces.

"*I was the commander of the platoon of the anti-tank guns. We were living outside the camp. We were supposed to go with our comrades to the camp. When it was actually bombed I was just on my way to the camp.*

"*Well, we saw these planes as they were coming and this happened around 7 o'clock. 7 o'clock Monday, and every weekday we have our formation, our assembly area, the whole camp and that's when we get news from the propaganda department. The information that they got was that all of us were going to be in the parade square exactly at 7 o'clock, so as a result they attacked the camp at 7 o'clock expecting to find us assembled in one area and then it would be a very good, nice massacre.*

"*But already after the bombing that had been conducted in ZAPU camps, the administration decided that we should vacate the camp and occupy defensive positions just around it. So when these war boys came, they could not believe it and could not find us in the square. I'm sure they were thinking that these guerrillas' timekeeping is strange. But I'm telling you, the whole square was riddled with bullets. It was these cannons that they're using called tank guns: when it hits the ground the bullet explodes. That whole square was riddled, just going on with strafing it, even though they couldn't see anything. We only survived because we were outside the camp.*

"How many people died? Three, one was a Cuban and then two comrades, those were the only casualties. It is said that one of their planes was dropped. I don't know whether this has been proved or not but the Angolans said that they found a plane just next to Benguela. One plane sank into the sea. And after it went into the sea the South African Defence Force, with their Navy patrolling around there, probably came to look for survivors.

"And then after the bombing we had to leave Novo Catengue for another camp. At that time Jack had left. I think the administration decided that he should leave and stay in Luanda. The bombing happened after Jack had left the camp and that's how he survived." (Comrade Meshengu)

Comrade Jack had been sent out of the camp against his will, during the alert prior to the bombing of the camp by SADF planes. Comrade Ronnie Kasrils describes how the bombs flattened Comrade Jack's former room. The collapsing roof and wall smashed what had been his bed to the floor.

During the time he was in the camps, Comrade Jack had managed to produce a set of 14 lectures plus additional material to be used by the comrades he had trained as political instructors.

After Novo Catengue, Comrade Jack helped initiate the process of establishing Mazimbu, the ANC school at Morogoro. In 1982, he lectured at the school. He also worked on the executive committee of the ANC Department of Education and as a member of the President's Committee.

In 1990, Ray Alexander and Comrade Jack returned to Cape Town after 25 years in exile. They had been offered associate fellowships at the Centre for Africa Studies by the University of Cape Town.

They returned on March 2. Thousands of ANC supporters, unionists and others from Mass Democratic Movement formations welcomed Comrade Jack and Ray at DF Malan Airport (now Cape Town International).

Comrade Jack said at the time: "This is a joyous occasion for my wife and myself. We were put out by the (Vorster) regime and kept out because we had fought for the rights of the people. We have come back and will continue that struggle."

He was the first to spell out the recently unbanned ANC's plans to turn itself into a functioning party, with branches throughout the country.

At the end of March, tributes were paid to Comrade Jack — and, in her absence, Ray Alexander — by a range of Mass Democratic Movement speakers at a meeting at the University of Cape Town, organised by the Union of Democratic Universities of South Africa.

In return, Comrade Jack paid tribute to the people of South Africa whose sacrifices had made his return possible.

After attending the Namibian independence elections, and paying a last visit to Lusaka to tie up loose ends, the couple returned to South Africa for good in August.

They became involved in political work. In October 1990 the SACP in the Western Cape formed a working group to re-establish regional branches. Both Comrade Jack and Ray were part of this.

In his final years at home, Comrade Jack devoted much time to writing. Now in his eighties, he did not have the vigour for a more active participation in the demanding politics of negotiation although he showed great interest in it.

On June 24 1994, he was awarded an honorary degree of Doctor of Laws by the University of Cape Town. Not much more than a year later he died in his sleep at home in Vredehoek, Cape Town.

Three prominent South Africans — Justice Albie Sachs of the Constitutional Court, Charles Nqakula, then-General Secretary of the SACP (now Deputy Minister of Home Affairs), and then-Deputy President Thabo Mbeki (now President) spoke at the memorial service held at St George's Cathedral on July 28, 1995.

What follows is a eulogy delivered by his eldest child Mary at his funeral service:

My dear pappie,

It somehow would be more appropriate to start my honouring of you as Dear Father. This is your eldest child and elder daughter on the occasion of your death. However, I have never addressed you as father. Perhaps the uncertainty of address is a reflection of the two-dimensional aspect of this communication: it is both an intimate expression of my feelings but also a public event. I will struggle to put into words what is incoherent, fractured and contained within myself. In the tradition in which you have trained me (and hopefully I bring credit to you) I will simultaneously pay tribute to you and situate our relationship in its socio-historical context.

Numerous books have been written over the past decade on the importance of the father-daughter relationship. Some of these have been psychological in intent and analysis, others have been collections of daughters' memories of their fathers. The typical Western middle-class analysis of this relationship revolves around the significance of the father in bringing the public or non-household sphere to the daughter, of showing her the world outside the home, of loving her and valuing her so that she can enter into equivalent relationships with other men, and perhaps most importantly, of affirming her as a person so that she can enter the world not as 'just a woman' but as woman/person. It is this latter aspect that is most frequently absent in contemporary father-daughter relationships. In your role as father you have done all this and more. What you also brought to our relationship was your nurturing of me, the physical care of me as a child, usually referred to as mothering. It is this added dimension that has both enriched and made more complex my interactions with men and with the world. There was a time when

I wished it was other, that my expectations of the men I was involved with would be less demanding. But I now see it as a wonderful gift and an experience that I only hope will become more common as fathers gain their right to nurture their children. For it is this dimension that will end the gulf between men and women and thus liberate human beings from gender-determined roles and forge the unity of the public and the private sphere. Thank you for bringing me consciously into the 'new world'.

The authenticity of all your actions, the varied hues of your personality, the appropriate balance between the space you gave me for exploration alongside the daily knowledge of your concern for my welfare and the single standard of justice in your dealings with all people are banners I proudly fly. The true spirituality to be found in all living things and the forms that living things produce, from the sloughed skin of a snake to the words of the bible, was a gift you gave me.

My mind can summon at will memories of pleasure you provided, intellectual excitement you stirred, emotional comfort you gave and hurt I caused you and hurt you caused me. My memory is rich with the emotional and physical feelings associated with your study, a place of retreat, a place of struggle and victory where I battled to acquire the motor skills to write, to deal with numbers, learnt to love Afrikaans, acquired the rudiments of Xhosa, never learnt to understand English grammar but learnt to read Dutch and German. In your study I lost fear of foreignness but most of all your study was a place that soothed me. A place where I was never required to state my business but could sit on the comfortable chair or on the floor and find acceptance and replenishment, both physical and spiritual. You shared your childhood with me in brief snatches as you doled out the motto sweets and liquorice — tales of Stilbaai, crossing the river and the shop across the river are as real to me as if I went on those journeys with you. The picture of an African woman by Graves that lived in your study now keeps watch over me in my study.

The rock pools with their marine life, the mountain and its residents: human, animal and vegetable were my true schoolroom and you the teacher of living and dying. You never tired of teaching, of sharing your pleasure in the oral story and song, the written word, prose and poetry: from the newspapers you read us in the morning to the bedtime stories at night-time. My knowledge of African mythology, the Latin classics and Greek writers were given to me by you. I know now as an adult how tiring that was and the commitment it required from you. Thank you — this valued gift you gave me I share with other children and enrich their sense of the world.

If these gifts were not sufficient, in addition you taught me respect for all people and all cultures, to find the humanity in people irrespective of class, race, gender, age or creed. Wherever you were you learnt the local language, spoke with the people, made friends and helped, in whatever way possible, to transform lives. You taught me to value people above ideology and question the commonsense/prejudice expressed by those around me. These teachings were not easy to give in a society riven by prejudices of colour, class, religion, gender and age. The knowledge was sometimes painfully acquired, being gracious to young white alcoholic men whom you brought to the supper table, recently released prisoners from Roeland Street gaol — you were a prisoner's friend — or being taught to be brave and courteous in my dealings with authority in uniforms and the Special Branch out of uniform.

For most of my life you have been there, neither distant nor intrusive but available, in the best sense of the word, for counsel, comfort and argument. I could berate myself for all the times I turned away from your instruction, and did not avail myself of your wisdom. I did what I was best able to do.

As a child I eavesdropped upon the Sunday night political classes held in our Cape Town home. I have attended conferences with you in Harare, Lusaka and Cape Town. Your intellectual enthusiasm and participation, the grace with which you conducted yourself as conference participant, was a delight for me to witness. I have been privileged to have you as a guest in my house, always courteous, helpful and unobtrusive. I feel privileged to have been able to share your joyous return to South Africa. I have heard you honoured publicly for your contribution to the struggle to make South Africa a united country where all could proudly proclaim their citizenship, honoured for your contribution to many people's intellectual development and the fostering of their intellectual concerns. You were a mentor to many and I wish that the gifts you gave me and others will be handed on from one generation to another.

My mother's account of your death process is deeply moving, compelling in its spiritual depth, romanticism and its graciousness. You, like your colleague Monica Wilson, departed this earth with utter grace — a true reflection of the very best in you. In the days since your death I have encountered another dimension of you — as father to the many young men and women who learnt from you not only their political education but in the words of Sandile 'each of us learnt how to become a person of integrity'.

I honour you, both as a man of simple tastes, wants and habits and a person of great complexity. I pay tribute to you as a thinker, an intellectual, a man who relished physical labour, a romantic, a cynic, a humorist. Those who knew you before you went into exile know of your belly-moving laughter, a laughter that you left behind. Its loss was a reminder of the pain you felt at being separated from South Africa. Wherever you were, you learnt the local language, spoke to the people and helped transform lives. I am sure you will continue to do that in spirit.

Hambe Kahle

2

'They have to bloody well think'
Jack Simons the teacher

Most of the comrades who were interviewed acknowledged how much Comrade Jack's teaching method helped them to learn and to grow into political activists capable of arguing their position and defending their views. Comrade Jack used a similar method everywhere he taught — in Lusaka and at Novo Catengue — but he was careful to tailor his method to suit each group he worked with. His teaching went alongside ongoing assessment of the course and of cadres' progress at Novo Catengue, reflecting his critical approach to education and his belief that improvements can be made if practice is examined. Teaching method and structured assessments produced a highly active, participatory education system in the Novo Catengue Military Academy.

Comrade Jack's methods owed a great deal to his personal gifts as a communicator and his encyclopedic grasp of his subject matter. They embodied his concept of the role of the communist intellectual: one who takes seriously, at whatever risk, the business of developing others. But they also incorporated — consciously or intuitively — the acknowledged principles of effective adult education, a subject which he became deeply involved in during his time at the University of Zambia. At the university in the 1970s there was intense discussion about adult education theory as part of a process of curriculum reform. Comrade Jack was actively involved in this debate.

Dr Anne Seidman, who headed the Department of Economics 1972-74, says:
"It was an environment that impressed us. A debate was going on about opening up dialogue with students and engaging them in assessed research,

rather than simply cramming them for final, all-important examinations. I remember discussions with Jack about creating an interdisciplinary foundation year course for the social sciences, rather than keeping the subjects in tight little boxes. Jack was definitely on the side of the angels."

Her husband, Professor Robert Seidman, lecturer and later Professor of Law in Lusaka during the same period, adds:
"The University of Zambia was trying to create a conducive environment for the younger African lecturers to get involved in active teaching and learning. One of the big inspirations was the educational philosophy of Dewey, which stressed problem-solving as a methodology for learning. Jack certainly used that 'Socratic method' of questioning rather than telling when he taught. As a Marxist, a dialectician, it obviously appealed to him. And I remember long discussions with him about the social functions of law, and the need to integrate law teaching with some consideration of social consequences."

Professor Neil Parsons was one of Comrade Jack's co-editors of *African Social Research* (the journal of the university's Institute for African Studies, and an influential publication in that period) and an assistant lecturer — and later lecturer — in history at the university. He remembers Comrade Jack contributing to the vehement debates about the structure of an African studies syllabus.

"Jack's notion of African studies was a variant of development studies, building on his own background. In that period, it was fashionable to shuffle off the idea of conventional academic disciplines ... but Jack's conception of integrated, active enquiry was far more than fashion ... His work was part of the last burst of real innovation at the university before the crash in the price of copper, Zambia's staple, made conditions difficult."

Comrade Jack was not only a gifted teacher, but an inspired trainer of trainers. That skill was the most significant loss when subsequent instructors tried to carry on his work in his absence, and the loss had important consequences. For all these reasons, the memories of his former students remain valuable today. They provide practical insights for any political organisation seeking to enhance its cadre development policy.

The syllabus
Even 20 years later, Comrade Jack's students remember clearly what they were taught.

"Jack Simons prepared political programmes almost single-handedly and the programmes were on the development of human societies, the primitive societies, going through the evolution of man and then primitive society, slavery, feudalism, capitalism, socialism and the theory of socialism. And he also dealt with the history of the Bolsheviks as an experience, the history of the CPSU, the

history of the USSR and the socialist community. We also looked into questions of developing countries, making comparison of one country to the other, looked into also the whole question of the development of the state and revolution ...

"Jack taught us the history, South African history and studying the pre-colonial era. I must say it was very very important for us because it imbued a sense of pride in terms of the lives that have been led by our people during the pre-colonial period. And of course then he got into the period of colonialism, removing all the falsifications in the history that we have learnt from Bantu Education or whatever ...

"Things were put straight for the first time. There were what is called wars of resistance from 1652. Jack made this point very, very clear: that our people resisted. If you look into colonial wars in the world, in South Africa you have had the longest in terms of years. Then of course he looked into those wars showing us how our people fought and why we lost — the question of disparity of weapons; the question of the economy, the question that our people were not united at that time.

"This pride in our fighters was important to inculcate amongst the cadres this tradition of fighting that we've had: the Dingaans, the Cetshwayos, the Shakas, the Moshoeshoes, the Makandas, the Sekhukhunes. These heroes during the wars of resistance, Jack dealt with very systematically and it helped a lot in giving confidence to cadres, the spirit for fighting.

"And of course the reasons for defeat were there, the weapons that the people were using and so forth, even the tactics. This, Jack took up to 1905 — the Bambatha Rebellion — in chronological order starting right from the Cape; from the Khoisans, the Khoi-khoi and how those people were exterminated by the Boers. That he explained because also it's important to inculcate hatred for the system of the enemy.

"And he built this up even when it comes to the history of Afrikanerdom, Jack also dealt with the history of Afrikanerdom starting from 1652 with the Dutch East India Company, coming up to the rise of Afrikaner Nationalism, the whole question of the Broederbond and up to the second World War to 1948, when the Nationalist Party got into power ... I must say you wouldn't know that Jack is an Afrikaner, the way [he made] the presentation of this aspect.

"He deals with the history of African Nationalism which is important because sometimes there is distortion from amongst our people to portray ... things like black consciousness [as] new in South Africa; this narrow nationalism of black consciousness. But when you get into our history, you see quite clearly that in fact the nationalism is as old as 1800 and something ...

"Jack deals with the birth of the ANC, people uniting, continuing the struggle by other means, politics. He takes the ANC from 1912; the development of the ANC from a small organisation of reformist-minded people and then into a strong organisation of militant, revolutionaries, the organisation that we are today.

"The period of the Fifties, he deals with that very well: the Youth League, *the roaring Fifties, fighting Fifties and the Freedom Charter, which is a very important aspect of political education. People must know what they are fighting for. And the Freedom Charter itself, although it's not elaborated — but even uneducated comrades of MK, you'd be able to use the Freedom Charter to rally our people around it, using the document to organise people. I mean, you can elaborate on the questions. Today people talk about mixed economy, people talk about market forces, people talk about all big questions and nationalisation. But the Freedom Charter is a very simple document: 'The people shall govern!' And people know that and we were able to use the Freedom Charter through this study series of Jack's.*

"And of course then Jack gets into the banning of the ANC, the setting up of Umkhonto weSizwe which is an important aspect, the history of MK. But that history is linked up with the whole history of our people. MK was formed in 1961. It was a necessity at that time when all other means and other roads had been closed. Peaceful methods had been exhausted and MK was set up. Then he shows the reasons for setting up MK and the attempts that were made initially to sabotage, and the aims of sabotage and the Rivonia arrests, then dealing with the post-Rivonia period, the difficulties during that time and so forth, up till 1976.

"All these questions were covered in the lectures of Jack, the rise of the South African working class, how unions came up; the development of capitalism in South Africa; the early strikes in the Twenties; the early unions, ICU, and then coming to the setting up of the Communist Party of South Africa itself ...

"He shows how the alliance comes about; that in fact it's not a paper alliance. It's an alliance based on the struggle itself on the ground, based on the history of the organisations; based on the common interests of the national democratic revolution. He shows that the Party has no separate agenda of its own outside the agenda of a national democratic revolution, then the Party goes to the higher stage, socialism. But Jack explains those things very, very well.

(Comrade Ntokozo)

The role of the teacher: Start from where the students are

That these memories remain so clear is in itself a testimony to the effectiveness of Comrade Jack's teaching. He did not walk into the classroom carrying some abstract vision of what his students might be like, and might know. Rather, he started from where his students were, and insisted that his trainee instructors do the same.

"Most of us had never stood in front of a big class to teach people — and worse, people who you were training with today, and then the next day you wake up and they're starting to look on you as a person to provide all the answers. That's where one really valued the approach that Jack tried to

inculcate in us: the need to approach and prepare your lectures; to try first and foremost to understand the people you are dealing with; and without making people feel bad, try to ascertain their educational level. And all the time getting them to participate before you introduce a subject in detail, so that people can feel they are beginning to discover things for themselves." (Comrade Reggie Mpongo)

"It was very very important for us that for the first time we were learning politics and of course removing all the distortions. When you are from South Africa you have a complete different picture, first of communism — that when you meet communists they are going to be people with horns and tail! There are all sorts of distortions. First we met Jack Simons, himself a communist, but of course he's a very simple person with a great sense of humour." (Comrade Ntokozo)

"To give some examples: Comrade Jack would simplify things like examples of the relationship between objective conditions and subjective factors, things that some of us had read and thought we understood. And his approach would be like: 'We are sitting here under a tree and there is the river there and the mountains there, which are the obstacles as an army if you wanted to cross the river and go over the mountains? There would be the difficulty of crossing the river, the mountains are steep, and problems of that nature. What would you then do to resolve those problems?' And people would come with ideas on how to cross that river and how to climb over the mountain, then Jack would say: 'That is the essence of understanding the difference between the objective conditions and subjective factors. Objective conditions are those things that we face in life which are not created by you; they exist on their own and in order to overcome them, you have to devise.' That simple way of explaining things made things very easy to understand for everybody, both those who had been to school and those who had not been." (Comrade Peter Mayibuye)

"Of course I must commend him in terms of his style, taking into account different levels of the comrades in terms of their formal education. Some comrades didn't have the privilege of getting even Standard VI, getting a secondary education, yet those comrades resolved to go and be part of the people's army Umkhonto weSizwe. Jack was able to develop all of us equally." (Comrade Ntokozo)

The political instructorate faced the serious task of educating 560 comrades whose education varied from illiterate to university students. This problem was very seriously addressed, leading to the eventual creation of an Adult Education Unit which operated in all the camps in Angola. Comrade Jack contrasted this with the lack of literacy teaching amongst the recruits in the 1960s, which left comrades ill-equipped to play leadership roles in the ANC or in MK. Everyone in Novo Catengue, from administrators to the trainees themselves, seems to have seen the need to overcome this problem.

"We arranged special classes for the comrades who had these problems. First we had literacy classes and I was taking part in that project, as well as teaching comrades basic mathematics and other arithmetic. Others were teaching them English, physics, chemistry — just basic stuff, so when we talk about phosphorus, say, when describing home-made explosives, a person knows what you are talking about ...

"We identified these comrades. We had their biographies and we would draw up a list. But even in class we could actually see that these comrades had a problem. And of course, when we conducted our classes as the political department, we had meetings where we'd do the planning skeleton and methodology: how to simplify the stuff; no big words. We'd actually teach the comrades, mix the language both in Zulu or Xhosa or Sotho, or simplified English so that the comrades understand it. And instead of just talking about what is a superstructure, we'd simplify it as much as possible for the comrades. When those comrades spoke from the floor in meetings, you'd never say: This comrade doesn't have a formal education when he is expressing himself. I thought the comrades had a lot of courage." (Comrade Ntokozo)

The use of mother tongue in instruction and discussion also helped to encourage the participation of less-educated comrades. The more articulate members of Comrade Jack's classes were called on to interpret what he was saying, and in informal discussions it appears that mother tongue was preferred as the medium of instruction. Comrade Precious and Comrade Thami have pointed to age as another factor contributing to widely diverse language and confidence levels. (The youngest trainee was 14; others such as Mavis Nhlapo were already at university.)

"Because of the language we used to discuss in our mother tongue. Because you find that when you are in a big group some people are shy to put it straight that I can't understand English, or I can't express myself properly in this language. So in our meetings we were free to use any language we understood best. So we used our mother tongue. It was easier for people to understand." (Comrade Precious)

Another obstacle to equal participation was the way many women had previously been socialised to be reticent and to confine themselves to "domestic" tasks.

"Women have a social background of not [participating, of being] just there to be looked at. So a lot of women did not participate effectively in political meetings. At school, they are always pushed aside. If there's anything to be done, it was always the boys who had to do all the work, and only a few selected girls. At home, they have to do the cooking — they don't have to do any studying. They are never encouraged to study; they always had to do all the home chores. So they were never really motivated to do anything constructive — not because they don't want to, but because they never had to learn to do that.

"So we needed to motivate ourselves and understand this background. OK, we are lazy to pick up books. We don't do any reading here. We sit and just chit-chat, gossip — let's do something! It's not because we can't read, but because we never learned to do that when we were still young. So we held meetings to explain our condition and get out of it. Naturally, when things happen we took deliberate decisions to say: So-and-so, you are going to do it! We were trying to discourage women from always jumping for what were traditionally women's jobs — like when there's some cooking to be done, then women volunteer. What we were saying was: Let's get them to the trenches — dig trenches! — don't volunteer to make the tea or something else! So our meetings were also about that. Then we also have problems of attitude amongst males ..." (Comrade Thami Ngwevela)

But Comrade Jack was not among these problematic males. And spurred on by his explicit commitment to non-sexism, the instructor cadre not only tried to overcome women's reticence by organising extra discussions, but also tried to find relevant materials about women's participation in other struggles.

"We developed some topics for them for discussion. Nothing incredibly systematic. I remember trying to collect books about women in various struggles so that there was that reading [available]. The commissar would meet with the women to discuss their specific problems and also to have a discussion on some specific topic. They would use examples of women in struggle and we had various books on this, but we didn't actually have a solid body of lectures that had been developed — just certain topics. We were constantly trying to come up with topics which would be interesting, particularly around literature that we could get our hands on." (Comrade Ronnie Kasrils)

Validate the experience of learners and use it as a resource

Comrade Jack did more than manage this diverse body of learners. He gave comrades confidence, by acknowledging their experience and using it as a resource in his teaching. At platoon level, he lectured from prepared notes, but did not read them verbatim. Rather, they were a guide to his input, which he signposted by writing key terms and themes on the blackboard. But immediately following his input, there was time for questions and then discussion within the class. His role was more chairperson than teacher; he corrected people only when they were losing their way, and summed up all the contributions at the end.

"Jack was a great listener. He didn't see himself as an expert; he also saw the participants as people with potentially useful ideas, and that's why at every lecture session there would be somebody taking notes." (Comrade Chris Hani)

"He'd pose the question very well and there'd be the contributions. Comrades

impressed me immensely. I could see how well this process had gone. Every one of these sessions, which would last a couple of hours in the evening, would be very positive: very good input. That's what he was able to achieve with very little input himself apart from raising a question, letting comrades then raise it and others come in at the end and sum up. [Then he'd] quote them and say: 'Well, I don't think we've covered this sufficiently. We need to do it a little more, and I think next time, so-and-so, you've got to come back and deal with that. We're going to give you 10 minutes before we get on to the topic next time, because I don't think you actually brought it out.' These comrades loved the guy, they absolutely worshipped him, respected him to the hilt."
(Comrade Ronnie Kasrils)

This approach was a radical departure from the authoritarian rote learning of Bantu Education that this generation of students had been fighting before they left the country.

"He campaigned a new approach for most of us who studied under Bantu Education, in that you as a student can also be an educator to the person who is giving instruction." (Comrade Reggie Mpongo)

This teaching method and the content of the lectures, as well as his intellectual perspective and personality, all reflected the way Comrade Jack had internalised his communist ideology and endeavoured to live it. In different ways, almost everyone interviewed for this book made the point.

"Everyone knew that Jack was a highly qualified academic, a professor for that matter, and yet here he was in the bush — in the wilderness — with everyone, and that created a sense of belonging to us. Also knowing that Mark Shope was part of the politics department — an ordinary worker — but [those two] were able to have an interaction amongst themselves. It sort of moulded our approach to dealing with other people." (Comrade Reggie Mpongo)

"He refused completely to have comrades, aides, working for him in his room; cleaning and washing. [He] completely turned them back, and that was very important for us as soldiers to know the correct revolutionary habits of not being dependent and so on. That [he could] manage and do that [raised the question]: What about us?" (Comrade Ché Ogara)

Establishing this condition of equality with the comrades he was teaching was not easy. As the only white person in the camp, among a generation of militantly black consciousness (BC) youth, the task of establishing easy communication was complex. Many of the trainees of the June 16 Detachment have commented on how his presence and attitude challenged their commitment to BC values. In the early stages, many of the more radical trainees would interrogate Comrade Jack about what he thought he was doing as the only white man in the camp. Some of these critics became admirers and close personal friends.

"Despite the fact that he was a professor, a great revolutionary and so on, he had that intimacy; he used to create that close atmosphere between him and his students where comrades could be completely free and open to ask — to confront him — and he was accessible to them." (Comrade Ché Ogara)

"Jack has got the working class language, down-to-earth way of life ... that's why he is understood by the people. Whether you were educated or not, you will understand Jack. He's got time, you know he is very patient. He can answer any question. It doesn't matter how nonsensical the question is, he will answer it by way of trying to educate you. That's how Jack is."
(Comrade Mark Shope)

For the committed educator, of course, there is no such thing as a stupid question. Comrade Jack welcomed all debates and inquiries — even those that might undermine his own position. Raymond Suttner was one of his students in Cape Town. Although he is now a socialist activist, he was then a liberal and was not aware that his professor was a communist. But he was impressed by Comrade Jack's teaching, and was later able to put it in a political context.

"What I learned was he really spent his whole life as a communist and as an academic. He taught me that when you deal with people's work, if you are a socialist, you really have got to take it seriously as a process of helping to build other people, even if they are going to develop in a way that becomes critical of yourself. I am critical of quite a lot of Jack's work now, but he wasn't threatened by it. He saw it as part of his duty even if the consequences were to expose some of his thoughts as erroneous."

This openness relates to another of the ways in which Comrade Jack developed effective learning and teaching; his creation of a democratic classroom climate.

Build democracy in the classroom
Although Comrade Jack was a strong disciplinarian — he insisted on regular attendance at classes, and that participants carry out the work assigned — he used discipline as a supporting framework for the tasks, not a weapon against the learners.

"The comrades, some of them, would be a little bit tense in Jack's presence. He'd come with very sharp questions, and that's where the tension would creep in. Of course, he couldn't abide it if the comrades had not prepared, or if [someone] was just reading notes from the book. So that little bit of tension would arise if the comrade clearly hadn't done the work, because Jack wouldn't

abide that. But he would always be very patient, not looking at the individual, usually eyes shut or looking down, concentrating like mad, this old man whom everybody respected." (Comrade Ronnie Kasrils)

"He has seen that his duty is to introduce the subject to us, and it's for us to find a way of adapting and explaining it to the broader community. One of his first methods would be to introduce a subject and then ask you to go and make your own research. Then the following class you present to the collective and the collective will make observations, criticise it, anything of what you have done. Then at the end his role would be to sum up and show shortcomings, and what have I done, and so forth." (Comrade Reggie Mpongo)

Classroom democracy extended as far as encouraging learners to be critical and push beyond a shallow understanding of received wisdom.

"I think Jack had that independence of approach which helped him to go much deeper into a problem than many other people. You would find Jack saying that it is not guaranteed that when the Freedom Charter is implemented you would have introduced such fundamental restructuring of South African society that you would have advanced — as some people would say — to some form of socialist orientation, creating the foundation for socialism. There is the possibility, even with the introduction of the Freedom Charter, that [you] would have a welfare state, capitalist in essence and everything else.

"He even challenged some of the things that he would find in material written by our own people, to help people think more. This would relate, for example, to what we were talking about of objective conditions and subjective factors. That objectively the Freedom Charter, for example, can create the basis for even better advance, but that it's not guaranteed: it depends on the subjective elements that are introduced, the manner in which power is transferred and the kind of forces within the liberation alliance, and so on ... I think it was that breadth and depth in his approach that helped people to think much more deeply about issues and problems ...

"His approach was to encourage people to be independent. He would encourage people to start but would want people to study so that they are able to deal with any problem without having to refer to books. And this independence went much further than simply understanding Marxism/Leninism as it exists, he would deliberately help people to think, even challenge some of the postulates that were found in the books. He would expect people to defend why they think what is found in the books is correct on any particular issue. He'd encourage you to talk about political economy, history and philosophy and everything else and periods when constitutional guidelines were being worked out and many other issues." (Comrade Peter Mayibuye)

"He made us understand political economy and was one of the people who,

when he spoke of the Soviet Union, was very critical, unlike most of us. I mean, that was the line. We didn't see anything wrong in it. But Jack was always critical in his approach. Most of the time, he spoke of some of his experiences in the Forties and this, in later years, began to make more sense. Then, it didn't make much sense to us. To us, everything was: If they support us, then they are the best people in the world." (Comrade Reggie Mpongo)

Although the lectures that Comrade Jack gave on Marxist theory relied strongly on the classic texts and on concrete examples of how these socialist countries had addressed certain questions, his approach makes them useful even in a later historical period.

"I think Jack has never been rigid. Jack has always been a debater. And I think that approach helped us in our preparations to face the problems that have arisen today in the international communist movement. And I think that sort of undogmatic approach has helped us to understand the need for the creation of fronts in the struggle against apartheid. Jack was a keen analyser of the politics of the whites and of strategies that were necessary to win over some sections of the white population ..." (Comrade Chris Hani)

In the context of a military camp, this democratic, collective and iconoclastic approach created an interesting dynamic.

"This also created its own problems. The structure of any army, its autocratic nature [mean that] concepts of democracy and all that are not part and parcel of it. In the army, it's one-man command. This created its own contradictions or conflicts within individuals, because the method he used was not a method applicable to other military subjects that were taking place." (Comrade Reggie Mpongo)

This method was, however, highly applicable to the tasks guerrillas would be faced with when they returned to South Africa and had to conscientise communities. And these provocative points, raised not as the diktats of a professor, but by a fellow intellectual in debate, were vital to another of the cornerstones of Comrade Jack's method: that learning must be active.

Involve learners actively in their own education

"The object of a class is to get students to study, and not to give the teacher an opportunity to exhibit his wisdom and eloquence. The students, not the teacher, should do most of the talking." (Comrade Jack's own preface to the draft Primer 1984. Reprinted in full on p53)

Activity was the keynote of Comrade Jack's classes, and if his students sometimes found it stressful, they also appreciated the capabilities it gave them.

"What Jack did was to devise his programmes in a highly active way. I learned a lot from this when I came down to Novo Catengue, in terms of what I had tried to do [at Quibaxe] not coming from an academic background and not having been used to, say, university systems and the like. On the one hand there was this core of instructors who were being developed who were having these seminars — up to about a score of them — and this was the key thing taking place. This is where Jack would be concentrating his key effort to develop them further. So they would be meeting virtually every evening and he would be putting them through their paces very rigorously: [turning] young militants into these very self-confident instructors and individuals who were very into theory and were beginning to grasp it in a creative way, not just parrot-fashion, not just by rote."
(Comrade Ronnie Kasrils)

"Jack would prepare these lectures and distribute them and he would call on any one of us to lead the discussions. So it was not a question of Jack coming as a lecturer in a lecture theatre and saying: 'This is what happened.' He would actually give us time to read and also lead the discussions. After that he would stimulate discussion. He would sit there, and we would debate amongst ourselves. In other words, after somebody made his presentation, he would ask questions, he would contribute, would contest ... He was stimulating participation by all of us in the discussions. And he would intervene now and again if he felt we were not coming out with the proper perspectives ..."
(Comrade Chris Hani)

Ground learning in students' own experience and practice

Comrade Jack made sure that every comrade was able to participate in this active learning by making sure that discussion was practical and concrete, and related to the learners' own current problems and questions.

"His aim was, on the basis of what they had learned, to utilise this for our struggle. How do you relate what you've learned at the Lenin School in Moscow to South Africa? So you've learned the labour theory of value, etc? How do you apply this to the mineworkers? We had come to understand that over the years we'd got comrades going abroad and studying — say at the Lenin School — and actually having difficulty in applying what they'd learned in a creative way to our situation. So he was setting his mind to this and doing it in a creative manner ... shooting out questions and saying: 'But how do you relate that? All very well, comrade, you're talking about the development from slavery to feudalism — what happened in South Africa? How do you relate that to South Africa?' And they have to bloody well think!" (Comrade Ronnie Kasrils)

"Those who were at university or in high schools tended to immerse themselves in Marxist literature or any other literature about the history of the ANC that

they could lay their hands on. This created a problem that we became aware of later when we came across a person like Jack. To give an example: in Luanda there were books like 'A Critique of the Gotha Programme' that we read and thought we understood. But later Jack started giving lectures and simplifying things and we realised that in most cases we were imbibing complicated things that we didn't really understand.

"Comrade Jack's approach was completely different. He had a capacity to simplify things to become clear even to people who had not gone to school. And in a way that would expose even to those who had tried to read some of the books, how unskilled their reading had been." (Comrade Peter Mayibuye)

"We were actually embroiled in serious discussions about the way forward, how to build our organisation, the underground organisation. Was it not possible to make use of the Bantustans, for instance, in building the organisation and using whatever space possible? This was a period where the trade unions were really also destroyed and we were beginning to discuss how to revive [them]; how to build a powerful youth movement making use of the black consciousness movement. Jack was channelling us towards the discussion of these vital aspects of strategy. In other words Jack was not only up-front as an academic in his lectures. His lectures were actually dealing with vital aspects of strategy at a time when the organisation, all the components of the liberation movement, had actually been destroyed" (Comrade Chris Hani)

"Comrade Jack with his syllabus brought about a revolution in the approach to teaching politics to our subordinates, the soldiers, and to all levels in the camp … Comrade Jack had the exceptional ability of really relating this political education and making it accessible to the comrades. He had a talent in simplifying and making sense of these basic concepts. I found that remarkable. The way he would relate to all of us at all levels, the patience he had, and the ability to cope and explain to comrades in a manner that all these terms really had meaning. Comrades could relate them to our day-to-day life; they could relate them to actual situations happening inside the country and internationally. All the time before he came, there was so much bookish [learning] amongst us. Some comrades actually developed attitude, playing with bombastic terms. But Comrade Jack was able to discern that." (Comrade Ché Ogara)

"With our work with Jack we were able to interpret Marxism. We were able to read Marxism on our own. Before we had come across it, but you don't have a method how to go through it. Through Jack's assistance we were able to read the Marxist books systematically. For instance, at one time we had a series on works, 'What is to be Done', 'The State and Revolution', 'Left-wing Communism: An Infantile Disorder'. All those books, we were able to study them and interpret those works in terms of our situation. This is what Jack taught us abut politics really, practically — that you can learn this but you must *be able to use it as a tool. Then we were able to get propagandists and organisers from among the comrades, were able to get agitators and political instructors."* (Comrade Ntokozo)

Build up resources for learners, but teach flexibly, whatever the resources

Although he had an effective bombast detector, Comrade Jack did not scorn reading and research well done. Indeed, he fought, cajoled and persuaded to obtain texts for his learners and encouraged them to use these texts. But he developed a teaching method that could work without extensive libraries. And even where the texts were available, they were to be used to spark creative thinking, not substitute for it.

"It was difficult for comrades who'd been away, hadn't had much access to our reading. He put them through the reading. Mzwai Piliso was fantastic in organising people everywhere to contribute books. There were a lot of Jack's own books in that library and Mzwai would bring books from South Africa, from Britain and from wherever our people were." (Comrade Ronnie Kasrils)

"Jack as an academic was not one who would use minimal resources. One of the criticisms he made of me at one point was I quoted someone who quoted something else. Why didn't I get to the 'something else' myself, even if it was correct? He was very careful about giving original sources. Both Jack and Ray, when I was in Zambia in 1968, asked me to send this and get that; bring this up and get that up.

"But I think that whatever Jack dealt with, he obviously approached with a broad perspective that would suffice on its own if he didn't have other resources. In other words, if the sources were at his disposal, he would use these broad insights to deal with the raw data, but in the camp situation, the overall methodology was probably what he wanted to convey most of all. You see, I think from what I've seen of his lecture notes, one of the problems one has in understanding our own history is to sort out this maze of wars, make sense of them, what they mean. Jack's got this skill in sorting out, in generalising about things. For that reason in some ways lack of access was not a serious problem because the main thing with all these frontier wars is for people to understand them as a whole and draw the lessons perhaps from specific ones. What comes out from what I've seen of Jack's account is always an attempt to create a specific resistance over a very long period — but that it takes different forms ..." (Comrade Raymond Suttner)

"What's interesting [in Simons' bibliographical suggestions for the lectures] is that in addition to the straight texts that would have been freely available — I see Darwin is included here — and also 'Time Longer Than Rope'. And of course that's Eddie Roux' book which was very critical of the Communist Party — very vivid — a very vivacious kind of a book and that again would have

been consistent with Jack's approach.

But again, Jack was very much against the idea of learning a text off by heart. The text, you would read and study to know what people were thinking and saying, but then you had to put the book down and argue the idea as an idea. He constantly brought in African reality — social reality — in relation to anything. If you were dealing with class and class struggle, he would speak about class in African society and class formation and class structure. So these works would be the formal texts. What was as interesting would be the text of life; of life experience." (Comrade Albie Sachs)

Test ability, not rote learning

Comrade Jack extended this unconventional approach to the examinations he was required to set. Candidates were allowed to prepare answers and to answer in speech, in the language in which they were most fluent. And the results were used to evaluate instructors' teaching, as well as candidates' learning.

In 1977 examinations were held in Novo Catengue:
"The Cubans who monitored Novo Catengue wanted an evaluation of performance of MK cadres to complete their reports to the Central Command. I decided to set a written examination, with measures to enable students unable to write English or their own African language. Those who 'passed' might have had an advantage, but political education took up only 60 hours of instruction out of a total of 200 hours per term of three months and probably had only a slight effect on the final rating. I adopted the practice used in the University of Zambia, Lusaka (where I headed the Department of Social Science and Social Welfare) of giving candidates an idea in advance of the examination questions. Multiple choice questions were for brief essays." (Comrade Jack Simons' written replies to questions, October 10 1991)

The process of examinations was a novel experience for both the examiners and the trainees.

"You see it was really something different and new from what we were used to in South Africa — the examination, the manner in which it was organised. It was not this formal writing exam, we never did exams in writing. Questions would be prepared in advance, all the questions and then they would be circulated to the detachment. We had special time of a month or so before the actual exams where every soldier would sit down every afternoon and evening, to revise those questions. It may be 15 questions on politics, broken up into international politics, national politics, Marxism. Then in the exam room, the comrade would choose from that or questions would be picked up from any one, maybe one from each sub-topic. Then comrades could express themselves in the best possible language." (Comrade Ché Ogara)

Comrade Ché had the benefit of both sitting for the exam and being part of the assessment of comrades taking the exam and reflecting on the results.

"... Firstly it was the assessment in a panel when the comrades sit down for an examination. There are a panel of three comrades, two or three, the commissar, the instructor, maybe Comrade Jack or Comrade Mark Shope. Comrades would make their presentation and after that we would make an assessment by allocating points, three up to five, five plus was excellent and so on. And then we would discuss. After the comrade's contribution we would take into account the education level of the comrades — that was very important — and generally the participation of the comrades in past lectures and so on. It was very important to assess the comrade from the time he or she began the lectures, the level at that stage, and then we would allocate marks. Sometimes we would find that the comrade who is educated and very eloquent, answers the same question as a comrade who when they started the course had never been to school. Sometimes you'd find that those comrades get a better mark than those (who were better educated).

"After that, a panel was formed to look into the question of posts, the assessment generally of the syllabus and all the facilities, the books, all factors related to the process of political education. We made our assessment on the need to improve. There were a number of defects in the programme. The special emphasis on national politics that comrades were lectured on, that had to be improved, for instance. There were general recommendations also on how to improve this training." (Comrade Ché Ogara)

(The text of the examinations of August and November 1977 are available and are included on Page 209)

Train the trainers

Every approach that Comrade Jack used, he also tried to inculcate in the instructors he was training. Again, his method was active, participatory — and highly demanding.

"We had our own special political course, to be upgraded in politics. We had our own short course, which Jack was involved in [as] the main instructor ... But unfortunately that group could not take its full course. Jack, as I explained, was a very strong disciplinarian and got angry when people didn't attend the classes. He felt they should be cancelled; that it should not continue. Those of us who were very interested in it suffered because of that. But then we'd also go to Jack's place, if he was not too occupied. [We'd] go to his room and raise a number of issues. Then he would advise us, give us direction and even recommend what books to read." (Comrade Meshengu, former military instructor)

"Jack made great use of the evenings and he would give different individuals

time off in order to build a core of instructors. I think that, apart from his general teaching, it was probably the greatest achievement there, and certainly something that I didn't do in the four months that I instructed at Quibaxe ... In teaching the political instructorate, Comrade Jack insisted that the instructors themselves prepare the input, reserving for himself the role of facilitator or chairperson. The topic would have been stated, people would have had to prepare and someone would be allocated to lead off. And we would gather there after dinner, in the dimly lit library which we had developed."
(Comrade Ronnie Kasrils)

Because Comrade Jack was training two corps of instructors — military and political — he made use of these two groups as a resource for one another. He used essentially the same method with military as with political instructors, but drew on the developing body of political instructors as coaches.

"He would give us topics on a particular issue individually. Then we'd go and prepare with the help of other instructors, including the politics instructors, because already we were aware of the method Comrade Jack used. Then you would have to come and present your report. After presenting the report, if there were any additions that have to be made from the floor [people would] criticise and then come to general discussion. So everybody made his contribution on how he understands a particular problem, the concepts and so on ... After that, then Jack would summarise and another comrade would be given a topic for the next time we met." (Comrade Meshengu)

Comrade Jack commented in discussion on the use of the term "comrade" when referring to MK students.

Reflecting his view of these people as his co-trainers, right from the start of their education, he said:
"Cadre is a military term of French origin, meaning squire. We should use it instead of comrade when referring to MK students."
(Author's discussion with Comrade Jack, October 1991)

"I could see how he had managed something which I didn't, this development of this pool of instructors. During the day they would give the lectures and we'd have something like say eight, nine classes going. We'd have about eight or nine of these young guys giving instruction. I would sit in with Jack to see how they were carrying out the tasks. Part of the group that were developed in this way weren't just the instructors but also commissars of different companies and platoons. They were also putting their platoons through discussions outside of the classes but of a different kind. You've got a formal programme in a class giving South African history or basics of Marxism, right? But at the level of the platoons, platoon discussions, let's say three times a

week or so, they're discussing latest events in South Africa or internationally and the commissar's handling that. So the commissar is now having to think on his or her feet and apply what's been studied in the class and what that commissar himself or herself is learning. And they acquitted themselves so well." (Comrade Ronnie Kasrils)

The legacy of Comrade Jack's teaching

Apart from this formal instruction, both at platoon level and in the special classes, Simons stimulated extensive informal discussion on whatever topic comrades were engaged by. He was also consulted by many of those tasked with preparing inputs for cultural evenings or political meetings as part of camp life.

Although he denied any responsibility for the setting up of literacy and adult basic education, it is clear that his ability to simplify material without dumbing it down was an influential approach which complemented the literacy teaching, and helped to overcome widely divergent levels of education and political understanding. This contribution was vital, because MK had experienced enormous difficulty in recruiting teachers interested in going into exile to teach adult basic education.

The Adult Education Unit grew out of Novo Catengue and it was only later that the comrade in charge of it, Mampi, received any formal training in literacy teaching.

"[Mampi] was the head of adult education in all our camps, not only at Novo Catengue. He started classes in Novo Catengue. When we thought he knew what he was doing, then we had adult education in other camps, which he did at a certain stage. We then sent him to the Soviet Union to do pedagogy ..."
(Comrade Mzwayi Piliso)

Ronnie Kasrils reflects on the spread and influence of Comrade Jack's activities:
"What I found with Jack in coming to Novo Catengue was a) that there was a very high level of understanding of basic Marxism and b) that he had created a core of instructors from the June 16 group in a very short period of time, and that was incredibly impressive ... But there was a lot of other activity taking place in terms of discussion groups and seminars at the level of the platoons or the company around key political questions. And then there was a third level of comrades with educational problems, literacy problems, who were going through a very basic reinforcing of what they had learned, and explanations were being given in a very clear and simple way.

"So I immediately called this place The University of the South because so much was happening in the sphere of political study."

"I'll tell you what my feeling is about the advantage that people who went through Comrade Jack's hands had. For instance there's a comrade here, Comrade Eddie Mabitse — we left the country together. We were in Lesotho together but it so happened he left at the beginning of '78. He then went to Catengue and he had the exposure, politically, of going through the hands of

Comrade Jack and Comrade Mark Shope. He had that kind of advantage.

"And for a very long time I could feel it, I mean we have been colleagues for a very long time. We got initiated into politics together, we were together at school and we shared a desk from Form One to Form Five. So in terms of our wavelength politically, we are almost at the same, our understanding, our depth of politics. But I must say that for a very long time after I arrived in Angola, in our exchanges I realised that even through a personal effort of self study, there was no way that I was going to raise to that kind of level that he was. When you talked to people who have gone through political education in Catengue, you always had this feeling that they had a proper understanding of politics, that you really envied, and which we could not unfortunately get from the instructorate that was available after he left. There was no way. To this day I still regret not having been in that first generation because I know that there are certain political subjects and issues that they would handle with ease; they don't struggle and they're not so abstract that you can't understand them; things were simplified to them; they had a very profound tutor.

"They could easily relate the Marxist classics to the South African situation. The way they come across in handling of Marxist concepts, it would be only if you have actually yourself read the classics in their raw form that you'd understand what they are saying in the context of the South African situation, actually came from the classics as this and that concept. I'm saying it sounds very original.

"They related to me some of the exchanges that used to take place during Comrade Jack's lectures, coming from these previously illiterate comrades. Even from those comrades who were not at school when they left here, who were part of lumpen proletarian youth, you could see that they were people who had a certain level of understanding regardless of the fact that they were not educationally advanced ...

"On the whole, those who left for Party school ... having gone through Comrade Jack's hands, were obviously ahead of everyone else. They were quite advanced, to an extent that, for instance the group that was sent to the GDR, in 1980, and supposed to be on a 10-month course, ended up spending only five months away and then they were told by the academy that they had to come back. The academy said send people who would benefit from the course, these guys are just wasting resources, they know everything. That was Jack Simons' group." (Comrade Thabang)

It seems that it was the capacity-building element of Comrade Jack's work that was the hardest to replicate after he left.

"He was passing on these skills to some trainees so they could train others. I think everybody has come to accept that after his departure, though these people were trained by him and continued using his methodology, there was a certain depth below which they couldn't go, which I think belonged to Jack

both as a person and as an experienced researcher, thinker and everything else. So although he passed on that information, he was not able to help it remain within the MK pool when he left the camp ... It was not very easy then to go and instruct after that experience. One would do one's own studies and use notes from Jack's lectures and then come and try to explain. But you'd find that the explanations are not always sufficient, not always convincing, as a learner who was trying to teach others, you'd find it difficult to engage the class in the same way that Jack did. So I think it was not possible to transfer that quality completely to all the individuals." (Comrade Peter Mayibuye)

Other comrades concur with Comrade Peter Mayibuye's point and believe that this process resulted in a decrease in the quality of political instruction once Comrade Jack had left the camps.

"When you look at that group of people afterwards, those people in the June 16 and Moncada detachments, after he had left the camp there seemed to have been a failure to develop continuity of cadreship. If you look, the movement more or less up to now still relies on that group of people who had worked with Jack. Afterwards there was never an attempt to give those people a chance to reproduce themselves either; if they were taken out of the camp for other tasks, a vacuum existed ... In 1982/83, just shortly before the mutiny, in our view, there was poor political education in the camp, so that some of the cadres coming into the country were failing to grasp the political process as it unfolded. At times they failed to adjust to working with various people — you know, 'I'm from exile, I know it all' — and those type of things. Some of the failures which we can trace now were due to political weaknesses and when you raise the issues, the response would be: Let's get the people who were once in the camps at the time of Jack to go back and assist. And naturally there was resistance because there's a danger of developing the mentality that they are indispensible, while they are asking: Why in this interim period was there never an effort to reproduce political cadres, instructors, etc?" (Comrade Reggie Mpongo)

These comments come from comrades who were part of the June 16 Detachment. A comrade who left the country with these comrades, but was delayed on the way, only getting to Angola when Quibaxe was being opened up as a camp, feels that he missed out on an invaluable experience by not studying under Comrade Jack.

"I would actually agree with Peter's observation about the gradual decline in the standard of political education in the camp as one generation of political instructors was replaced by another. When we arrived in 1978, our political education was handled by people who were prepared by Comrade Jack. And I think on the whole they performed fairly well, although obviously they couldn't be the man himself. And of course a lot of them were really still being introduced to politics and had to mature with time. But you could see that

people were really working hard to impress and to actually show depth of understanding in their lectures.

"The simple way in which matter was being put to them, and where certain things were very contextualised — I think that was lacking with the generations that came after. It was maybe the lack of this profound understanding which led to their inability to simplify the material. Then you have people just reading, getting these Marxist teachings but unable to actually contextualise them or even to use those concepts for analysis. A person can know about and lecture on what dialectical materialism is because he has read it from the book and the instructor has helped him read it. He can discuss and argue what is written in the book in terms of his understanding. But he can't necessarily use that instrument in real interpretation of things. And as a result, the generations that followed, in terms of their Marxist understanding, tended to become too abstract." (Comrade Thabang)

Thabang gives us an insight into the practical teaching process and resources that were used in Quibaxe and other camps:

"We didn't have the lectures themselves made available to the trainees. The politics department had these lectures and they would be the property of the politics department. It is only when one got drawn into the commissariat and the politics department that you then got exposure to the lectures. If you don't have them in the camp you can check with the regional commissariat in Luanda or you can check with the politics department in other camps and try to rebuild that collection. But what I'm saying is that these were only the property of the instructorate. They used these lectures in their preparation for their classes, together with the material that was available in the camp's library.

"The lectures were handled on the basis of instruction. A person would come into class, say the theme of the day is this and after explaining what the theme is about, then go into the details, and sort of lecture. From there, there would be a question session when people could respond to things that were said by questioning or by making their own contributions. That's how the classes were handled with us.

"It differs from one individual to another. Some comrades were known to have been very good. With others you'd sit in his class and you could feel that he knows the matter but he's struggling in terms of putting it across. For the instructor to be able to simplify things he must also understand the stuff. When the instructor is not profound in his understanding that also tends to lead to unhealthy attitudes. If he doesn't have the patience or he doesn't appreciate what his responsibility is, he might actually take offense at times. The person would be, let's say, a matriculant or would have done his Form 3, and would be helping somebody who'd done Standard 6 to understand something very basic. That kind of a person, he's not an educationist."

Comrade Chris Hani has provided an overall reflection on political instruction from 1977 onwards:

"The political education work which took place subsequently in Angola came at a time when I was no longer in Zambia, nor in Angola; I was in Lesotho. But I would see it as a continuation of the work he had begun in Lusaka (in 1969). I think the greatest contribution by Jack lay in the fact that he was dealing now with real raw material from inside the country. The young comrades who had just joined the movement and read the tradition of the Black Consciousness Movement, and some of them had no political tradition at all except anger and bitterness from the traumatic experience of the Soweto uprising.

"So Jack actually laid the political foundation stone for the comrades who rose to become leading and outstanding commanders and commissars of Umkhonto weSizwe. I would think that those lectures served to strengthen the comrades who were at the centre of rebuilding the army in the Seventies and Eighties. And I think if there was this outstanding achievement in commissariat work, Jack made a singularly important and central contribution. Not only for the comrades who got political lectures during this period in Angola and other places, I think basically our orientation, especially as a Communist Party, had been unquestioning loyalty to the Soviet Union and the Communist Party of the Soviet Union ... I think that unquestioning loyalty blinded our creative political initiative. We did not question certain things, the methods used in the implementation of socialism in the Soviet Union, especially the post-Lenin period and onwards. We simply absorbed what they told us and followed a position which has now become really dangerous. With most of our people who went to Soviet political schools, Party schools, both ANC and the Party, there was, I think, a failure to objectively apply the theory of Marxism-Leninism to our own situation. We felt that there was a perfect model that could not be improved on or criticised — and all along we were guided by this approach. When the Soviet Union intervened in Czechoslovakia, we went out of our way to justify that intervention. We felt it was in the interests of socialism. I can't remember until very late our Party questioning a single action of the Soviet Union. We took for granted that the one-party state was correct and we felt that the means justified the end. And I think this was a basic weakness and I think we're trying now to overcome those weaknesses, thanks to what has been happening in the Soviet Union.

"But what is happening in the Soviet Union is dangerous in the sense that demagogues like Yeltsin want to throw the baby out with the bathwater and are actually saying that the whole period of socialism was negative. And that's not true. The Soviet Union was a backyard country when the revolution triumphed. There has been a lot of achievement in education, in social welfare, in scientific achievement and generally I think we all agree that tremendous strides have been made, but again we accept that serious mistakes were made. And if all of us communists from different countries had been critical of these mistakes at the very beginning, I think socialism would not have been faced with the sort of

volatile problems that it is facing today." (Comrade Chris Hani)

Some comrades who had studied with Comrade Jack were asked how they perceived their political training in the light of developments in Eastern Europe and the Soviet Union. Comrade Thabang commented on the fact that there were comrades who, at the end of their basic training, were sent to the Soviet Union and GDR for further political training, and returned to play a political instruction role within the camps. What effect did this have on the level of political instruction?

"Political instructors were creamed off from this group that were sent to Party schools or people would be taken from political departments for further political upgrading. In a way it did help to improve the level of quite a number of instructors we had. But at the same time, people can tend to have the impression that political education and then Party school does magic to people — and it's not true. Maybe people have different experiences, but from what I've seen, those who actually benefit from Party school and who come back much more advanced, are the people who were quite impressive in their level of understanding before they left. They were able then to actually benefit from this exposure. Before, what has happened in certain instances is that we have had comrades who have gone to Party school but who came back almost the same. Perhaps it wasn't easy for them to grapple with what they were given or perhaps they as individuals did not make an effort to read. For a person to be dynamic he's got to be a person who's himself an active reader, an avid reader. You don't just become dynamic from what you are taught in class. People who impress are those who always make an extra effort to do their own self-study, because that's the only way that one actually gets more ideas, more knowledge: by reading. But if you're just going to Party school and then you sit in the lecture hall, and you're given a long lecture about how Engels ended up writing Anti-Duhring and what-have-you, it's going to be difficult even to understand what's being said.

"One cannot be absolute because of course some comrades who come from the Party school are able to explain things much better than people who have not had this exposure, in a quite impressive way. They would enlighten a lot of us. But at the same time I would still say that it would always be with limitations if a person hadn't previously had a very sound grounding in class politics and in understanding the South African situation in that context of that politics [such as those who had passed through Comrade Jack's hands]."
(Comrade Thabang)

And although the point was not made explicitly by anyone interviewed, there was an implicit contrast between the active, democratic, critical and participatory methods used by Comrade Jack and the more structured, formal training of the Soviet experience. Comrade Thabang spoke of "sitting in a lecture hall, listening" and Comrade Thami Ngwevela expanded on this point, contrasting her training in the Soviet Union with her experiences in Novo Catengue with Comrade Jack:

> "I don't think there was any particular conflict with the way it was done in the Soviet Union, but it's a different country, they use different methods of teaching. The first point is that we were using translation in the Soviet Union and we also were taking different subjects at a much wider level than we dealt with in the camps. In the camps we were dealing with Marxism and Leninism as it applied to the South African situation and in the Soviet Union it was Marxism-Leninism linked up a lot with the history of the Soviet Union itself, the rest of Europe, and I think the influence of the theory in the rest of the world, to the third world, Latin America, North America and so on. You learnt, for example, the history of the world communist movement, the various communist parties, the history of the Soviet Union itself. We also did political economy of capitalism and socialism, philosophy, the theory of human evolution, debate on the conflict of human sciences with religion or political sciences with a religious understanding of the world. We also did a short course on public communication, like how to speak on the radio ... And a lot of these things, they used to illustrate by going to museums, going around the country to see monumental places and pictures, through cinemas and slides."
>
> (Comrade Thami Ngwevela)

The strength of Comrade Jack's approach seems to have been in the development of an independent, active, analytical ability which stayed with his students for the rest of their lives. His emphasis as a teacher was as much on learning process as on informational content. When he left — and for trainees sent to other institutions abroad — the focus seems to have switched back to content; to "covering" certain areas.

For political educators today, the lesson is clear. No matter what is taught, it is the "how" which determines effectiveness. As Comrade Jack himself wrote: "The students, not the teacher, should do most of the talking."

3

'Make the People our Forests and Caves': Reflections, documents and debates on political education, 1969–2000

At the time of the 1969 lectures, the ANC's strategic debate revolved around the relationship between internal and external work, and around what factors would ultimately determine social change. Nearly a decade later, the debate had changed. At the time Comrade Jack's lectures were used in Novo Catengue, the ongoing debate in the camp between Cubans and South Africans was about the balance between political and military instruction, reflecting different understandings of the strategy and tactics appropriate for the South African revolution.

These were two historical phases of a debate which is still going on; now, about how to build political awareness in the post-1990 younger generation, many of whom have only the faintest memories (or none at all) of the repression and resistance which brought the ANC into existence.

This chapter lets Comrade Jack's "graduates" speak about those debates, and about how their educational experience at his hands shaped their perspectives.

"The document on Strategy and Tactics adopted at the Morogoro Conference discussed at length the relationship between the political and military struggles, emphasising the primacy of the former.

"You can't have an army that is ignorant. [It must be] political, in depth. I used to say to young people: when you have an AK and they are shooting, using the AK must be a political decision. The first bullet that comes out of that gun is a political bullet. You must know that as the ANC we are not fighting against white people but against the system. Our bullets must not go into people who have

nothing to do with the system." (Comrade Mzwai Piliso)

At Novo Catengue, the camp instructorate was divided into two sections, political and military. The programme allocated different amounts of time to the two sections although, as Peter Mayibuye notes, sometimes the boundaries were blurred.

> *"When we talk about tactics — one of the most central aspects of military instruction — we're talking about how to master the terrain, form battle groups, how to position people for combat, organise marches, place sentries, use moving and stationary columns and so on.*
> *"But political instruction was given as much, if not more emphasis. In addition to formal classes you'd have a review of the news in the morning, a session analysing the news in the evening, plus special instruction for people who were to become instructors and occasional seminars on particular topics in which a whole company – even two companies – would participate. Then you would have news analysis sessions within platoons maybe once or twice a week. So in terms of emphasis, political instruction was the most important. What made MK different from other liberation armies was that understanding that the person behind the gun is more important than the gun itself. And this shaped the unique strategic approach of the movement as much as formal consideration of military tactics."* (Comrade Peter Mayibuye)

This approach meant that even military instructors had to deal with political issues in their classes, so that no false divisions between subject matter developed.

> *"Usually we were just military instructors who had gone for specialist training. The little politics that we managed to get was about the ANC — that we were introduced to briefly when we left the country — and international politics, which we were introduced to in the Soviet Union. Consequently, our training wasn't very political. It was people like Jack Simons who strengthened us and helped to upgrade our political level. There were several departments, artillery, politics and tactics, firearms. We were in the same unit as Comrade Jack, with him representing the Political Department, and we used to gather to work out common approaches. Because it happened that while we were teaching military topics, questions were posed by our classes that we needed to be able to answer at the same level as the political instructors. Those meetings were to develop such a common approach."* (Comrade Mshengu)

In Comrade Jack's diary, there are repeated references to the Cubans feeling that MK soldiers should be trained militarily and then sent back into the country; that the extensive political education was incorrect. Simons felt that there was some validity in their view, in that more emphasis should have been placed on rapidly equipping comrades to return to South Africa. But he felt that this rapid process should include both military and political training.

As for the MK graduates themselves — whether military or political — they seem to have felt that the ANC's politico-military strategy was correct and that the balanced training they received at Novo Catengue had been most appropriate.

> "Even in the military, we had those differences with our Cuban comrades. They wanted quick training, and then the whole batch should be sent away and another batch [trained].
>
> "Their main emphasis was also on guerrilla warfare. This came from not understanding our struggle. At times, sitting together as military instructors, informally discussing these matters, they would say: 'I don't know what your population is, but you are more than 30 million. And you are oppressed by so few people. How is it possible when we went with our [small force] and won our revolution that way. What is the situation?' Even with the bombing, the Cubans could not believe that the SADF had the capacity to fly from those bases of theirs in Namibia right up to where we were. I remember the major who was there, the Camp Commander, who used to be based inside the camp. Luckily, when the bombing happened, he went outside the boundary. You see, even a senior person like that couldn't believe it. Even militarily, they were not aware of how strong South Africa was.
>
> "So in politics, there used to be a problem when it came to the allocation of hours to the Political Department. The Cubans felt politics should only get two hours, with tactics, firearms and so on allocated six hours or more. That used to be a very serious argument, but gradually, the Political Department, with the help of the commissar, explained it to them. And as time went on they were able to understand.
>
> "Some of the people they brought were not even really military men. Some were militia, not proper military. But later another batch was brought: colonels, majors, lieutenants, who were serious military men. They could sit down and discuss business, and we were able to sit down with them in a comradely spirit and iron things out so they understood." (Comrade Mshengu)

> "There was a kind of strain in the understanding, partly because I think they were basing themselves on their own experience in Cuba and on all the struggles in Latin America they were assisting. Most important to them was training people to be good guerrilla fighters, good in the kind of fighting that hinged on the [Red Base] approach of establishing ourselves in the bush and try to expand continuously on some small liberated explicit areas. That approach wasn't necessarily, but it was implied, in their approach.
>
> "And of course this conflicted with the approach that people like Comrade Jack adopted, and generally with the way our people saw ourselves operating when we came back. Looking back, the ANC approach was correct — although the existence of this generally correct theoretical approach doesn't mean that it was consistently reflected when people were deployed ... Over some years we adopted an approach of simply deploying people to carry out an operation and that would be a victory in itself. Hitting a police station: that would be a victory irrespective of what mobilisation was linked to it, whether long-term survival had been considered, or whether it contributed overall to building an underground structure that combined all aspects, not just military things.

"Emphases changed. Some kind of parallel approach grew up: creating political underground structures here and military underground structures there, which became problematic in time. So those operating in underground political structures would reach a level where they'd say: OK, we understand the politics; we have to distribute leaflets. But the enemy needs to be confronted. Meanwhile those operating in military structures would be saying: OK, we understand how we operate, but how is this linked to the process of liberation; how is it linked to activities of the masses? And out of that experience, the emphasis would change and ultimately people came to understand the need for what we called an integrated approach." (Comrade Peter Mayibuye)

The late Chris Hani, former MK Chief of Staff, had worked in MK, ANC and CP structures and was in a strong position to evaluate the educational approach the ANC adopted.

He agreed with Mshengu and Mayibuye:
"The emphasis of the Cubans was on military work, and very little on political work. I think they were influenced by their own experience: the experience of Castro and their men — except for Che and a few others — had come there deeply patriotic, but I think they lacked deep political consciousness. They hated the Batista regime, and wanted to replace it with a bourgeois democratic government.

"Now most of our comrades felt that people who had been trained in Angola needed the skills of political organisers in addition to military skills. They knew they were going into a situation where the political movement — the ANC and the Party — were virtually non-existent. So they had to seize the opportunity to build these organisations as well as carrying out military operations.

"Secondly, looking at the terrain of South Africa, we felt there was no chance of just sending a group into the countryside to survive in some thick, dense bush and use that as a base for military operations.

"Rather, our feeling was that they must organise the people politically, and the people, if you like, would become the forests and the caves and the camouflage of the incipient guerrilla movement.

"So that's why, from our point of view, we needed to put a lot of emphasis on politicising cadres. We needed to strengthen their conviction that ultimately their cause would succeed; that there would be serious obstacles en route; and that these obstacles would be overcome by politicising the people in large numbers so that they became not just spectators but participants in the struggle.

"Our position was absolutely correct. And I'm happy that we stuck with that position ... that we didn't just lay emphasis on producing and reproducing guerrilla fighters. We stressed that members of the ANC, the Party and even MK should work very vigorously in the mass democratic movement, so that the MDM should be our shield and our military work could combine dynamically with our political work. If we have achieved a lot now, it's because — despite setbacks and errors — that was our strategy." (Comrade Chris Hani)

Hani's assessment emphasises the character of the South African movement —
and the political education that underpinned it — as "home-grown" for South
African conditions. Integral to its theory was the capacity to debate, challenge and
learn from fraternal experiences that these differences with the Cubans illustrate.

By the mid-1980s, the central role of political education had been enshrined in
ANC policy. This was made clear in the report of a four-day Department of Political
Education workshop held in Lusaka in February 1988. In a paper presented by Reg
September, then Secretary of the department, the "Report on the Commission on
Cadre Policy, political and Ideological Work" presented to the Kabwe Conference in
June 1985 was quoted. This important document resulted in the setting up of a DPE
structure to combat many of the shortcomings identified in political instruction. It
echoes both the theory of political education described by Simons and the feelings
expressed by his Novo Catengue graduates about the relationship between political
and military work.

Among the main points made in the document were:
*"Above all the main direction should be the training of cadres to exercise
political leadership and be organisers. They should be well versed with the
political and ideological forces inside the country. They should be able to
transmit independently ANC policy to all sections of the people at home
internationally. The movement should set up its own political school.*

*"Political education is the life-blood of any revolutionary movement. We
should have a political education programme aimed at constantly improving
the political consciousness, knowledge and skills of our cadres. Every member
should undergo a course of basic political training.*

*"A serious deficiency in our educational programme is that there is no
authority responsible for political education. We should set up a Department of
Political Education whose functions should include:*
• The appointment and monitoring in every region of political officer;
*• The drafting and implementing of a syllabus of political education and
ensuring fulfilment;*
*• The preparation of such material as may be found useful for conducting
political classes.*

*The theory of revolution ... is to be taught in such a way that comrades do
not only regurgitate the theory, but apply it to the concrete South African
situation and to the specific tasks assigned to them.*
• The South African state and political economy.
*• The ideological and theoretical understanding of the relationship between the
concept of national liberation, class struggle and the emancipation of women.*
*• Experience of other revolutions."To ensure the successful fulfillment of the
programme on political education, the commission recommends that:*
*Cadres liable for selection as political instructors should be committed for a
minimum of two years.*

*Every region must have a circulating library which must contain relevant
literature and works that would supplement the political education cadres
receive. Steps should be taken to develop the reading of progressive literature.*

This can only be achieved through the creation of reading groups. A comprehensive list of reading material must accompany the political programme. Special attention must be paid to material from inside the country and to the experience of other revolutionary struggles.

Teaching aids such as films, videos, tape-recorders and projectors must be procured for such study groups. The use of documentary films, especially from socialist countries, must be encouraged. Films produced at home must be used as part of our education programme, and not only viewed as entertainment films.

Recommendations for political and ideological work in the army:

1. Ideological work constitutes an essential factor in creating the nucleus of a people's army which will be ready at all times and under all circumstances to fight for and defend the gains of our revolution. In the words of our President OR Tambo: 'In building up our political army we aim therefore not only at the overthrow of the fascist regime, we aim at the building up of a politically conscious and revolutionary army, conscious of its popular origin, unwavering in its democratic functions and guided by our revolutionary organisation.' We recommend that the movement implement in full the principle of political guidance and leadership over the army to ensure strict control and accountability through the relevant structure of our army.

2. The Commissariat, in conjunction with the Department of Political Education, must ensure through its organs, continuous, uninterrupted political work within the ranks of the army. It must work on a comprehensive programme of training and education of political activities in our army, viz. commissars, instructors, propagandists, etc. Emphasis should be put on producing field workers at grassroots level. In this regard short term political courses should be introduced, based on our own experience as an army and as a movement. Opportunities offered by fraternal countries abroad should be fully utilised in this regard.

"Veterans and stalwarts of our movement should be fully utilised for the purposes of conducting short courses, lectures, seminars etc. for selected groups and the membership of our army in general.

"To ensure that our political programmes meet the demand of producing the required cadre, the problems of political literature and training facilities must be solved decisively. In this regard a proper mechanism should be worked out to supply the army with the required literature, particularly literature from the home front.

"There is a need to establish an effective and dynamic link between the rear and the front.

"We must pay particular attention to the all-round improvement of the material, cultural and spiritual well-being of the soldiers especially in the camps. We should solve the problem of how to combine the improvement of the material, cultural and spiritual life of a soldier with the strengthening of his or her political conviction."

(Extract from the "Report on the Commission on Cadre Policy, Political and Ideological Work", presented to the Kabwe Consultative Conference, June 1985)

Comrade Jack had taken his rightful place on the Secretariat of the Department of Political Education, bringing his vast experience as a political instructor into this new approach to cadre development. And teaching lived on not only in the army but among imprisoned guerrillas inside South Africa. It was still remembered after liberation.

Thandi Modise was one of the women cadres he trained in Novo Catengue in 1977. Modise wrote to him in 1991:

"You will most probably have difficulty in recalling which one of your girls I am. That is not important — I just want to thank you for keeping me sane and fighting! Yes, you did because I would fight to recall all the lessons you gave us and pass them on to other comrades in jail. It was also these 'passing-on' of the bits I remembered that comrades kept on digging for more; reaffirmed their roles in the struggle and are now fighting on.

"I am happy and honoured, comrade, to have attended these lectures. Perhaps I could ask you for these same lectures for my youth group at home?

"Amandla! Thandi Modise." (Letter from Thandi Modise, 17/10/91)

Racism and Revolution: The Lectures 1969-1976

Introduction 1984

(This was the draft introduction to the original primer, worked on by Comrade Jack and Marion Sparg.)

Communists are notoriously addicted to theory. Every member is expected to have more than a nodding acquaintance with a wide range of basic concepts. Among these are the conflicting interests of labour and capital, commonly called the class struggle; contradictions of capitalism as revealed, for instance, in recurring economic crises; modern imperialism and its offshoots — colonial rule, national oppression and war; pre-requisites of social revolution, fundamentals of socialism and the content of worker democracy, otherwise known as the dictatorship of the proletariat.

When presented in the philosophical context of historical materialism and dialectical materialism, the items of a communist curriculum are more than enough for a full-length university course in the social sciences. Yet only a handful of members have the good fortune to attend a Party School. The rest must study theory as best they can, in between the daily round of making a living, raising families, attending branch meetings and carrying out assignments.

It is the duty of leading Party units to organise study classes on current affairs as well as on the basic concepts of Marxism-Leninism. The idea is that members should be able to interpret events correctly and relate them to Party programmes, policy and pronouncements. Communists naturally vary a great deal in degree of experience, analytical capacity, theoretical understanding and readiness for a prolonged study course. Some members with only a rudimentary school education are able to absorb basic concepts like a sponge sucking up water, while a university degree is no guarantee of ability to grasp the abstract concepts of dialectics. Whatever their degree of understanding, however, communists are always under pressure to keep abreast of events and of the development of the Party line.

That obligation, I suggest, is largely peculiar to the Communist Party's style of work, pattern of organisation and cultural heritage bequeathed by the founding fathers — Marx, Engels and Lenin — whose combined published works run to more than a hundred fat volumes of text, footnotes and biographical references. Apart from professional scholars, whose business it is to study this enormous output, few people other than communists are prepared to take up this daunting challenge.

Marxism-Leninism is par excellence a theory of social change by way of revolution. Peoples and parties that have no stomach for revolution are bound to steer clear of the precepts contained in the Communist Manifesto and the collected works of Lenin, Stalin and other great Communist thinkers, which are being printed and reprinted over and over again in many languages, in many countries. This book will gain its purpose only if it spurs the reader to read the greatest political strategists of all time.

The best way of learning the theory of Marxism-Leninism is to study the books of Marx, Engels and Lenin, to study the chief sources of Communist theory. Its principles have nothing difficult about them that the workers cannot understand.

The object of a class is to get the students to study, and not to give the teacher an opportunity to exhibit his wisdom and eloquence. The students, not the teacher, should do most of the talking. The best method of running a class is to get the students to prepare themselves in advance by reading the particular section that is to be discussed at the next meeting. One student should be given the task of opening the discussion and explaining in his own words what he has read.

It is for the teacher to see that the discussion is to the point and on the right lines, and that every member of the class understands each point before passing to the next. This the teacher can do best by putting questions to individual students. The teacher should think out questions before going to the class. Both he or she and the students should make use of the books included in the list at the end of this volume, and other suitable reading material.

This is a course of instruction for freedom fighters

Purpose: The purpose of the course is to give freedom fighters a proper understanding of their task and goals. In order to do this, they need to acquire a thorough grasp of revolutionary theory and tactics. This course therefore contains both general political education and discussion of the particular nature of the South African revolution. Only people who have dedicated themselves wholeheartedly to the liberation of their country will be admitted to this course. Any member of the class who shows himself to be lacking in sincerity or who does not take the course seriously will be excluded. Wholehearted participation in the course means regular attendance, willingness to study any literature prescribed, and readiness to take part in and lead any discussions when required.

Course outline

I. What is political revolution?
  • The difference between the evolutionary and the revolutionary approach.
  • The meaning of social reformism.
  • Examples of great revolutions in history.
  • Is the African National Congress (SA) a revolutionary organisation?

2. What is a revolutionary situation?
  • The idea of a revolutionary social class.
  • Class consciousness.
  • The objective conditions for the formation of a class.
  • Are Africans in South Africa a class for itself?

3. The revolutionary struggle of the capitalist class:
  • Feudal society.
  • The rise of capitalism.
  • The English revolution of 1650.
  • The French revolution of 1790.
  • Is South Africa feudal or capitalist?

4. The working-class revolution:
  • The growth of the working class; its struggles against the capitalist classes.
  • Formation of trade unions and working class political bodies.
  • The Russian revolution.
  • Is the South African working class revolutionary?

5. National liberation movements:
  • The struggle against imperialism in North and South America.
  • National independence movements in Asia and Africa.
  • Is the national liberation movement working class or capitalist?
  • The social character of national liberation in South America.

6. Revolutionary struggles against imperialism:
  • Developments in national liberation after WW11.
  • Lessons of Cuba and Algerla.
  • Revolutionary wars in Korea and Vietnam.
  • What can we learn from these countries?

7. The struggles of oppressed minorities:
  • Comparison of the position of the Negroes (African-Americans) of USA and
    the Africans of Southern Africa.
  • Tactics and aims of American Blacks.
  • What is meant by Black Power?

• Can the American blacks liberate themselves?
• Conclusions for South Africa.

8. The history of national liberation in South Africa
   • The history of power struggles.
   • The rise of the African National Congress.
   • The programme and tactics of the ANC.
   • The history of the SACP.
   • The slogan of the 'black republic'.
   • Relations between the ANC and the SACP.

9. A revolutionary programme for South Africa
   • What are the antagonistic classes?
   • The class structure of the white minority regime.
   • The class structure of the movement for the overthrow of white supremacy.
   • What will take its place?
   • African power in politics and economics.

Note: It proved difficult to locate many of the comrades who were part of these classes in 1969. Some have since died. For example, Flag Boshielo, who initially took notes on the series had been a volunteer in the 1952 Defiance Campaign. He became an MK commissar and was killed by South African security forces when he was crossing into the country through the Caprivi Strip. Other comrades have also died or are scattered around South Africa. For this reason, not all of the material was written up. This section documents all the material that is available: essentially the first two lectures and several appendices based on discussion points from these and from Lecture 3.

Lecture 1: What is Political Revolution? (June 1 1969)

By revolution we understand a transfer of political power from one social class to another. A social class is a section (part) of society and is separated from the rest of society by common economic interests and a common ideology.

The most basic class division is that between those people who own the means of production and who form the capitalist class, and those people who do not own the means of production and who belong to the working class. Means of production include all those elements other than labour which are used to produce wealth: i.e. goods and services; the land itself and what we get out of it (raw materials); tools and machinery; the building where these are kept (factories, plants); and finance capital i.e. money (which is stored-up capital).

If the colonialists belong to the capitalist class, what social class did Africans form at the time of independence? Whether there were social classes among Africans before independence can be answered only through a detailed study of different parts of the continent. There were cocoa farmers, landowners and traders in West Africa

— Nigeria, Ghana — who formed the nucleus of a capitalist class. It is possible that there were the beginnings of a capitalist class in South Africa, but it is clear that on large parts of the continent, Africans were predominantly peasants, wage workers or minor functionaries.

A capitalist class exists only where goods are being produced for a market. There are no capitalists in the traditional village where people grow foodstuffs and make things to satisfy their own needs. Therefore it can be said that the African independence in most parts of the continent meant a transfer of political power from one social class to another.

But although we can agree that African independence has meant the transfer of power from one class to another, this does not mean that the new African governments have carried out a social revolution. They lacked the two key prerequisites for such a revolution: a revolutionary party and revolutionary theory.

African nationalism and its political expression (e.g. UNIP in Zambia, KANU in Kenya, Nkrumah's NCPP, etc.) concentrated on the transfer of political power — i.e. achieving independence — and did not develop a programme of economic and social change. These parties did not have a revolutionary policy. Additionally, when they achieved independence they inherited the old colonialist system and went on working along the old lines. They did not destroy the old state machinery to build a new one. They took over government and ministerial houses and other privileges. They became a class of bureaucrats. The tendency in many African countries has been to maintain the old economic as well as political system. There has been continuity and not revolution.

Why do revolutions take place? (Continuation of Lecture 1: 3 June 1969)

We have seen that revolutionary struggle means the struggle for the transfer of political power from one social class to another, and the use of this power by the revolutionary class to bring about changes in the social system and make itself master of the productive forces.

But revolution is a destructive way of bringing about social change. A country that has gone through a revolutionary struggle suffers a great deal. Why, then, do people risk their lives and their safety for the cause of the revolution?

The theory of revolution was worked out first by Karl Marx (1818–1883), Friedrich Engels (1820–1895) and Vladimir Illych Lenin (1870-1924). All revolutionaries of the nineteenth and twentieth century have drawn on these founders of scientific socialism for ideas about the aims and methods of revolution. We shall also study their writings as well as the contributions made by revolutionaries in more recent times.

The Marxist theory of revolution centres around the principle of conflicting social classes. *The Communist Manifesto*, which was first published in 1846, contains the famous statement: "The history of all hitherto existing societies is the history of class struggles." Marx and Engels, who wrote the manifesto, summarised in these few words the essence of their theory of social conflict and change.

The theory can be outlined briefly and simply. Every class society consists of the owners of the means of production on the one hand and the workers on the other hand. The workers sell their labour power for a wage to the owners (or are forced in a slave-owning society to produce without receiving a wage). In both cases the product of the labour belongs to the owners. They sell the product for a profit. The smaller the wage, the greater the profit.

This is the source of the antagonisms which give rise to class struggle. The antagonisms take different forms in different societies. In the words of *The Communist Manifesto*, however, "whatever forms they may have taken, one fact is common to all past ages and that is the exploitation of one part of society by the other".

The exploited part, the workers, are forced by their conditions of life to unite in defence of their common interests. They form trade unions, co-operatives and political parties in opposition to the class of owners or capitalists. The working class combines in the first place for the improvement of their wage standards, the conditions of employment, and their living conditions. They try to bring about reforms within the existing society. This attempt to bring about reforms is a necessary and important stage of the class struggle.

If we look at the history of the ANC in South Africa, we realise that, for the greater part of its existence, it was a movement for social reform. The aim of the ANC from the first days of its formation until the end of the Second World War, was to obtain political and economic rights and freedom of movement, organisation and free speech within the existing social order. The goal was to bring about a free and equal society without colour bar or discrimination; and to do so by constitutional methods of struggle.

This was also the aim of the working class parties of Britain, France, Germany and the USA. The labour parties or social democratic parties of these countries did not aim at revolution, but at social reform.

The first real revolutionary party in the present era was the Bolshevik section of the Russian Social Democratic Party. Writing in 1899, Lenin challenged the theory of social reformism. The real task of a revolutionary social party, he declared, was "not to set up projects for the transformation of society, not to preach sermons to the capitalist and their admirers about improving the position of the workers, but the organisation of the class struggle of the workers for the seizure of political power and the organisation of socialist society" (Our Programme).

Revolutionaries in other countries held similar views, but it was only in Russia that they succeeded in reaching their goal.

What is the explanation for the success of the revolutionary party in the old Russia? We can distinguish two main reasons. One was the formation of a revolutionary party with a clear programme of struggle by revolutionary methods. The other reason was the condition of the workers and peasants of Tsarist Russia. They were excluded from the centres of power, both politically and economically, under a despotic government that denied them the opportunity to bring about social reforms.

In the advanced capitalist countries of Western Europe; the working class was given the vote at different times between 1860 and 1890. They used the vote in order to obtain the right of collective bargaining, the right to state education, the right to unemployment insurance, old age pensions, and subsidised housing. Because of these concessions, the workers in the advanced capitalist countries lost sight of their revolutionary goal and accepted social reforms within the capitalist system.

The condition of our people in South Africa is like that of the workers and peasants of Tsarist Russia. That is why the national movement of Africans, coloureds and Indians has taken a revolutionary road.

(Appendix i to Lecture 1, June 8 1969)

The meaning of social reformism

Revolutionary theory declares that it is impossible to bring about complete equality of rights and opportunities between all persons in a capitalist or any other class society. A distribution of political power by means of adult suffrage will not provide the conditions necessary for a genuine democracy as long as the ownership of the means of production is in the hands of the capitalist class. Genuine democracy includes, for instance, the right of workers to take part in the management of industry and in the making of economic decisions. None of this is possible under capitalism.

It is argued today in some socialist countries that the balance of world forces is moving against capitalism. According to this viewpoint, workers in the democratic capitalist countries can, through pressure, bring about important changes in the structure of capitalism, changes that are more far-reaching than ordinary reforms. It might be argued, for instance that the national economy could be supervised and directed by representatives of the workers, by the employers and the state, and that this would be a half-way house between capitalism and socialism.

An opposing point of view is represented today most strongly by the leaders of the Chinese Revolution. They call this policy of socialism through constitutional struggle "revisionism". They argue that revolutionary parties which take part in the parliamentary system lose their revolutionary aims because such parties have to appeal for votes to a wide cross-section of the population.

Furthermore the critics of the constitutional struggle insist that the ruling capitalist class will not surrender power without struggle, but if necessary will do away with democracy and introduce a dictatorship. This actually happened in Fascist Italy and Nazi Germany.

A third objection to the theory of constitutional progress to socialism is the aggressive imperialism of the USA. It is now the chief pillar of capitalism throughout the world. Without it, socialism would have swept through Western Europe and Asia. Therefore, the critics say there can be no changeover to a classless society, except through struggle against US imperialism.

This controversy between reformism and revolution is perhaps the most important issue facing all revolutionary movements today. The question cannot be decided without a close examination of the history of revolutionary struggle and theory.

However, it is useful at this stage to remind ourselves of the experience of our own organisation. The ANC was formed in 1912 with two houses, the upper one consisting of chiefs. Many of the leading traditional rulers of our people, notably in Lesotho and Swaziland (and even the Barotse) actively assisted in the formation of Congress. This assistance was welcomed by the founders because of the influence that the traditional rulers had over the peasants.

In 1927, however, the South African parliament introduced the Native Administration Act. This Act reduced the chiefs to the position of Indunas in the Native Affairs Department, tax collectors, policemen and running dogs for the magistrates. This meant that the chiefs could no longer take part in politics. In 1928 the ANC elected James Gumede president — the most radical leader the ANC had ever had up to that time. In 1935 James Gumede was defeated when he stood for re-election, largely because of opposition from the chiefs. The point is that the ANC could not be a revolutionary movement as long as it included persons who, like the chiefs, were responsible to the government and depended on the government for jobs and status.

(Appendix ii to Lecture 1, June 11 1969)

The American Revolution

The American Revolution in 1774–1783 is not usually included in the list of great revolutions that have changed the mainstream of historical development. This is because the results of that revolution were to create a capitalist society which was neither democratic in the fullest sense — since it left slave-owning in the South — nor wholly progressive — since it very soon developed a strong imperialistic tendency.

In spite of these characteristics however, we shall take special note of the American revolution because it represented an early and important struggle against colonial rule. It therefore belongs to the category of movements for national liberation against a foreign imperialism and has a special meaning for us in relation to the emergence of independent African states.

The first question we ought to examine is why the colonists in America revolted against the British. Most of the colonists were of British origin. The ruling class in the American colonies belonged to the British aristocracy and were loyal to the monarchy. How, then, can one explain the determination to cut imperial ties even though this meant a long period of armed struggle against imperial troops?

The answer is to be found mainly in the economic policies of Britain towards her colonies, and the growth of the colonial economy. The British colonial policy of this period is known as Mercantilism: the colonies existed in the eyes of the British mainly for the benefit of British manufacturers, traders and shipowners. The colonies were taxed for the benefit of the British Crown. They were prohibited from manufacturing goods in competition with British goods (such as textiles, iron goods and clothing) while in addition all imports and exports to and from the colonies had to be carried in British vessels.

There is a parallel between this situation and the position of the so-called "homelands" in South Africa. They, too, exist for the benefit of white employers (mine workers, manufacturers, traders) in the towns. They, too, are allowed only to export raw materials (including labour) and are forced to buy manufactured goods from the white-dominated towns.

The parallel ends there. Our movement struggles for the elimination of white colonial rule throughout the country and for the return of all parts to African rule. The American colonists, by contrast, demanded the right of self-determination and secession — the two principles of national liberation in a colony dominated by a foreign power.

The colonists launched the struggle under the slogan "No taxation without representation". They moved into action in December 1773 in what is known as the "Boston Tea Party", by dumping a cargo of tea belonging to the East India Tea Company into Boston Harbour.

From then onwards conflict between the colonists and imperial troops multiplied until the first shot was fired in April 1775. A month later, George Washington was appointed commander of a continental army representing all the 13 colonies. The war had begun in earnest.

The next important event was the adoption of a Declaration of Independence on July 4, 1776. The Declaration said that the colonies "are, and of right ought to be free and independent states". Further, that "all political connection between them and Britain is and ought to be totally dissolved". The USA had been born.

After many ups and downs the colonists won the war. They received the support of the French and later also of Spain and Holland — all enemies of the British. But the real reason for the victory was the determination of a small group of revolutionaries who had courage and stubbornness to overcome all difficulties. By treaty between England and US in 1783, the existence of a new, independent US was recognised.

What would the colonists do with their newly-won independence? That was now the burning issue. The Declaration of Independence contained one great promise: "We hold these truths to be self-evident — that all men are created equal." What kind of equality would be granted to the people of America?

The colonies were divided into classes — the working people, small farmers, big farmers, shopkeepers and manufacturers. In the Southern States were free men and slaves. Perhaps the American Indians were segregated in reservations, or subjected to attack by land-hungry colonists. What kind of reality was there to be for the workers, Indians and slaves? The short answer is that the American Revolution did not do away with classes. On the contrary, the new state soon developed into one of the most highly developed systems of exploitation in modern times.

There were some important gains made. The vote was extended to a large section of the population. But adult male suffrage was adopted only 50 years after the revolution and then only for whites, and Indians and slaves were excluded from the franchise.

Class-conscious workers demanded concessions and when these were refused, organised armed risings against the rich. As a result the merchants, manufacturers, slave-holders and money-lenders came together in 1787 and drew up a constitution which would protect the owners of property against the proletariat. The present US Constitution has really not moved far from the constitution of 1787. It too is designed to prevent the working people from obtaining power.

This was done in 1787 by creating "the separation of powers", dividing the government into three parts: the House of Representatives and the Senate; the President (who is the head of government); and the Supreme Court appointed by the President. The system of election was so organised that it would be impossible for a left-wing, radical party to obtain control through constitutional means.

The great American Revolution had achieved its purpose of independence from imperial rule. But the revolution did not bring about a change in class structure. It left the capitalists in control. Today the US is the mainstay of capitalism and the leading imperialist power.

We can draw the conclusion that independence from colonial rule is not enough to bring about a revolutionary change which will transfer power to the great mass of people. That is the lesson which the peoples of Africa will also learn in due course.

(Appendix iia to Lecture 1: June 15 1969)

More about the American Revolution

The American War of Independence is often called the American Revolution. It was in fact an armed struggle for independence or secession from British imperialism. We have to ask whether it was in fact a revolution — that is to say, did the war bring about a transfer of power to a new social class, and did that class use its power to reconstruct the state in order to bring about a radical change in the social order?

To answer this we need to look at what the social classes were that took part in and led the American War of Independence. The American colonists of 1775 included wage workers, small farmers, plantation owners, merchants, manufacturers. The small farmers were in many cases peasants, in the sense that they worked their land without hired help, that is, members of the farmer's own family, his sons and daughters did all the work, but they were not peasants in the African sense. African peasants did not in most parts grow regularly for the market. The African peasant did not own his land. He was not an individual proprietor. He was a tenant of (co-owner in) the community.

The American farmer on the other hand had all the instincts of a capitalist. He wanted to make money through the sales at the market. He owned his land and, if he wanted, he could obtain more land.

The main reason for the American War of Independence was economic. The British, like all other colonialist powers practised a mercantilist policy. This meant that the colony existed only for the benefit of the imperial state. Britain claimed a monopoly of shipping between herself and the colonies under the Navigation Acts. Secondly, the British imposed taxes undemocratically on the colonies (hence the revolutionary slogan "No taxation without representation"). Thirdly, the British tried to choke the rising class of American capitalists by preventing them from producing or exporting manufactured goods. Britain wanted the colonies to produce raw materials for and buy manufactured goods from British industrialists.

Although some parts of the mercantilist policy were changed after the American War of Independence, British imperialism continued to demand a privileged position in her colonies, both in Asia and Africa. The common complaint that Britain kept her colonies backward illustrates the way imperialism limited the development of the economies of the Asian and African countries.

The colonies had legislative councils of the same kind as the Transkeian Legislative Assembly. They could make local laws with the approval of the British Crown. But the British parliament was the final legislative authority in the colonies. The American War of Independence was fought for political power, so that the Americans could achieve economic power and make their own laws. The leaders of the War of Independence were the industrialists, the merchants, the manufacturers, plantation owners, farmers. Workers supported and fought in the war, but they were not the leaders and did not make the constitution. The constitution was drafted by property owners to defend private property.

What emerged from the American Revolution was a capitalist society with a strong imperialist inclination.

It is clear that the American War of Independence did produce a political revolution — a transfer of political authority and power from the imperial state to the colonial state. In the same way it can be said that African independence involves a political revolution. We must not underestimate the importance of African power. But this does not constitute a socialist revolution.

The American revolution was essentially the result of contradiction between a colonial capitalism and an imperial capitalism. The defeat of Britain opened the way not to a socialist revolution, but to the emergence of a great new industrial capitalist state. As we now recognise, the American revolution was a great triumph for world capitalism.

We must also recognise that the American war was a struggle between an imperial power and a national bourgeoisie fighting for national independence. It was a progressive war in so far as the imperial power represented an old order of society based on the exploitation of colonial territory. This distinction between the imperial state and an oppressed colony contains elements of feudalism. It is this feudal aspect of imperialism that gives wars of national liberation a revolutionary character.

(Appendix iii to Lecture 1, June 18 1969)

Feudalism

What is feudalism? The word appears often in the literature of revolutionary theory, and most of us probably have a general idea of what it means. Many of us know, for instance, that feudalism is regarded as one of the major stages through which human society is said to have passed before reaching capitalism.

For instance, Engels wrote in *Socialism, Utopian and Scientific* (1880): "The bourgeoisie shattered the feudal system, and on its ruins established the bourgeois social order, the realm of free competition, freedom of movement, equal rights for commodity owners, and all the other bourgeois glories. The capitalist mode of production could now develop freely."

The rising capitalist class fought its revolution under the slogans of "Liberty, Equality, Fraternity". What these words meant you can see from Engels' explanation.

The capitalists fought for the unlimited right to exploit labour without restriction; and the unlimited right to make as much profit as possible. So feudalism was a system that imposed restrictions on the freedom of action of the capitalist. In the fully-developed feudal society of the 13th and 14th centuries we find the following characteristics:

1. Society is largely agrarian. The great majority of producers are peasants who not only grow their own food, but also make their own clothing and utensils. This is very like the system of production in Africa where pre-colonial villages were economically self-sufficient.

2. The peasants were subjects of a feudal lord — a member of the aristocracy. They lived on his land and made payments in kind to him in exchange for certain rights, especially the right to use the land. They worked for him and paid tax or rent in the form of grain and other goods. The relations between peasant and feudal lord can be regarded as a development from the tribal system. In fact, many feudal lords were the descendants of the tribal chiefs of an earlier period.

3. A number of small towns existed where merchants traded goods and where articles were manufactured for the market. The producers were organised in guilds — which were not trade unions, but rather associations of guild masters designed to regulate entry into trades and crafts such as spinning and weaving, metal working, leather working, dying and furniture manufacture. Each guild consisted of employers, journeymen and apprentices. These artisans often combined agriculture with their manufacturing activities.

4. Political power lay in the hands of the king and the lords of the manor (manor was the term for the estate over which a lord had sole command). We might compare this system with that dominated by a paramount chief, such as Shaka, and his relationship with the chiefs of the various clans constituting the Zulu kingdom.

5. An important part of feudal society was the Catholic Church headed by the Pope. The church was not only a religious body, but an important political and economic institution stretching across much of Europe. The church owned vast areas of land from which it drew revenues, and it claimed spiritual authority over all monarchs.

This system underwent great changes during the Middle Ages (from about the 12th century onwards) as a result of trade, the introduction of new methods of production, and the growth of a distinct class of manufacturers. These changes created social dislocation and tension. The peasants (called serfs) revolted against their lords. The merchants and manufacturers in the towns came into conflict with the feudal aristocracy, and the lords struggled against one another and against the church.

The Communist Manifesto describes these conflicts in the following passage:
"Freemen and slave, patrician and plebeian, lord and serf, guild master and journeyman, in a word oppressor and oppressed, stood in constant opposition to one another, carried on an uninterrupted, now hidden, now open fight; a fight that each time ended either in a revolutionary reconstitution of society at large, or in the common ruin of the contending classes."

Three important developments took place in the course of this struggle.

One was the revolt against power of the Pope and the Catholic Church (which we know as the Catholic Reformation) led by Martin Luther and John Calvin in the 16th century.

The second was the English Revolution under Cromwell in the 17th century.

The third was the French Revolution of 1789. Religious and political revolts together contributed to the growth of national states and the transfer of political power to the capitalist class. That is why *The Communist Manifesto* says: "The bourgeoisie historically has played a most revolutionary part."

The capitalist revolution occurred because manufacturing and trade developed to a point where the old feudal system became an obstacle to progress. The industrial revolution made possible more effective methods of production and created a demand for new markets. But merchants and manufacturers needed freedom from restrictions to take advantage of these.

At the same time, overseas colonisation in America and Asia brought Europe into contact with huge new areas it could exploit. But court and aristocratic privilege and monopoly governed the award of trading concessions. So manufacturers and merchants demanded freedom from the rule of the feudal aristocracy, which in turn tried to defend its privileges and powers against them.

France at the same time of its revolution was divided into three "estates": the nobility, who lived on revenue obtained from the serfs and peasants on their lands; the clergy, who obtained their money also from the land and from the church dues; and the third estate — the rest of the population.

This third estate, which had no political power whatever, included financiers, merchants, manufacturers, artisans, farmers, labourers, artisans and professional people. It thus consisted of many different classes, but all had a common interest in removing the privileges of the king, the nobility and the church.

When the revolution took place, therefore, the entire third estate combined in armed struggle against the remains of the feudal aristocracy. This was a national struggle. It was accompanied by national slogans, and it led to the formation of the national state.

The capitalist revolution took place because the system of government, laws and institutions inherited from the feudal past were unsuited to the needs and demands of the capitalists. The old order was based on the idea that power and privilege belonged to a class by reason of birth. The capitalists wanted to substitute a social order in which political power would be determined by economic power. For that reason the capitalists demanded equality before the law, the abolition of inherited privileges, free competition and free markets.

The same kind of conflict exists also in South Africa. Here, too, political power is the monopoly of a minority faction of the population which claims that power by reason of its birth — just like the old feudal aristocrats. The white colonists attempt to maintain a rigid social system inherited from the pre-industrial period. The exploited African masses produce wealth for the capitalists, but are excluded from the state apparatus like the capitalists of England and France under feudalism. Our people are struggling against an obsolete and degenerate social system. Our struggle is for the establishment of a new social order which will free our people for unfettered development, for equality before the law, for the abolition of the privileges of birth and for the right of all people to full and equal opportunity.

(Appendix IV to Lecture 1 June 22 1969)

Feudal aspects of South African society

Feudalism is a type of society in which the rights, powers and obligations of every person are determined by status (that is, by the legal, economic, political and social position of an individual in relation to the rest of society).

Under feudal conditions, a person's status is fixed at birth. Men and women are born into a particular status group and, in principle, remain there throughout their lives.

A status group is not the same as a class. We define a class in relation to the means of production. Basically, those who own the means of production are one class, and we shall call them capitalists. The rest of society, which lives by selling its labour power for a wage or salary, is the working class.

Feudal society can also be divided into two classes of this kind. The owners would include the feudal lords (who were in the position of chiefs ruling huge tracts of land), the church (which in those days was also a big landowner), the yeoman farmers, the manufacturers and merchants (or guild masters) in the towns. The other class included serfs and free workers both rural and urban.

But the free burghers (town manufacturers and merchants), serfs and free workers were all part of the third estate which thus included different classes. The bourgeoisie fought their revolution under the slogans of "Equality before the law; freedom from restrictions on economic growth", and not for an equal share of political and economic power between different classes.

In South Africa, one can distinguish status groups that follow the lines of difference in skin colour. The law creates a difference in status between whites and all persons who are classed as non-white, but it also legislates differences between the various groups classed as non-white, e.g. Africans, Malays, Japanese, Chinese, coloureds, Indians.

But if we divide South Africa into economic classes, a different pattern emerges. Class groups are not identical with racial categories. The working class includes members of all racial groups — whites, Indians, coloured, Africans, etc. This is true also of the owning class. There are African landlords, Indian merchants, etc. The economic classes cut across the colour lines.

South Africa combines an industrial economy based on capitalist ownership with feudal-like institutions. Africans, coloureds, Indians are members of the industrial economy. Their status however, corresponds to that of the third estate in feudal times. Our revolutionary struggle is being fought against feudal restrictions as well as capitalist exploitation, and that is one reason our struggle is exceptionally difficult.

(Appendix V to Lecture 1, June 25 1969)

A note on castes

We have seen that the South African society cannot be explained in simple class terms. In order to distinguish between the different positions of the various sections of the population — African, whites, coloureds, Indians — we have used the term status groups. This is necessary because the class divisions cut across the ethnic communities, known here commonly as races or colour groups.

In order to distinguish between these two ways of classifying people — class and status — we have looked at the structure of feudal societies, where people were divided into hereditary estates: the nobility, the clergy and the commonality. In that case, too, the class divisions between the owners of the means of production and the propertyless cut across the estates. The commonality (third estate) included, for example, manufacturers, merchants, wage workers and serfs.

This kind of intersection of class and status groups is found also in India, where the status groups are known as castes.

The Indian pattern is of great importance to us — perhaps even more than the feudal society. This is partly because it still exists today and partly because there are strong similarities between the Indian system and our own structure.

I might add here that it is believed with a fair amount of justification that the caste divisions in India were originally colour divisions. Historians are of the opinion that several thousand years ago light-skinned invaders known as Aryans attacked and conquered the indigenous population and in the centuries that followed the invaders and the local population blended. But their descendants retained the status differences in the form of castes related to occupations.

In theory there are four main caste divisions: Brahman (the priests), Kshatriya (the soldier), Vaisya (the merchants) and Budra (serfs). In fact, there are many hundreds of castes and sub-castes which are distinguished by a few simple tests.

First of all a caste is endogamous; that is, the members of a caste must marry within it. They cannot take husbands and wives from other castes. If a woman has a child by a member of a different caste, he will not be regarded as its father. If a man marries a woman of a caste lower than his own, he is likely to be expelled from his caste.

This is not a set of legal rules. The system is enforced by religious taboos and social pressure, but the endogamous rules are obeyed in much the same way as South Africa's ban on marriages between whites and other sections of the population. The difference is that South Africa uses the criminal law, police and prisons to enforce its caste-like system of endogamy.

Secondly, a person belongs to the caste into which he is born. That, as we have seen, is the caste of his parents or, if they are not married, of his mother. In principle it is not possible for a person to change caste. It is common enough, however, for members of a caste to move to an area where they are not known and to pretend to be members of a higher caste, just as coloureds are known to leave the Cape and settle in the Transvaal, posing as members of a more privileged group.

If a person lives with people of a lower caste and identifies himself with them, he will in practise be regarded as belonging to that caste and his children will also be so regarded. Here again we can find a parallel in South Africa. A "native", in terms of the Native Administration Act of 1927, includes any person, whether African, white or coloured, who lives in a reserved area as a "native" and under the same conditions as "natives".

Thirdly the differences between castes are clearly seen in the way in which Indians prepare and eat food. A superior caste will not eat food together with members of a lower caste or eat food cooked or served by a lower caste person. Similar taboos apply also to smoking and drinking.

South African social divisions are not so strict. The law makes it difficult, but does not prohibit different groups from sitting together and sharing the same food. It is a universal practice as we know for Africans, coloureds and Indians to prepare food for whites.

At the same time we must not blind ourselves to certain factors connected with meals which are similar to the Indian caste system. There is strict segregation between whites and other persons in all public eating places — that means restaurants, hotels, cafes, dining cars. It is only in a person's own home that it is possible for Africans, coloureds, Indians and whites to sit together for a meal; and this sharing of meals takes place in what is probably only a very small proportion of homes. For most white people, segregation during meals is as strict as the corresponding caste distinction in India.

Fourthly, another similarity between the Indian and South African systems of stratification is its relation to occupations. Although some members of a caste will not work at the occupation referred to by the caste name — not everybody who belongs to the tanner caste is a tanner — there is a certain correspondence between caste name and occupation. For instance Brahmans are traditionally priests, and priests today are still drawn from the Brahman caste.

At the bottom of the scale are the so-called repressed castes or harrijans or "untouchables". Fifteen percent of the Indian population of over 400 million people are untouchables, and their position needs some explanation. The principle underlying all these complicated rules is pollution: the notion that a person is made unclean when he comes into physical contact with a person who is of a lower caste than himself. The idea of pollution often adheres to certain activities, e.g. tanning hides, removing excreta, wasting corpses, handling meat.

Traditional harrijan occupations are connected with dead things like corpses and meat, or with human refuse. People who work with these are at the bottom of the scale. Other people may also fall into this low caste if they serve the harrijans — a barber who cuts their hair, a drummer who entertains them.

The startling feature of the Indian social system is that most members of the lower castes accept their social position, even though the Indian government and Indian law since independence are supposed to have wiped out caste inequalities. In law, no person should be discriminated against because of his caste.

Lecture 2: Class Consciousness (June 29 1969)

The structure of the South African society is such that it imprints and nourishes an acute awareness of the physical difference between human beings.

Racism is a disease in South Africa. It is a disease that grows out of the exploitation of black and brown by white, out of capitalism wedded to colonialism. Racism is one of the major obstacles to our emancipation.

First of all, the division into colour groups by law and by customs produces an acute colour consciousness. This is most conspicuous in the white group and in the coloured group. The reason is that the white group identifies its superior economic, political and social status with its skin colour. They say: "I am superior because I am white" — by which they mean that their white skin entitles them to a monopoly of power and privileges.

To justify the system of oppression, whites claim that they are superior by nature (by birth), or as a result of God's will, or by history — meaning that they reached the present stage of civilisation long before the dark-skinned peoples. We can refer to these arguments as biological, theological and historical.

These arguments are false. There is no ground for the statement that whites are superior in any sense, except for the envious one that they have seized power and monopolised it for themselves. In other words, the white man's superiority is the same as that of a burglar with a revolver who forces the unarmed householder to deliver his goods. The white man robbed our people of their cattle because of his superior arms, and his superiority has rested ever since on gunpowder and armed forces.

The white man does not only rule by force however. In order to remain in power he has to persuade the millions of oppressed people that he, the white man is superior. He has to condition them into accepting their state of inferiority. In order to do this, he has to create in them a feeling of their inferiority. He not only makes all the oppressed people feel inferior but he also tries to create divisions among them. For instance he encourages the coloured people to believe that they are superior to the Africans. As a result, the oppressed are divided into colour-conscious groups.

This fostering of colour consciousness divides the population into hostile colour groups and holds up or delays the growth of class consciousness. People look upon themselves not as members of a class but as members of a colour group. They are inclined to defend the interests of their colour community, rather than the interests of the class; and that is why workers of different colour groups — whites, Africans, coloureds, Indians — are organised into separate trade unions and compete against one another for jobs. Class consciousness develop as an historical process under capitalism.

This process is described in *The Communist Manifesto* as follows:
"When industrialisation takes place, workers are massed together in factories and workshops. They come from different areas, perhaps from different countries, and are unknown to one another. They compete for jobs and clash

with one another for that reason. They discover, however, that competition among them enables the employers to starve the workers and make them work long hours. The workers learn that they can only improve their wages and improve conditions through combination — that is, by trade union action."

Trade unions are the first organised form of conscious working class activity. There comes a stage when workers regard the defence of their trade unions as more important than the defence of their wages. This is a political attitude. The loyalty to trade unions is based on the long-term expectation of obtaining an adequate standard of living. The trade union is an instrument of struggle between the employers and workers. In the course of this struggle, the workers develop political consciousness. They realise that they cannot guarantee their standards of living by economic struggles alone. When this point is reached where the workers are politically conscious, they form political parties. Their aim is to take over power and to introduce socialism.

Although class consciousness has also developed in South Africa under the conditions of capitalist exploitation, class consciousness has competed with colour consciousness. The result is that trade unions and working class parties have been divided along colour lines. These divisions have weakened the class struggles and the national liberation movement.

Colour consciousness

Colour consciousness is a divisive strategy of the ruling class. This class inflames racial passions, incites workers of one colour group against workers of another colour group, and in this way discourages united action among the oppressed against race discrimination. This divisive strategy is being carried to even greater lengths in the policy of so-called "ethnic segregation" amongst Africans themselves. When people are divided according to languages — Zulu, Sotho, Tswana, Venda — as in Soweto's Daveyton township, they are being taught to see themselves as members of tribes and not as members of a single African nation. The system of Bantustans likewise has the effect of creating a tribal consciousness in Africans. Colour consciousness is the enemy of class consciousness and tribal consciousness is the enemy of national consciousness. That is why South African whites propagate colour consciousness and tribal consciousness.

(Appendix i to Lecture 2, July 3 1969)

The Marxist concept of alienation

Our people suffer from many kinds of oppression — class oppression, national oppression, racial oppression. This last, as we have seen, bears certain similarities to the oppression of the untouchables, the Harrijans in India's caste system. It might even be said of South African society that it includes the worst features of capitalism, feudalism and a caste society.

This is strange, because all these forms of oppression ought to be incompatible with a fairly advanced industrial society. Our people work, in their hundreds of thousands, in mines, factories, workshops and in many other modern kinds of economic activity. How is it possible for the ruling class to impose such a medieval form of class rule, with so much obvious discrimination, on an advanced industrial proletariat?

We explain the perpetuation of white tyranny in terms of its coercive apparatus. That is to say, we point out, quite rightly, that the government uses fascistic methods of control. It has banned our organisation, it has imprisoned or executed our leaders; it operates a strict curfew, tortures its political opponents, and operates a vast system of espionage to uncover all attempts to organise against it. South Africa has been turned into an armed state with the sole aim of suppressing the national liberation movement and all forms of class struggle.

The powers and activities of the police state are indeed a formidable obstacle to our emancipation. The recognition of this fact will not weaken or discourage our determination to achieve freedom. The ferocity of oppression is a challenge to our movement, a challenge for us to find weaknesses in the regime and to organise our people for the revolution. The key to success is organising our people to carry out our mission, and so we must equip ourselves with a very clear and detailed understanding of the nature of the South African society. We must also try to understand why it is that our people have not developed the revolutionary consciousness which alone will enable us to destroy the system.

"There can be no revolution without a revolutionary situation, there can be no revolutionary situation without a revolutionary consciousness, and there can be no revolutionary consciousness without a revolutionary party."

Karl Marx was the first great theoretician of revolution. In working out his theory of revolution, he began with the idea of "alienation". The idea comes from the same root as "alien" — meaning foreigner or stranger. Alienation, as used by Marx, means estrangement — the condition of being a stranger to one's own society.

Marx traces the idea of estrangement or alienation to the growth of class divisions, first under slavery, then in feudalism and finally under capitalism. Alienation began, he said, when a propertyless class arose — a class that was excluded from ownership of the means of production, and was therefore unable to control its labour power and the products of its labour.

Marx argued that creative labour was an essential part of human nature. A human being who could not take part in creative activity, he argued, was not a complete being. Therefore when slaves or serfs or wage-earners lost control over the productive system and over the products of labour, they ceased to be complete beings. They were alienated from the human species, in Marx's words, and therefore from their society.

Alienation in this sense can be seen very clearly in modern factories where the individual worker is engaged in making only a small part of a finished product. Mass production led to large-scale division of labour and a high degree of specialisation. The worker sells his labour power for a wage in order to live and is employed on jobs that are mechanical, repetitive and monotonous. In capitalist society, says Marx, the worker becomes a slave to the productive system, and the things that he makes confront him "as something alien, as a power independent of the producer".

> *"The more the worker spends himself, the more powerful becomes the alien objective world which he creates against himself, and the poorer he himself — his inner world — becomes; the less belongs to him as his own.... As the worker puts more of his life into the object of his labour, the less his life belongs to him. Hence, the greater his activity, the greater is the worker's lack of objects. Whatever the product of his labour is, he is not the master. Therefore the greater this product, the less is he himself. The alienation of the worker in his product means not only that the labour becomes an object, an external existence, that exists outside him, independently, as something alien to him, but that it becomes a power on its own confronting him; it means the life that he has conferred on the object confronts him as something hostile and alien."*

This passage is not easily understood. Let us try to understand it by looking at our own condition. It has often been said that Africans, coloureds and Indians are treated as aliens in the land of their birth. Solomon Tshekisho Plaatje, the first Secretary General of the ANC, once wrote that Africans became outcasts when the Native Land Act of 1913 was passed. He meant that they no longer had security or a permanent home of their own; they were strangers in their own land.

Our people are treated as outcasts wherever they find themselves. They have no political rights; no right to freedom of movement, occupation, speech, and organisation; they cannot form trade unions or combine in any way to protect their interests. They are like serfs in all these respects and are therefore alienated from themselves and from society.

They are also not allowed under the white man's regime to form themselves into a single united nation. Elsewhere in Africa, where people are free and independent, Africans are engaged in nation-building. The white regime in South Africa, however, forces our people to live in separate compartments, to recognise only traditional tribal leaders, and to think of themselves as tribalists and not as members of a single united nation. Our people are being alienated from our national destiny.

Finally, they have lost control of the means of production and the fruits of their labour. Robbed of their land, exploited through skilled work, denied the right to settle and build homes in the towns, we have become a landless, homeless proletariat. Our condition is far worse than that of the working class of other industrial countries. We suffer a great degree of alienation as workers.

These different kinds of alienation have created a vast state of insecurity. In practical terms, this means that our people are engaged in a ruthless struggle for survival against the police state. They are rebellious but they are not yet revolutionaries. It is the mission of our organisation to create in them a revolutionary consciousness, to put and end to their alienation, and to restore in them self-respect, national cohesion, and working class dignity. All this can be done only in the struggle for the achievement of African power.

(Appendix ii to Lecture 2, July 9 1969)

The state in revolutionary theory

The state is the political organ of society. That is to say, it is the section of society which possesses power and uses power firstly in the maintenance of cohesion (keeping the parts together) and enforcing obedience to law; and secondly in dealing with other states both in war and in peace. According to the Marxist theory, the state only exists where there are class antagonisms and a class structure. Engels wrote in his book *The Origins of the Family, Private Property and The State* that the state has grown out of society. It is the product of conflicting economic interests, and that it places itself above society.

To understand this expression "above society", we might look at traditional African society and ask ourselves whether it had an organised system of state power. The answer is yes, in some parts of Africa, especially along the Western coast (today's Nigeria) where the Islamic Emir States were feudal states of an advanced kind.

In Southern Africa, however, political authority was predominantly exercised by chiefdoms on behalf of the people as a whole. Everybody was entitled to land. Therefore there were no antagonistic classes and no state in the Marxist sense. This does not mean there was no political power. Some African societies, like the Zulu kingdom, had a well developed form of government with a standing army and a very tough policy of enforcing obedience. But the soldiers came from the people and did not form a professional army. The power lay with the people.

When Engels talks of the state being above society, he means that political power has been taken from the people and placed in the hands of a special agency, which includes the makers of laws, the judges, the police, the prisons, the bureaucracy. These agencies of state power are above society in the sense that they are not controlled by society.

The bourgeois writers argue that the State is above society because it is neutral and harmonises the interests of all classes. Even in South Africa the racists have the impudence to say that they represent all sections of the people; that they are the trustees of the black people and that their policy is intended to do away with conflict between the races.

But this is a false argument because no person can be trusted to exercise power in the interest of another who is unable to defend and represent himself. No slave owner ever did true justice to his slaves. The South African government represents the white population and rules the country in the interests of the whites. We can therefore describe the South African state as an instrument of white domination.

Using the slogan of white supremacy, the government in South Africa defends the interests of the capitalist class. The government protects the white bourgeoisie against the competition of African, Indian and coloured workers and merchants, landowners, manufacturers. In other words, the government gives the white capital a monopoly over the means of production. In so doing it prevents a bourgeois class developing among Africans, coloureds and Indians. This prohibition takes the form of racial discrimination and is basically a means of strengthening the grip of the white bourgeoisie over the economy. At this stage, then, white domination is class domination. The South African state is an instrument of class rule.

If white workers receive privileges under the system, it is only partly because of their struggles. They are also being bribed to take part in the oppression of Africans. It is the job of the liberation movement to win the white workers to our side. We can succeed in doing this if we offer them something which they do not possess today — a share in the means of production.

As we have seen, South Africa's class system is not a simple one. It is a class system to which we can also apply the terms multi-racial and multi-national.

All three types of social cleavage — national, racial or colour, and class — are potential or actual causes of social conflict. The Nigerian war* , for instance, is a war of competing nationalisms. Negroes (African-Americans) in the US are fighting against colour or racial oppression. As for the class war, it is a constant element in all capitalist societies. Every strike by workers is a form of class struggle.

Each area of conflict is related to a particular set of demands, which may vary from one country to another, but which always have a distinctive element. The class struggle is concerned with the distribution of wealth. The first aim of working class organisations like trade unions is to improve wages and conditions of work. By the final stage, however, workers struggle for power — that is, for the socialist state.

In the area of race conflict, the first aim of the oppressed racial group is to achieve equality. This means initially equality before the law (removal of all legal racial discrimination against the oppressed). As the Negroes (in the US have discovered, however, equality before the law does not guarantee real equality. They continue to suffer large-scale discrimination, which is enforced by the courts, the police, employers and more generally by economic inequality. The slogan "Black Power" reflects the Negroes' demand for real equality under a black man's rule. The national struggle involves a conflict between competing nation/s and national groups.

> Stalin, in his *The National and Colonial Questions,* defines a nation as:
> *"A group of people who occupy a common territory, speak the same language, share the same traditions and culture, psychology, outlook, have the same economic system and who are politically independent or aspire to have political independence in their territory."*

Most of these characteristics might also apply to a tribe. So what is the difference between a tribe and a nation? Is it size? No! Compare the populations of Lesotho or Botswana with that of the Transkei. The difference is not size, but group consciousness. The nation is a group which is aware of itself, expresses this awareness in flags, national anthems, literature and other symbols of this kind and which attempts to achieve or defend its independence.

The struggle for national freedom may take several forms, e.g. the struggle for cultural autonomy. The right of self-determination, on the other hand, means that the nation must be able to decide the conditions under which it participates in the greater multi-national society. Finally, secession means breaking away to form an

---

The Nigerian Civil War over the secession of Biafra raged from 1966 to 1970

independent nation state — the most extreme form of national power.

In South Africa all three forms of struggle — class, racial and national — are taking place at the same time. What are the forms of power to which the oppressed peoples aspire?

(Appendix iii to Lecture 2, July 16 1969)

National self-determination

What is a nation? Perhaps the clearest and most precise answer to this question comes from Joseph Stalin in his essay on the national question, written in 1913. He wrote the essay because the contradictions between class parties and national movements in central and eastern Europe, including Tsarist Russia, were spreading confusion in the working class.

As Stalin puts it: "The way that nationalism swept onward with increasing force, threatens to divert the working class masses." The Social-Democratic Party (the forerunner of the Bolshevik Party) found it necessary to work out the relation between the class structure and the national structure.

Above all, the social democrats wished to prevent bourgeois nationalism from gaining control of the various national sections of the working class. We can find a parallel in South Africa where Afrikaner nationalism did succeed in diverting Afrikaner workers from class struggle.

Stalin sets off by defining a nation and comes to the conclusion that it is "a historically evolved, stable community of language, territory, economic life, and psychological make-up manifested in a community of culture".

You will note that this definition lists a number of characteristics and that it emphasises the time factor. The nation is a group that grows as a result of an historical process, through the growth of markets, the spread of a common language and culture, the acceptance of a common set of ideas and values and a common aspiration. Though Stalin does not mention this last aspect, its occurrence marks the emergence of a mature nation. A nation is mature when it claims political independence.

This claim takes form at some point in the history of a nation firstly as a demand for cultural autonomy — the right of a people to live according to its own traditions and customs — and secondly as a demand for the right to self-determination.

Stalin defines this as "the right to determine its destiny", and adds that "no one has the right forcibly to interfere in the life of a nation, to destroy its schools and other institutions, to violate its habits and customs, to repress its language, or curtail its rights".

In Stalin's thesis the working class must set itself the aim of international class solidarity, and of liberating workers from the control of the national bourgeoisie. For this purpose it is necessary to combat all forms of national oppression and to demand the right of self-determination for all nations.

Only when national oppression has been eliminated will it be possible for workers to recognise their interests and create a genuinely international movement. In other words, the recognition of national rights is an essential part of the development of a world working class movement.

The problem of the relationship between the two forms of struggle — class and national — took the form in Tsarist Russia of a demand by various national minorities (Lithuanians, Caucasians, Ukrainians, Jews) to form separate sections of the Social-Democratic Party under a federal structure.

To understand this, let us imagine that the various provincial sections of the ANC (the Xhosa in the Cape, the Zulu in Natal, the Sotho in the Free State and the Tswana, Pedi, Venda in the Transvaal) were to demand that the ANC should be organised along federal lines to give each section some autonomy within the organisation.

Stalin put the question in this way:
"We know whither the division of workers along national lines leads. The disintegration of a united working-class party, the division of trade unions along national lines, the aggravation of national friction, national strike-breaking , complete demoralisation within the ranks of the social-democratic movement - such are the fruits of organisational federalism".

A similar situation has always existed in some or other form in South Africa. What is called "provincialism" here is partly the existence of separate "national groups", usually referred to as "tribes". The original purpose of Congress was to weld peoples of different national cultures into one single nation — to give them a sense of unity and a common purpose. That purpose, as we know, was to liberate our people from white domination — which was, in fact, national oppression.

This has been an easy task. Differences of language, customs, traditions and status have enabled local or provincial leaders to weaken the cause of national unity. Congress has always had to face and overcome the differences of regionalism such as Stalin refers to in his analysis of the old Russian society.

"The only cure is organisation on internationalist lines. The aim must be to unite the workers of all nationalities in Russia into united and integral collective bodies in the various localities and to unite these collective bodies into a single party."

Why is it important to have one single organisation in order to overcome the separatist elements of languages and cultural differences? "Because," says Stalin, "when a worker moves within his organisation and continually meets comrades belonging to other nationalities and with them fights a common struggle under the leadership of a collective body, he becomes deeply convinced that workers are in the first place members of one class family, members of the one army of socialism."

That has also been the experience of the ANC. It is only by participation in the struggle as members of one single organisation, that the different sections or organisations have recognised their common destiny as a single nation which demands the right to govern ourselves, the right to rule our country.

The oppressors have learnt the strength of our national unity and wish to destroy it. For this purpose, the bourgeoisie is trying to turn the clock back, to force our people into separate, regional or national moulds. So long as the whites can divide our people in this way, so long will it be impossible for us to combine our forces in

a single concerted attack on white supremacy. National divisions in our ranks are therefore merely a reflection of white minority policies, and a danger to our cause.
(Appendix iv to Lecture 2, July 23 1969)

A case of uneven development

The bourgeois writers who have produced the great bulk of material on South African history, looked at the past record from the viewpoint of the white settlers and the government. These writers were far more concerned with the quarrels between the Boer and the Brit than with the resistance of the Africans to the white invaders. Only one or two writers — notably Eddie Roux in *Time Longer than Rope* — have tried to see our history from the side of the liberation struggle. As a result, our understanding of the background is inclined to be shallow and lopsided. This is a great pity, because the distorted picture is likely to encourage illusions and incorrect attitudes with regard to the current problems of our struggle.

There are several outstanding features of the history which people usually overlook because of this incorrect emphasis. For one thing, how many of us realise that the resistance to colonial invasion and conquest went on for a longer period down South than anywhere else in the continent?

The first contacts between the colonists and the vanguard of our people took place in the area of the Tsitsikama forest round about 1706. From then on, there were sporadic clashes between Boers and Africans, leading to the first armed clash in 1779. For the next hundred years, whites and Africans struggled for the upper hand in the Eastern Cape. The Africans were pushed back, but their stubborn resistance succeeded in preserving most of Xhoseni for the use of the Xhosa-speaking peoples.

A second important point is that it was the arrival of the British which tilted the balance against the chiefdoms in the south-eastern region. The British came as representatives of a new industrialised civilisation, of an expanding imperialism. It was they who conquered our people, but they also liberated the slaves, introduced the principles of equality before the law and introduced the franchise on equal terms for all racial groups.

Because of this, it seemed likely to the people of the Cape — both the Xhosa and the Tswana-speakers — that they could belong to a common society with the whites and coloureds.

All of them participated in parliamentary politics, voted for the same candidates and fought their battles within the limits of the parliamentary system. Leaders in the Cape, men like Soga, Jabavu, Rubusana, Dr Abdullah Abdurahman, Sol Plaatje, were respectable, educated, middle-class persons who identified themselves with one or other of the white political parties.

To do so was all the easier because the Cape was undoubtedly the most developed area, at least up to the end of the century. It had the largest population, the biggest area, the most advanced system of education and the highest income per head. However, its agricultural system, though more developed than elsewhere, was not sufficient to support the steady growth of the economy. But the discovery of diamond mines from about 1875 onwards gave the Cape a new stimulus for growth.

Kimberley attracted Africans from all parts of the continent south of the Zambezi and laid the basis for African nationalism. Also during the 1880s, a class of educated Africans had emerged, who were able to produce a wholly African newspaper, *Imvo Zabantsundu*. These educated Africans were employed not only in the church, but also as clerks, journalists and civil servants in the lower grades.

All this took place at a time when the rest of South Africa was in a fairly backward economic and social position. White settlers in the Transvaal and the Free State were farmers with little capital. They robbed the African of his land and forced him to work under a system of strict racial segregation that was taken over from the days of slavery. Large areas of the Transvaal and Natal were still occupied by chiefdoms which retained much of their old independence.

The conditions in the north underwent a radical and rapid change as a result of the discovery of gold and the development of the Witswatersrand mines from 1885 onwards. In the next 20 years, it became obvious that the Transvaal was bound to be the main industrial centre of South Africa. In spite of these great mining developments, and in spite of the defeat of Boers by the British, the Boer system of racial discrimination remained. All the northern colonies — Natal, Free State, Transvaal — excluded Africans from the franchise and gave whites the monopoly of power.

Industrial colour-bars, pass laws, land segregation and discrimination in every field of social life applied in the north. It was here, and not in the liberal Cape that African nationalism took shape. The founders of Congress did not come from the educated and politically conscious Africans of the Cape. The ANC was very largely a movement of lawyers, clerks, ministers of religion, writers and politicians in the northern provinces.

It was not long, however, before the African citizens of the Cape lost their privileges. In the early 1920s, they began to recognise their common destiny with their people in the rest of the country. The Hertzog government, which took office in 1924, steadily extended segregation patterns throughout the whole country until one uniform system of discrimination operated in all the provinces.

The most significant steps taken in this direction can be described briefly by certain acts of parliament: the Native Labour Registration of 1911; the Native Land Act of 1913; the Native Affairs Act of 1920; the Urban Areas Act of 1913; the Native Administration Act of 1927; the Native's Representative Act of 1936; and the Native Trust and Land Act of 1937. These were the milestones along a road that led to the racial enslavement of our people in all parts of the country.

The important aspects of this mass of racial legislation must be born in mind. One is that the Africans in the Cape lost the right to buy land freely. They were as segregated and discriminated against in terms of land rights as the people in the Transvaal. Secondly, the removal of the Africans in the Cape from the common roll left them without an effective voice in parliament. The removal of the privileged status that the Africans possessed in the Cape opened the way to unity between African national leaders in all the provinces.

National unity is brought about by material conditions that develop a common consciousness in people who often have different traditions and backgrounds.

National consciousness, like class consciousness, is not a quality that comes to us by nature or birth. It is the product of history, of the conditions under which men live. African nationalism was a product of alien rule, of the exclusion of Africans from the centres of power, of colour-bars and racial discrimination.

To the extent that Africans suffered equally under the white man's rule, they were bound to develop an awareness of themselves as members of an oppressed nation. The extension of discrimination to the Cape was therefore the condition for the growth of a national consciousness no different in the South from that of the people in the north. Differences of language, customs and traditions remained, but they were overshadowed by the sense of being bound together in one single cause for liberation. It is this single purpose, this common understanding that is essential to the building of a nation.

(Appendix v to Lecture 2, July 27 1969)

Tribe and Nation

We have seen that both tribe and nation are territorial groups of people who share a common background of origin and traditions, speak the same languages, are aware of themselves as a distinct political and economic unit and want to preserve their separate identity in relation to other groups. Both tribe and nation are historically evolved. Generally speaking, we can agree that the nation is the later development, and that in many parts of the world it grew out of an amalgamation of tribes.

Apart from this difference in the stage of development, there is one important quality that distinguishes a tribe, and that is its dominant kinship structure. A tribe consists of the persons who are related (or believe themselves to be related) to one another through common ancestors. Most tribes consisted of three layers of kinsmen:
• those who were members of the ruling family or clan;
• people who claim to be descendant from the families of the followers of the ruling family, but were not of royal blood; and
• people who joined the tribe later on (e.g., who migrated from some other tribe, or who were conquered in war.)

Whatever their origin, members of the tribe were linked together by a series of kinship ties that cut across districts, sub-districts and provinces. A modern nation, by contrast, is composed of peoples of different origins.

This diversity is very evident in the United States of America, perhaps because it is the most recent of the big nations. Nation-building consists in developing common interests, values and attitudes — economic, political, religious, cultural — among peoples who, though of different origins (and, perhaps, races) occupy the same territory and are subject to the same government.

One of these common interests, whether real or imaginary, arises in opposition to other nations. Americans of all kinds take part in wars against other countries and in so doing develop feelings of patriotism and solidarity with one another. External pressure tends to consolidate people and develop a feeling of oneness. For instance, the Portuguese and Rhodesian attacks on Zambia create a national consciousness between the many different tribes. But alongside these common national interests, there are also internal common interests, e.g. trade unions, co-operatives, and working class parties which in a similar way express the common interests of workers of different kinds.

(Appendix vi to Lecture 2, July 30 19/69)

Some colour bar acts

South Africa's legal system is a reflection of the relations between the various nationalities or, as they are usually termed, race or colour groups. This is a special feature of colour-caste society, and differentiates it from "normal" class society. In a class society, all persons are supposed to be equal before the law. The statutes of England, for instance, do not explicitly state that the capitalists have special powers over or privileges distinct from the working class. Those privileges come rather from property rights, from their ownership of the means of production and from their position as employers of labour.

The South African statute book, in contrast, is loaded with discriminatory laws. There is no pretence here of equality before the law. In fact the South African social system is openly based on the principle of inequality. More than 300 years of slavery, forced labour, wars against our people and seizure of land, have gone into the making of this unequal colour-bar society.

All the colonies that came together in 1910 to form the Union of South Africa enshrined inequality in their statutes, but not to the same extent. The Cape came closer than any other region to the ideal of equality before the law. Cape liberalism was real, even though it did not extend to economic or social equality between different colour groups. In the other colonies of Natal, Orange Free State and Transvaal, on the other hand, there was not even a pretence of equality. The law discriminated openly and grossly against all persons of colour.

The Act of Union of 1909 represented the triumph of the northern provinces and their principle of inequality over the Cape principle of equality before the law. The new parliament was exclusively white in terms of the constitution, which provided that only white persons were capable of being elected to either the House of Assembly or the Senate. The ruling party, the South African Party, was led by Botha, Smuts and Hertzog — three Boer generals who had fought against the British for independence and white supremacy. Hertzog later broke away from Smuts and Botha over issues around Afrikaner rights in 1912, and formed the Nationalist Party in 1914. The first parliament consisted of white supremacists representing farming, mining, commercial and professional interests. The discriminatory legislation reflected the interests of the main capitalist groups.

One of the first acts was the Native Labour Registration Act of 1911, which gave the mine-owners an effective monopoly over the recruitment of African workers, and also provided for a large number of disciplinary measures (enforced by fines and imprisonment) against African workers convicted of insubordination against their employers. This Act retained and extended the old colonialist traditions of compulsory and enforced labour.

Two years later, Parliament introduced the Native Land Act of 1913, which did more than anything else, besides the colour-bar itself, to arouse African opinion and to consolidate the people against white supremacy. The Land Act set aside (or "reserved") 10 000 000 morgen of land for African occupation — about 7% of the total area. It prohibited Africans from buying or leasing land from any non-African outside these scheduled areas, except with the permission of the government. Since the African population could not expand its territory, the reserves would inevitably become overcrowded. The 1913 Land Act therefore supplemented the 1911 Labour Act by driving peasants in the overcrowded reserves to find employment in the mines.

However, the Appeal Court decided, in the case of Thomson and Stillwell vs Kama, that the prohibition of the acquisition of land rights did not apply to the Cape, because one of the qualifications for the vote in the Cape was the ownership or lease of land valued at a certain minimum level. Africans were entitled to the vote on the same basis as anyone else, and their franchise rights were protected by the entrenched clauses of the South Africa Act. The court held that legislation which denied Cape Africans the right to acquire land reduced their franchise rights, and was therefore unconstitutional.

The introduction of additional discriminatory laws was suspended during the First World War. Various Bills were introduced at this time, but none was actually adopted. The enactment of colour-bar laws began again after the war ended, with the enactment of the Native Affairs Act of 1920. This created a Native Affairs Commission which was supposed to look after the interests of Africans and provided for the introduction of local "Native" Councils in all the provinces. The Act also provided for the holding of annual conferences of chiefs and other hand-picked persons who would "advise" the government on matters of concern to Africans. This Act created a segregation mentality amongst whites and also encouraged Africans to think of themselves as a people separate and apart from whites.

The 1923 Parliament passed the Native (Urban Areas) Act. This has been one of the main instruments for our oppression and a cornerstone of the system of racial discrimination. This is the Act under which the movement of Africans into towns, their residence in towns, their conditions of employment and their lives as townsmen are regulated and controlled by white bureaucrats. It is under this Act that pass laws are enforced, that Africans are forced to take out service contracts, and that the police raid with their pick-up vans. It is this law that has become an instrument for the disorganisation of African family life, the persecution of trade unionists and political leaders, and the conviction of 500 000 Africans every year for pass offences. It is under this law that Africans have been rigorously segregated from other colour groups.

The very next year saw the enactment of the Industrial Conciliation Act of 1924, which provided for the recognition of trade unions and their representatives on industrial councils and conciliation boards. In other words the Act introduced machinery for the settlement of disputes between workers and employers — machinery which was the direct outcome of the Great Rand Strike of 1922. But the Act excluded Africans from this machinery and denied them the right to form or belong to registered trade unions. It therefore created a division between African workers and the rest of the working class, since coloured, Indian and white workers had the right to take part in the wage-fixing machinery under the Act. This was responsible for a wide division in the ranks of the working class, the effects of which are still felt even today.

(Appendix i to Lecture 3, August 3 1969)

The strategy of the liberation struggle

In earlier lectures, we concluded that the Native Representation Act of 1936 marked a turning point in the development of our movement. The Act:

• removed Africans in the Cape from the common roll;
• gave them three white representatives in the Assembly;
• introduced four white senators to be elected by Africans in all provinces; and
• created the Native Representative Council (NRC) of 12 elected and four nominated Africans plus six government officials (22 members in all).

This act brought sharply home to Africans that constitutional struggle for equal political rights was impossible under white supremacy. Congress had set itself the goal of extending the Cape franchise to the north, but events had moved in the opposite direction. The northern policy of an all-white franchise was being introduced into the Cape.

Since all attempts to extend African rights by agitation, mass campaigns of propaganda had failed, new methods of struggle would have to be adopted — or so it seemed to some members of Congress.

During the next 10 years (1936-1946) questions of tactics and strategy became a central point of debate in the movement. This period saw:

• the emergence of the All-African Convention (AAC), as a result of the Hertzog Act;
• the formation of Anti-CAD (Anti-Coloured Affairs Department) in the Cape and of NEUM (Non-European Unity Movement), both direct responses to the decision by the Smuts government to establish a separate Office for Coloureds;
• the formation of the African Youth League, which rejected the conciliatory and constitutional approach of the earlier period; and
• the protracted dispute over a proposal to boycott the NRC.

The arguments for and against the boycott reflected the uncertainty of the leaders about the methods of struggle that were to be adopted against a regime that refused to make any concession to African claims.

Two factors stopped the movement from coming to a clear-cut decision. One was its involvement in parliamentary elections under the Hertzog Act, including elections to the NRC. The other was the outbreak of World War II, when Congress once again proclaimed its loyalty to Britain and to the white government's war policy. For these reasons the issue of tactics, although kept alive during the war, was never finally settled.

It was not Congress that pushed the movement towards a revolutionary path of struggle. The pressure came from outside: from the great Miners' Strike of 1946 and from the Indian Passive Resistance Campaign of the same year.

The result of the Miners' Strike was the long-awaited refusal of the NRC to carry on the farce of what Mosaka called the "toy telephone"*.

The boycott movement had failed to take root because it involved many different and conflicting interests. African leaders could be elected to the NRC, or take part in election to the Senate and Assembly. Coloured politicians, on the other hand, were not eligible for election to any of these bodies and also bitterly resented the government's attempt to segregate them under the Coloured Advisory Council (CAD).

The coloured radicals of this period in the All-African Convention were nationalists. They wanted to emancipate their people from white domination and put an end to racial discrimination — and in this respect resembled the African nationalists. Unlike Africans, however, the coloureds were a minority group. To achieve emancipation, the AAC hoped to find a mass base among Africans. Its strategy was therefore two-fold: to consolidate the coloured and African masses under their leadership, and to detach them from the whites.

These coloured politicians tried to fight on two fronts, both against all whites — racialists, liberals and communists — who were lumped together as the *herrenvolk* (master race) and secondly against those African and Indian leaders (in the Congresses) who rejected their attempts to gain control of these organisations. The AAC was the instrument through which the coloured leaders of Anti-CAD and NEUM attempted to become the leaders of the African masses.

In order to attract the young radicals of the African and Indian Congresses, the coloured leaders adopted a posture of extreme militancy. They claimed that the boycott was a revolutionary form of struggle and demanded co-operation on the basis of their 10-point programme.

The programme was in fact a moderate demand for democratic rights and contained no traces of any revolutionary socialist objectives. By insisting on the acceptance of the 10-point programme and the boycott, the Unity Movement was able to resist every attempt by Congress to mobilise people across racial categories for a mass campaign. The objective result of the NEUM's position was to hold back the Coloured youth and some sections of African intellectuals from participating actively in militant struggle against white supremacy.

(Appendix ii to Lecture 3, August 12 1969)

Some colour-bar acts (continued)

The Industrial Conciliation Act of 1924 was a concession to the white workers who for a long time had battled for trade union rights. A second important concession was the 1926 Mines and Workers (Amended) Act. As the name indicates, this was an amendment of the original 1911 Mines and Workers Act, under which colour-bar regulations had been applied to the mines of the OFS and Transvaal. The regulations prohibited Africans from doing a large number of specified jobs in the mining industry. But the Supreme Court had ruled in 1924 (in the case of Rex vs Hidrich-Smith) that the colour-bar clauses were unlawful because they had not been authorised by parliament.

* *Paul Mosaka was a councillor on the NRC who made this comment to explain how he felt about talking to deaf ears.*

This case was a direct result of the Mineral Strike of 1922, which led to the defeat of the white miners and the downfall of the Smuts government. The Nationalist-Labour Party government that took its place acknowledged its debt to the white miners. It repaid the debt with the so-called "Colour-Bar" Act of 1926, which restored the colour-bar in the mining industry but confined it to Africans and Asians. The Act merely confirmed what had been the standard practice on the mines since the beginning of the century; but it also locked the door for African advancement in all jobs other than those classified as unskilled. Today our miners, although they have accumulated more than 100 years of experience, are still restricted to the most burdensome, most dangerous and worst paid jobs in the richest industry.

The next — and in some ways the most vicious of the discriminatory laws — was the Native Administration Act of 1927. The germ of this piece of legislation could be found in the old colonial systems (such as that of Natal) where the governor had absolute and dictatorial powers equated to the rights of a paramount chief over Africans.

In fact a paramount chief is precisely what the Governor-General was, according to the Native Administration Act of 1927. The Act proclaimed him as the supreme chief of "natives" in Natal, Transvaal and OFS, and gave him powers to divide or shift tribes, groups and individuals from one area to another and generally push Africans around as he thought fit. These were the powers that the government was later to use to great effect against the leaders of the liberation movement (and, indeed, against all opponents of the regime, including free-thinking chiefs and other traditional leaders, who were exiled to various places).

The Act authorised the government to extend the wide powers of detention without trial which were laid down in the Natal Code to other parts of South Africa. In addition, the Act included the notorious Hostility Clause, which created the offence of "saying or doing anything that would cause friction between white and black persons". In fact, this clause was never used against the white racists, but only against leaders who protested against white domination and demanded equality. Among the many who were prosecuted and banished under the Hostility Clause were Clements Kadalie, S Mahabeni, SP Bunting, E Roux, Johnny Gomas and Mrs Bhola.

Another provision in the Act was to have serious consequences for the movement. This was the section giving the government powers to appoint and dismiss chiefs, and turn the chiefs into minor officials whose position was defined by regulations denying them the right to take part in political activities. From this time onwards, the chiefs, with few exceptions, were turned into instruments of the white supremacist government and ceased to lead their people in struggles against the oppressor.

For the next ten years, Hertzog battled away at his so-called "Native" bills, designed to bring about the complete segregation that he and his party had declared was the only hope for a white South Africa. He finally succeeded in 1936, after the formation of a coalition government with Smuts and the merger of the South Africa Party and Nationalist Party to form the United Party. With this increased support, Hertzog was able to get the two-thirds majority in both houses that he needed to take away the common franchise Africans had possessed since 1852.

The Representation of Natives' Act of 1936 removed Cape Africans from the common roll and placed them on a separate roll, allowing them to select three white members of the Assembly and two white Senators. Africans in the other three provinces were allowed to elect two whites to the Senate. In addition, the Act created the NRC which had only advisory powers and proved to be a useless body.

The adoption of this act, as we have seen, led to the formation of the All African Convention (AAC) and marked the early stages of the transformation of the ANC from a talking shop into a genuinely militant organisation. For the next 10 years or so, leaders of Congress continued to participate in the affairs of the NRC but with increasing reluctance as they recognised its futility in lifting the burden of increasing discrimination against our people. It was only when they understood clearly that the white supremacists would never voluntarily agree to an extension of the franchise, and would never accept Africans as citizens with equal nights, that the movement broke with the long tradition of constitutional protests and parliamentary methods.

The other of Hertzog's "Native" bills that came onto the statute book was the Native Trust and Land Act of 1936. This is often hypocritically described as a kind of compensation for the removal of Africans from the common roll. The Act added a limited area to the land set aside for occupation by Africans under the Native Land Act of 1913. But the area was still less than that promised back in 1914 by the Beaumont Commission which had been appointed to carve the country up into white and black areas. It had taken the government 20 years to carry out — and then only in part — its earlier promise.

What else did the Act do? It extended the prohibition of land purchased by Africans to the Cape where our people had formerly enjoyed the protection of the entrenched clauses of the constitution. It brought all the scheduled and reserved areas under the control of a so-called Trust which was nothing other than the Native Affairs Department (NAD). From then onwards, peasants in all the so-called reserves were exposed to the bullying methods and petty persecution of the white bureaucrats of that department.

Another blow inflicted by the Act was contained in Chapter Four, which laid down new conditions for squatters or labour tenants living on the white-owned lands in Natal, Transvaal and OFS. The Native Land Act of 1913 had turned the squatters into labour tenants — people who could occupy land on the farms only if they worked for the white farmer for not less than 90 days a year. The Native Trust and Land Act of 1936 went further, and included measures to transform the labour tenants into wage labourers by introducing a graduated tax on farmers for every labour tenant on their land, and by limiting the number of labour tenants to a maximum of five families per farm. These regulations aimed to give farmers access to farm labour on a more equal basis.

This was on the eve of World War II, which was to absorb the energies of South Africa and most of the world for the next seven or eight years. During this period South Africa's racists, who were pro-Nazi, organised sabotage on a large scale against the war effort. The government, fighting both an internal and external enemy, was careful not to provoke the African masses. However, it did not hesitate to use war emergency powers to outlaw strikes among Africans and to take other steps to stop Africans using this comparatively favourable situation to launch a militant rights campaign. When the war ended we were in no better position than before. Shortly afterwards, when the Nationalist Party came to power we began to experience the full weight of the most ruthless racial tyranny that we had ever experienced.

(Appendix iii to Lecture 3, August 10 1969)

The relevance of strategic debates in pre-revolutionary Russia to our struggle

In our last lecture we saw that our movement went through many stages before arriving at the decision to embark on armed struggle. It can be said that this decision was forced on us by the atrocities of the ruling class and the white dictatorship. The decision was therefore defensive in character. Congress and its allies have been fighting a defensive battle for most of the present century. We have been trying to resist new forms of oppression and new restrictions on our rights and freedoms.

The main reason for our defensive position was the vicious policy of the government, which rained blows on our heads without giving us a chance to breathe. As far back as 1928, laws were used to exile and ban our leaders and handicap our organisation. But more important was the failure of our movement to work out and apply a strategy of attack — a way of mobilising the people to achieve our political aims. We recognised that we needed to mobilise people in this way. This is shown by the attempts to campaign against the pass laws and, perhaps more importantly, by the passive resistance movement of 1946 and the Defiance Campaign of 1952.

Moreover, there is no doubt that questions of strategy became the dominant issue in the movement after 1960 and that these debates resulted in the formation of MK. But even allowing for these developments, we must recognise that the movement gave less attention to problems of strategy than they demanded, and that, as a result, we had not developed a revolutionary organisation before the formation of MK. (The M-Plan was a first step in that direction, but was not carried out except in the Eastern Cape.)

Other revolutionary movements have faced the same problems of aims and methods. Any party that seeks to overthrow a dictatorship must stand up to the threats of imprisonment, torture, exile, constant raids by the secret police — the same difficulties that we have experienced ourselves. No such party can survive unless it discovers means of evading the activities of the security police, of rallying the people in spite of oppression. States vary in terms of efficiency and ruthlessness, but all try to crush their opponents without mercy. People accept the dangers.

For instance, when discussing the problem of the workers and peasants in Tsarist Russia, Lenin wrote:

"The main obstacle in the struggle of the Russian working class for its emancipation is the absolutely autocratic government and its irresponsible officials. Basing itself on the privileges of the land-owners and capitalist interests, the government denies the lower classes any rights whatever and thus fetters the workers' movement. That is why the struggle of the Russian working

class for its emancipation must give rise to struggle against the absolute power of the autocratic government."

This quotation appeared in a draft programme for the Social Democratic Party and was written by Lenin in prison in 1895-96. He wrote the programme in invisible ink between the printed lines of a newspaper that was then smuggled out. The programme was one of the basic documents shaping the ideas and organisation of the Russian revolutionary movement.

Lenin insisted in his programme that while his party should support every social movement against the autocratic government, the party must retain its independence of action (its own programme). As he put it, "the emancipation of the workers must be the act of the working class itself".

In the same way, we can and must say that the emancipation of the oppressed people of South Africa has to be the act of the oppressed peoples themselves; and that their struggle for emancipation must take the form of a struggle against the absolute power of the white supremacist regime.

In the years following 1896, the Social Democrats in Russia debated at great lengths both the aims and the strategy of their movement. Two points of view emerged.

According to one opinion, the social democrats should conduct a constitutional struggle on a programme of social reform. The opposing school — of which Lenin was a prominent member — insisted on a revolutionary organisation. The issues were debated vigorously by Lenin in his famous pamphlet *What is to be Done?* written in 1901-2. The pamphlet in fact dealt with an inner-party struggle. It was Lenin's view that such struggles "give a party strength and vitality", and that a party was weak when it lacked clear and distinct aims.

Lenin raised the question of political organisation in Russian circles by distinguishing between a mass party and a party of professional revolutionaries. He rejected the view of the constitution group that the Social Democratic Party should be a broad organisation of workers, with open elections, published reports and open meetings.

He argued against a broad mass organisation and in favour of hard core of professional revolutionaries for the following reasons:
• There must be continuity of leadership in a revolutionary movement.
• A mass movement draws to itself people who are likely to be misled and who hold divergent ideas; therefore there is a need for disciplined and conscious leaders.
• To have leaders of this kind the organisation must consist mainly of people professionally engaged in revolutionary activity.
• Because of government repression and the activities of the secret police, it is necessary to confine the membership to professional revolutionaries "who have been professionally trained in the art of combating the political police".
• Only a revolutionary organisation of this kind will attract workers and people from other social classes into active struggle against the regime.

(Appendix iv to Lecture 3, August 17 1969)

The organisation and methods of a revolutionary party

A revolutionary party is by definition a party that rejects the existing order of society. It is a party that has a revolutionary programme; that is to say, a programme of replacing the existing order with a new order. Such a programme is not possible without a theory of society that provides a guideline for its future development.

As Lenin put it in *What is to be Done?*:
"Without a revolutionary theory there can be no revolutionary movement."

Both the theory and the movement arise out of specific social and economic conditions that result in a whole section of the society (whether a class, a race, a national minority or a religious group) being alienated from that society, rejecting it, and being determined to reshape it in a new image. Revolutionary theory provides that new image.

Socialism was the theory of revolutionaries in the industrial countries of Europe during the last century. Socialism contained a rejection of capitalism and raised the vision of a new type of society where the means of production would become public property under the control of the working people. Socialism therefore meant the substitution of workers' power for capitalist power. Every country in Europe saw the emergence of a socialist party in one or another form during the course of the century, but not all the socialist parties continued to be revolutionary.

Some revolutionaries became reformers. Instead of seeking the overthrow of the capitalist system, trade union and socialist party leaders struggled for concessions within the framework of that system. This was possible because of the introduction of a broad franchise system in the second half of the century. Working class parties arose which competed for votes and for seats in parliament. The ballot box seemed to be the easiest and quickest road to socialism itself. The result was that the socialist vision became blurred and was identified with "national" interests — as though there could be a common interest between capitalists and workers. With few exceptions, the workers of Europe were led into wars by the leaders of Europe and fought not against the capitalists, but for them and against other workers in imperialist wars.

Russia was an exception to these developments in Europe. Circumstances there were very different from those in the western countries. Russia was slow and late in making the transition from feudalism to capitalism. The defeat of Napoleon's armies in 1812 by a great national effort had, in fact, given the Tsarist autocracy and Russian feudalism a new lease of life, and postponed the inevitable arrival of industrial capitalism. Serfdom, for example, was not abolished until the 1860's and even then, although technically illegal, it continued to operate in disguised forms until the end of the century. Although at the end of the nineteenth century Russia was the fifth most industrialised country in Europe, it was still mainly agricultural and backward. The great mass of the people was illiterate and superstitious; mines and factories largely employed migrant labour, and political power was concentrated in the landed aristocracy. The government employed a large secret police to suppress revolts and destroy opposition movements.

In those specific circumstances, a revolutionary theory was able to take root and grow without the diversions caused by the parliamentary collaboration of labour leaders which occurred in the western capitalist countries.

Under those circumstances a revolutionary party was able to maintain its image and concentrate on overthrowing and destroying the existing regime. Revolutionary socialism came late to Russia — only towards the end of the century — but it came with a tremendous force which was to change both Russia and the rest of Europe in a span of only 30 years.

Writing in 1902 Lenin divided the history of the Social-Democratic movement into three periods:
• In the earliest period social democracy took root, but without a working-class base; the movement was confined to a small handful of Marxists.
• Later, social democracy becomes a mass movement, but without a core of revolutionary theory and leadership
• Then there was a period of disunity and diversion. The proletarian struggle spread to new groups, but the leaders failed to keep pace with the masses.

The opportunist Social-Democrats lagged behind in theory and in practice and tried to justify their backwardness by invoking arguments about "spontaneism" and "economism". (By spontaneism, Lenin meant the belief that the masses if left to themselves would make the revolution without leaders; by economism he meant the theory that trade unions and workers should concentrate on economic demands such as wage increases and leave politics alone.)

Lenin finished this survey by remarking that the movement was entering a fourth period which would lead to the consolidation of revolutionary theory. The party, he argued, would emerge from the crisis in the full strength of theory. The opportunist leadership would be replaced by a genuine "vanguard of the most revolutionary class".

In looking to the future, Lenin was clear-minded about the problems. The Russian workers, he pointed out, had a real advantage in having been able to draw on the experiences of the mature working class movement of Western Europe. On the other hand, Russian workers had to fight a monster compared with which the capitalist government in a constitutional country was a mere dwarf. History, he said, had placed before the Russian workers a task that was more revolutionary than that facing the workers of any country. If they completed this task, the Russian workers would become the vanguard of the international revolutionary proletariat.

In explaining the early history of the revolutionary movement, Lenin said that a revolutionary consciousness had to be brought to the workers from outside, i.e. by intellectuals who identified themselves with the workers and who, through education, could acquire knowledge, ideas, experience which were unknown to the masses. "The history of all countries shows that the working class, exclusively by its own effort, is able to develop only trade union consciousness." The revolutionary theory of socialism on the other hand, "arose quite independently as a natural and inevitable outcome of the growth of a revolutionary socialist intelligentsia".

In the same way we can distinguish between the emergence of working class consciousness among our people and the growth of a revolutionary national consciousness.

South African working people became class-conscious in the period after the First World War as reflected in the rise of the Industrial Commercial Workers' Union. It was at this time that the workers began to form a class in themselves, to become aware of their own special interests as against the interests of the ruling class. But they could not become a class for themselves — in the sense of developing a revolutionary image — without assistance from outside. That assistance had to come from revolutionaries who were developing theory in organisations. To provide such theory and organisation is our task in the struggle that lies ahead.

(Appendix v to Lecture 3, August 24 1969)

5

'The University of the South'
MK camp life and political instruction 1978/9:
Extracts from Jack Simons' Diary

It is not often one has the chance to read about the experience of the camps in Angola first hand. Through interviews with comrades who were there as trainees and instructors, we can reassemble parts of the jigsaw of camp life. But Comrade Jack kept a record of his daily experiences while in Novo Catengue and so has given us an invaluable personal record to supplement the oral history.

He kept two diaries, but unfortunately only the second has been traced. The first covered the period from about September 3 1977 to March 8 1978 — the six-month stint when he set up the classes and wrote the lectures which appear in Part 2 of this book.

He went back to the camp at the president's request in December 1978, and recorded this diary. It is included verbatim, although edited for brevity, clarity and relevance. Comrade Jack used a kind of personal shorthand in writing the diary, and also referred to a number of individuals not mentioned elsewhere in the text.

19/12/78 Tuesday Flight to Benguela booked for 20/12.

20/12 Wednesday Mistake in booking. Talk to Jessica about Afrikaans on radio unit. Flight to Benguela (timed 15.00 today) put off — mistake by booking clerk. Plane left 11.30 this morning. Next flight is same time tomorrow (Thursday). But likely that plane will be fully booked.

21/12 Thursday Leave Luanda 11.20. Arrive Benguela. No transport. [*To Novo Catengue — editor*] Walk to sea.

23/12 Saturday Walk to town. Long queues at shop. Nikita Maleka (Commissar) says clerk gives preference to light skins. 2.15. Last night's music. Dilingo jives. Fond of music, ebullient — quick to laugh. But enormously committed. As is Piliso. Others here: Dr Peter and Commander Julius. In charge of Benguela residence. Commissar Nikita Maleka, 41. Impressive professional. Nikita 1975. Then a "gunrunner" for a Chinese: took guns into Lesotho and brought out diamonds. Police caught him in possession of case of 12 pistols at Ficksburg. Taken to Jhb. There he asked to see a magistrate to make sworn "confession".

His story: was arrested in Jhb (not Ficksburg) when on way to police station to deliver arms in response to broadcast message that persons surrendering unlicensed weapons would be allowed to go free. Magistrate accepted this version and refused to give statement to police. Charged with illegal possession of arms. Sentenced to eight years. HL lodged an appeal. Bail fixed at R1 000. Indian friend put up bail. Obtained service of Maisels who advised him to skip and helped him to escape into Swaziland. Made his way to Maputo. Joined ANC. After spending a year in Mozambique, went to Dar and from there to SU [*Soviet Union – editor*] for military training. Returned and posted to Benguela. Brought up as Moslem. Speaks Arabic, Gujerati, Urdu and Sesotho. Great grandfather came from East Africa, settled in Lesotho. Family has remained Muslim.

24/12 Sunday Bad night — mosquitoes. Sore throat — perhaps malaria — or flu? Leave for Luanda — meet Liz Matos when going to plane. Arrive at 6pm. No car. Early walk. Queues lined up outside few shops open — 8.00 on a Sunday. Main article bought was the "bun" which is popular substitute for bread (though I did see some loaves). Also toys and other articles (clothing) which I assume were Xmas gifts. Officially the day is not recognised (nor is Sunday as a day of rest) — yet the atmosphere is that of a holiday. [Note: Cuban Medical Residence opposite displayed conspicuously for passers-by to see, a picture of Castro surrounded by many coloured electric bulbs — a modern shrine to the national saint. Old habits persist under modern cloak!] There is much poverty here.

Jamaican song often played in residence:
Too many people are suffering
Too many people are sad
Too little people have everything
We make the wealth

Poverty is pre-revolutionary but is made worse by shortages. More equality, but less to share. Young Pioneers on street (about 12) with posters, wanting lifts from motorists. But only two drivers stopped — one a motorcyclist.

Too many people don't care:
You stinking hypocrites
(another Jamaican song)

10.15. Nikita is eating breakfast; I'm drinking tea. We are joined by two girls, one speaking Afrikaans (ex-Namibia [SWAPO]). She explains that bread (*pano*) is issued only to persons with ration cards, each allowed four shillings worth (about 40 buns) regardless of size of family. Persons without cards don't get a share — even if they are workers. This arrangement causes resentment, fighting broke out in some queues. I saw FAPLA [*Angolan army: editor*] units helping to control the crowds outside shops.

25/12 Monday Luanda. Conference postponed awaiting arrival Lusaka contingent. Xmas day quiet in town (7.45am). No workers to be seen except Cubans who are putting in a high security wall around their residence in Almeida Rd. Some trucks on road but this is clearly a public holiday. I was a bit later than usual: 7.15 instead of 6.30, but even so found most of residents abed.

What an absurdity! I arrive here Monday night, am kept waiting until Thursday for plane to Benguela, leave Friday midday for camp, spend barely three hours there, return to Benguela, stay there until Sunday (24th) wait five hours at airport for plane, arrive Luanda 18.00 (no one here. I get Protocol to phone residence for car) and am told on arrival that meeting will take place on Wednesday since all who must attend have not arrived (nine awaited from Lusaka). Even allowing for confusion and delay caused by our services, one wonders whether this failure to co-ordinate and schedule events is unavoidable. Do we have to generate a frenzy of action, an impression of great urgency to compensate for tardy, slow-moving pace of operations? As regards, I don't know what I'm here for. No one has told me more than that the President gave the instruction. [*Simons was in fact there in order to attend a joint meeting of the National Executive Committee and Revolutionary Council: editor*]

26/12/78 Tuesday Two hours' walk. City at work, quiet, subdued. Party of Cuban builders working on construction of concrete block-slab and reinforced steel building. No Angolan labour on site. Why do Cubans undertake construction without Angolan participation?

Last night an abortive cinema show — abortive because projector or operator failed to perform. Film is CBC-televised account of SA ... this kind of breakdown — we put up with it 40 years ago: must we still endure?

27/12 Wednesday. ... Last night (Tuesday) was CBC film on SA — unfortunately without audible sound track. Hence missed most of propaganda effects. There followed Soviet film (with Portuguese dubbing) on heroic exploits of a partisan group against Nazi invaders.

28/12 Thursday What I thought was malaria (it started in Benguela) has turned into a vicious head and chest cold. The first this year (1978). Miserable night ...

31/12 New Years Eve ... Rather quiet ... I give Ray's letter and the book (Magubane's photos of Soweto) to Steve Dlamini. Tomorrow I'll hand the Benguela fruit to Mac — who evidently wants to take her something from me. Others leaving for Lusaka tomorrow are Thabo, Joe Nhlanhla, Tom Nkobi, Florence Mphosa, Joe Gqabi.

2/1/79 ... We agree on commission of five — delegates to nominate for appointment by President. He tells me after lunch that I am one of the five. I urge that I am more useful in camp. He agrees. [Wrong to cancel visit to Novo where people have been waiting for more than month to start classes.] (...) [*Simons in fact was not deployed on this commission of the Revolutionary Council, but was made a fulltime "consultant": editor.*]

... The business completed OR [*President Tambo: editor*] announced that 1979 would be The Year of the Spear, commemorating 100th anniversary of Isandhlwana, ... a "swearing-in" ceremony for those who had not yet taken the oath to "defend the revolution with the Spear of the Nation till victory or death". Some very old members were sworn in for the first time: Yusuf, Reggie, Dan Tloome and myself!

I'm too phlegmatic to be stirred by such a ritual, but admit that I found it a touching occasion. We (some of us) wound up the evening by attending the Cuban 20th Anniversary of the Revolution, lots of people, food and drink, but I don't take kindly to these mass social events and was pleased when OR insisted on my leaving with him at about 9.30. The more so as my cold (which started in Benguela Saturday 23rd) has moved to the chest. The party had the usual effect of congesting my bronchial tubes. Added to the cold, the effects were painful — coughing, wheezing and gasping for breath all night.

Instead of leaving today for Benguela, we learn that seats are being booked today for tomorrow's flight. (Our chaps made no effort yesterday!) Not ideal — the Luanda residence — for awaiting planes.

4/1 Thursday Due to arrive Novo 20:30. At airport from 12:30 to 18:00 yesterday — only to find that flight was cancelled. Public suffers great inconvenience — no apology or explanation. While waiting we are told that food is laid on in restaurant. After standing about until the huge queue has been absorbed, we find that we have to pay for meals. Not having money, we return to the restaurant for a quick snack. Great lack of funds — transport has packed up, largely because reckless drivers smash cars. Back in Luanda residence at night, I write to Ray and pack the letter in a container which I hand to Agnes, with strict injunction to forward it at first opportunity to Ray. This is my third letter. She has acknowledged receipt of the first two — plus the Magubane book and the Benguela fruit.

5/1/79 Friday Start work. Arrived at Novo last night at 8.30. Moved into quarters: room formerly occupied by Ronnie. Moved about — spoke to the batch of students with whom I'll be working. Gave them a short talk on Vietnam and sorted out some problems of classes with Raymond Nkuko and Arthur (Commissar). See Larry Isaacs (*here called Castro Morris*) who seems to be running *Dawn*. Also Khumalo — veteran trade unionist who came from [Robben] Island and insisted on receiving MK training (though he is much older than other students).

Cuban relations deteriorated. Not many Cubans in military course ended November. Students attend political classes and do guard duty. Mzwayi says that Cubs are under impression that we regard struggle as primarily political — which is the case — and feel they are superfluous (one does not want to fight). Dr Peter is upset at being ignored [by] Cub doctor; Gwen in clinic complains of no co-operation.

6-9 Preparing for oath ceremony. Waiting and taking oath.

6/1/79 Saturday Peaceful sleep — no medicaments to ease breathing. Novo Catengue's air is good. Early walk along river bed, traces of heavy rains, pools of standing water ... Revisiting familiar routes and trees. Happy return to NC. Work schedules taking shape. I foresee 3 classes, each 2 months:

1) Returned group to be given advanced course on SA.

2) Instructors' class — about 12 selected to take place of present instructors who will go abroad (GDR)

3) Preparatory class — for about 20 students chosen to study in SU. Departure unknown — might be in a month or two.

Parade this morning in preparation for oath-taking ceremony on January 8 with President presiding. Strange — people recruited into MK and never required to apply formally for membership. Last year I argued that those who wished should be enrolled in ANC. I was then under impression that allegiance to MK had been ritualised. I was wrong.

But what of the others, who passed out of training prior to this new procedure? Will they too be called on to swear loyalty with the Spear of the Nation till Victory or Death?

I suggested that the written process be read and explained to all oath-takers. This is to be done — this afternoon and tomorrow. No electricity available (we had none last night). Jokingly, someone said "sabotage!"

7/1/79 Sunday Waiting for presidential party. Expect them at 14:15hrs. In evening, a bus-load of cadets arrives, but no President. No one knows if he arrived from Luanda or is still waiting for a flight.

Delay has taken much of the zest out of the proceedings. Students had to cancel their usual weekend football games, fruitlessly, as it turned out. People bear up well — don't complain — but effect is depressing. At yesterday's "rehearsal", camp commander (Julius) admonished the students on the need to maintain high standards of conduct in keeping with the oath. Referred to misconduct of one person at Benguela, who sold a pistol for money. Warned against dagga and liquor. Had much to say about the penalty for rape.

Mzwai followed in similar vein, stressing that oath-taking subjected soldiers to the code laid down, breach of which could be punished even by death.

More was said about students who cross the mountains (carrying blankets) to visit villages for liquor, dagga — perhaps women. I heard similar complaints more than a year ago. Yet am told that standard of discipline is high.

Conversation with Castro — Morris Semang (Larry Isaacs) — who seems to have made a great adjustment. Cubans to be giving instruction (at platoon level). Am told he is working on editorial staff of **Dawn**. He has no criticism of conditions in camp. On the contrary, approves wholly of the camps and MK administration.

8/1/79 Monday The great anniversary of ANC, plus swearing of allegiance to MK. But Presidential party does not arrive until after nightfall. Delayed by closing of airport at Benguela for repairs to tarmac. I'm out walking and escape the meal laid on in the Cuban mess. Parcel from Ray, and letter.

9/1 Tuesday Taking of oath. Proceeds slowly. Only 150 out of 250 sworn in by midday when President adjourns proceedings. Says he has tummy upset — probably due, he suggested, to rich food provided by Cubs (Hardly diplomatic).
We resume at 4pm after heavy rain — and complete another 40 — leaving 60-70 to do (I count 53). President is hardly fit, but finds stamina to talk to Political Department on Isandhlawana Centenary Celebration — and to sit through two hours of singing by camp choir. He conducts two songs with great verve and energy. That is evidently close to his heart.
    Monday night's culture evening was entertaining but not up to the standard of performances staged during my first stay.

10/1 Wednesday Oath-taking ceremony is hurried through by 8:00. President and party take off after a short speech — to Lobito where a plane is waiting. He takes with him two instructors, and Dudu, as his private secretary, a sign of dissatisfaction with the attention he gets in Head Office. Send letter to Ray (4th) via Cas.
    Dilingo gives me draft Military Code. I'm to "touch up" style. I've done the job, but wonder why it was not given to H/O personnel.

11/1 Thursday Work in earnest began today. Met political instructors a.m., the "special group" (ex Moscow) p.m., and an audience mainly of instructors and heads of departments at night for a talk on Zambia and the southern African situation. Tiring. Perhaps because I've not been working at this pace for some while. I hope I have the required stamina.
    My main responsibility is "special group". I quizzed them for two hours on their Soviet experience in the sense of academic work only. My opinion is that they do not obtain new knowledge or insight into SA struggle. But this is a premature conclusion. I need to work more closely with the group and also I'm probably biased!
    Note comment by Chico (printer) that members of the group returned with expensive goods — watches, radios, clothing. Is this advisable?

12/1 Friday Camp commissar leaves (for a short visit I'm told) as before, when Mark was withdrawn, I'm left to organise classes on my own — with only four instructors. Commander speaks to detachment on discipline and morale, citing cases of delinquency: a guard sleeping at his post; a combatant trainee who "loses" his pistol; another (or the same) in possession of 1 000 kwanza; and another 200 given to a fellow student to buy liquor (at B?). Difficult to comprehend content and purpose of the lecture, which appears to have been unpremeditated.

In evening Jabu (art) informs me that he did not receive art material which I thought had been sent to NC. Check with Wolfie. Also none of the books donated by Mrs Roberts.

13/1 Saturday Heavy and continuous rain — far more than at same time last year. Many roofs are leaking badly. New sheets are needed.

Am told that instructors will be pulled out early next week — sudden. No time to prepare substitutes, who are members of "special group" and without lecturing experience. I'll have to prepare material for them — on "MK series" — without sufficient data.

Two long walks today. Rains have brought vegetation to life. Much green and many flowers, purple and yellow predominate. Mosquitoes, hornets and flying ants invade room at night. One has to keep windows & doors closed. Stifling.

16/1 Tuesday Big upheaval — last minute as usual. All political instructors withdrawn, plus choir (temporarily), which disrupts my classes. Have to find replacements for instructors immediately — from among "special group".

Received tin of tobacco from Yusuf — welcome gift, letter from OR & one from Wolfie, who says he's on his way here. Reports that he could not call No. 250 for mail.

NC is now virtually a "transit" camp (perhaps because Vorster disclosed his knowledge of its whereabouts). Guard duties & essential services are maintained, with temporary units (such as "special group"). But we must maintain classes for detachment — two weeks on Isandhlwana.

My workload is all the greater because instructors have to be trained and to teach at same time. My letter to Ray (5th) handed to Commander — with revised version of Military Code.

19/1 Friday Heavy rains which bring to surface multitude of flying objects! Mosquitoes (how they bite me in bed!), flying ants, moths, hornets — plus crawlers: the lizards, cockroaches, beetles that invade the room in a flash if the door or window is ajar.

I therefore sleep with door and window tightly shut. No air-bricks. Foul hot air. Wake up early (as today 4.30) soaked in sweat.

Letter from Ray (6 & 8 Jan) last night, with MG [*Monthly Guardian: editor*] & newspapers. Must check whether she has had my letters — 31/12 (1 & 2), 4/1 (3), 10/1 (4), 16/1 (5).

Long staff meeting. Minutes read & recorded. Outline number of activities — teaching course for next month; ANC meeting; conference; briefing sessions; work on course for new detachment. Some of my 1977 innovations have fallen away — like evening classes for platoon leaders. Should be revived, but only when lectures have been written.

Castro (Larry) a useful contributor, as is Andrew (Ace). Meanwhile I grapple with SA history — "Wars of Resistance" for current classes.

Chief of staff asks me to give the talk on Isandhlwana on Monday 22. I suggest a student — but he explains that occasion demands a "senior" representative, to match the Cuban speaker.

20/1 Saturday Wolfie came yesterday (next door). Walked with him through bush and along riverbed. Hope he likes it, good effect his being here, on morale of administration, logistics, art, library. Shows interest in their work and is helpful.

Instructors returned from Luanda, will mark time until they leave for study course. In agreement with administration, I'll keep services of "trainees" — & invite instructors to sit in on classes of "special group".

Much rain today kept me from my afternoon walk. Wolfie and I stroll around camp and visit workshop. Very orderly, more so than at last visit 1977.

23/1 Tuesday Wolfie left, making up his mind (which wobbles) at last minute. Took with him letter to Ray (6th) — unfinished, because he'd said he'd leave tomorrow. (Letter was started on Friday 19/1)

Vusi added comments on heroes of today (very appropriate, & neglected by me)

Only two Cubs attended — Commissar and Interpreter (Director not in camp) — & had not prepared an address (though copy of mine was given well in advance). In past, Cubs would attend on such occasions — perhaps only for entertainment, though two or three sang with our choir (1977).

"Chief" had longish talk about relations yesterday. At an earlier period (I was not then in the camp) the major (who is Director of School) & his top men would meet company commander weekly to discuss "problems" & sort out difficulties. Also, Cubs would invite 4 or 5 of our staff people to spend weekends in Lobito seaside cottage. There were occasional political discussions between Cubs and MK personnel & generally a fraternal spirit. This was more pronounced during absence of Director, when commissar was in charge & encouraged interchanges of this kind.

The Director returned & swept such arrangements aside. At weekly meetings he would declare "no problems", so meetings came to a halt. Trips to Lobito were off — for our people.

The Cubs moved into present quarters (to give our administration more room) & isolated themselves.

Various examples given of failure to inform us of difficulties (e.g. breakdown of water supply, when Cubs filled drums & complained of non-co-operation on our part. Director says: you seem to think we Cubs are here to work for you) or to discuss new development in camp (e.g. work done on spring near old tank, which I observed & commented on to Chief — he did not know). Thami said there is isolation & some antagonism. If not resolved, we must expect to run into a crisis. (But we are not doing anything to ease relations — accept the situation & keep up running caustic comment on Cubs — their separate kitchen, eating arrangements, trips to Lobito) e.g. when water supply was cut off, we did not approach them with offer of assistance.

I doubt estrangement is due to personality clashes. Our people blame the Major — think a new man in his place would change things for the better. I doubt this. The isolation is being institutionalised & in my view is political in origin.

The Cub trainers & administration are under impression that MK is not being seriously prepared for combat — but is more a political organisation. They feel we lack drive — allow long periods to elapse between transfer of detachment after completion of training & arrival of new batch.

Wolfie did an excellent job — visiting all departments concerned with supplies & units — editorial, printing, women's section, art, library. Most sympathetic, takes notes and gives assurance of support — though no promises. Administration very impressed — so much so that Chief wanted me to begin my address by acknowledging presence of "Comrade Wolfie" — on ground that as Chief Logistics Officer, & coming from HQ, Wolfie was senior to all — even to Cuban Commissar. But refused to accept this pecking order, & "recognised" Wolfie after Cuban Commissar & Chief of Staff.

What a revelation of the deferential attitude to Lusaka Head Office: source of authority and power!

Isandhlwana series is drawing to close. Next step is to write up material in form of lectures, available for reproduction, booklet perhaps? "Old" instructors have been assigned this task & should be working on it now.

The Special Group to embark on series "National and Class Struggles in SA" — to be run as seminars. New instructors to work on ANC constitution and Freedom Charter — theme of next week's classes.

25/1 Thursday ... (Commissar Arthur back from Luanda with parcel — Ray's letter (& letter from family), 2 newspapers, Guardians, & "supplies" — avocado (rotten — thrown away), vitamins, bran — none of which is required — wrong.
Cubans obtain clear water for themselves from spring on mountainside — making 2 or 3 trips a day. Clear that they can't supply whole camp, but they should have talked things over with our people who put up with muddy water, but lack sensitivity — or regard for our own sentiments. As in treatment of patients in the detachment.

My appetite is diminishing. Not, I think, because of physiological deficiency. I simply don't relish the eternal diet of canned fish & spaghetti — prepared in a way I find unappetising. I eat mashed potato & now egg dish — kind of omelette of powdered egg — but have no desire to eat much. Can't really blame the diet however. Logistics & kitchen do make special effort to keep me happy!

26/1 Friday Lukas (Chiko) who went to Luanda as "security" with choir (& who was on truck that overturned) says that OR spoke to students there about NEC/RC meeting [*National Executive Committee and Revolutionary Council meeting: editor*], & that additions were Joe Gqabi & Jack Simons (which the audience seems to have found entertaining!)

This evening was visited by Company 1 Commander (excellent officer who was in charge of party going to Luanda). He came to talk about his notion of how the war would develop — intensified military activity leading to general rising — like in Russia Oct 1917. Although wrong (though I did not say so). Bolsheviks had developed a small but tight, influential party organisation, skilled in agitation & propaganda inside & capable of giving leadership. We have to build such an organisation, as the NEC meeting revealed.

27/1 Saturday 8:30 p.m.Instructors' briefing session today. Comparison of ANC constitutions. Yesterday presented the political background, ranging from Bambatha Rebellion to formation ANC & then the developments leading to the constitutions of 1919, 1943, 1958 — with postscripts on formation of MK & subsequent events.

We had to find formula to account for the reformist character of the 1919 constitution. Was it an indication of defeatism? E.g. no reference to land division & absence of clear demand for political representation.

Mavis (bright girl) argued that constitution should be seen as having two main aims: unity of Africans & rallying them against discrimination within prevailing structures.

Andrew (Ace) made another valuable contribution. The constitutions represent stages in the maturing of African nationalism:

1) 1919 operating "within" the system, the founders believed in educating the ruling class (or race) by persuading — bring about removal of colour bars, obtaining some kind of political representation, redress of grievances by constitutional action. But the first step was to unite & educate African masses.

2) 1943 constitution marks a big advance. ANC now wishes to change the structure, notable by securing political rights on basis of equality, re dividing the land, securing workers' rights, & dismantling colour bars. Though the intention is to "reform", the changes proposed are so sweeping as to be revolutionary in content.

3) 1958 constitution, drawn up during Treason Trial, after Congress of People & with imminent threat of illegality, is terse but conspiciously revolutionary. Speaks of "liberation", asserts that Africans must liberate themselves, seeks abolition of discrimination (absolute equality) & by implication majority rule under universal franchise. Calls for a scrapping of old society & creation of new one — as set out in the Freedom Charter. Not yet revolutionary enough. Does not put forward specific demand for overthrow of state — i.e. white minority regime; makes no attempt to analyse power structure. That perspective is developed later — after banning of ANC & call to arms. This is the "post script" which ought to form the 5th part of the programme :
1) aims
2) membership
3) methods
4) organisation
5) armed struggle.

28/1 Sunday Mzwai came last night. Paper by Sizakele (June, 1977) on courses of study to equip our people for governing the country after the Revolution. Mzwai says

I've been put on the Manpower Development Commission — but will remain here in Novo until further notice. How I'm to function on a committee sited in Lusaka is a mystery. But I've written to OR, in reply to his letter of Jan 15 on this matter & the other two points he raises: General Economic Commission & Freedom Charter.

Received from Commander a letter asking that Mavis and Oria be sent on mission to represent ANC women in GDR on 20 Feb. Occasion is centenary of Bebel's work on women. Florence (who writes to Mzwayi) says she has no-one suitable in Lusaka & that she has already forwarded the names of the two girls! I'm to "prepare" them for the conference — at which Oria will give a 15 minute talk. Met the two this morning & discussed the assignment. After that I drafted my reply to OR's letter of 16th on three issues raised: Freedom Charter; Manpower Development; Economic Survey. Andrew (Ace) is typing the letter & Mzwayi will take it — also a copy for himself as member of Manpower Commission.

29/1 Monday Letter to Ray (7th — the sixth went with Wolfie on 23/1) handed to Mzwai who leaves today. His address to Detachment — 8:15 to 10:45 in broiling sun — was about Vietnam, united front at home, Bantustans &, in reply to question, Freedom Charter & recent questions.

He also announced changes in adminstration. His health is deteriorating. Julius Mokoena, his 2nd in command in Personnel, was appt'd camp commander in Novo, & now returns as Personnel Leader. (Maybe Mzwai will be a sitting member of Manpower Comm, to which I have been appointed — by verbal intimidation). New commander is Thami Zulu, former Chief of Staff. His place is taken by Nkosi, Commander of Company I, who has risen from ranks over heads of men senior in rank, age & service, like Moss, Ordnance & VC (Vusi), Records & Admin Sect.

On Vietnam, he stressed unity & flexibility — tracing emergence of Liberation Front (NLF) in South & establishment of socialist republic in North. This was set out in some detail & presented as model. Spoke of Joe Gqabi's address in camp & reminded us that detachment was to have discussed Joe's insistence on working with organisations opposed to apartheid: Bishop Tutu, who testified in trial of 12; Inkatha (200 000 strong) with question mark about Gatsha.

As for unity with PAC — No! a thousand times no. It was vacillating, insincere & controlled from outside (i.e. Europe, America or China — not specified). Drew parallel with Patriotic Front — unity imposed from above on ZAPU & ZANU, without common ideology.

Referred to OR's talk with Sobhuza who asked: what is ANC doing about "little organisations"? — SASO, SASM, BPC & others. They were children of ANC — not competitors. ANC was not your property — it belonged to peoples of Southern Africa. He, Sobhuza, was a foundation member.

Asked whether FC was open to revision, he said it belonged to the people, adopted in Kliptown 1955, & endorsed by ANC & Congress Allies individually & separately. Could not be tampered with unless people were consulted & agreed. (A constitutional quibble or a loyal adherence to principles adopted when ANC was legal?)

As regards operations, he dwelt on clash 3 weeks ago when 7 combatants were attacked. One of the 7 deserted to the enemy, alerted a farmer, who called in police. The renegade (who slipped away on pretext of toilet needs) accompanied police when they attacked, & revealed pre-arranged signal & positions. Commander was shot dead. The remaining five detached themselves & are now in safety. He warned against agent provocateurs or infiltrators. All of us had to flush them out & report. Our safety & success demanded vigilance.

Cited case of Camp Commander (or Chief of Staff) at Benguela who sold pistol for wine & women (August) at a time when we had no bullets or weapons. (Case was reported also by Camp Commander at time of oath ceremony.)

In conversation with him after meeting, Mzwai in reply to my question, said we could discuss FC & forward suggestions, but amendments could not be made unless people at home were consulted.

In talking to detachment, he disapproved of Labour Party's public statement of support for ANC. This was not correct United Front tactics — exposed LP to reprisals. (His objection does not take into account impact of Hendrickse's statement on public & its possible significance on rejecting Leon's proposed alliance with Inkatha.)

Mzwai again referred to my inclusion on MDC. I am expected to draw up a brief for modus operandi — starting with a register of qualified adherents, members & supporters at home and abroad who might be drawn into activity. I mentioned my letter to OR & said I expected a directive on its basis.

(Mzwayi to Detachment: "Comrade Jack won't be with us for another 10 years"!)

A new name. [*For "South Africa" — there was a brief debate around finding a new name for a liberated South Africa: editor*] ANC suggested Maluti but hesitated. Nguni name is Ulundi. Meanwhile Makiwane group (in ANC at time) appropriated Maluti as their own. I suggest Malundi — Nguni suffix. He said this was mooted at time but no action taken. No objection to "floating" Malundi in camp.

3/2/79 Saturday 9am. Have been laid up in bed since Tuesday morning — malaria — horrible. [*Simons had suffered recurrent malaria for some years: editor*] For the first two days I ran a high fever and was hardly able to move my legs (as in the bout in 1973, when I picked up the bug in Dar Es Salaam.) A number of injections (2 a day) plus quinine tablets (6 a time) enabled me to recover somewhat. My stomach was upset however; I vomited several times (again today, but slightly) and have no taste for food. There is an epidemic of malaria in the camp. 79 cases reported from Monday to Thursday. Hard to understand — especially as Cubans seem to be immune.

9:15 pm. Relatively good day. Manged to eat breakfast (oats) & lunch (fish & macaroni) though in small portions. No supper.

Nurse Alice (ex-Baragwanath) a charming person, took my temperature this evening & pronounced it normal. But I am weak & fear a relapse. No exertion tomorrow or later unless I've regained vitality.

Many veterans — including Commander Thami Zulu & Khumalo, veteran trade unionist & ex-Island inmate — most of my departmental staff, succumbed. Most recovered after 3 or 4 days. This is my 5th!

4/2 Sunday Better — much. Received Ray's letters of 23/1 & 29/1, with cashews & two avocados (both rotten).

5/2 Monday 8.30 am. Good night, best since last Monday. Walked yesterday for half hour with Alice — good results, though exhausted. Showered this morning & went for breakfast to mess. Another sign of progress.

Letter sent to Ray this morning via Commissar Arthur (Mavis, Oria & Lindiwe go in same truck). I think this is 8th letter.

6/2 Tuesday 16:30. Attend 1st class since Monday a week ago (29/10). Very good perfomance, both the paper & discussion. Sound Marxists are coming up — not concerned with hair-splitting or abstractions & able to apply concepts — also to SA.

Slowly but surely getting back to normal. Though usual after-effects of drugs (e.g. swollen rectum & bleeding piles) are painful & likely to persist. Haven't a great deal of energy however for strenuous work — backache (result of being in bed for long stretch) forces me to rest after an hour or so of writing.

7/2 Wednesday 12:30. Back from class: Andrew's platoon, good discussion — as yesterday. Much interest in "nationalism", as dealt with in classics & in relation to our situation. Most of members participate & we do manage to resolve problems, reconcile differences & arrive at conclusions. Another month or so, combined with instruction in the platoons, should be enough to produce a good working team.

After-effects of malaria slowly ebbing ... But I've developed backache in lumbar region — painful.

8/2 Thursday Slow progress. Appetite picking up (helped by tinned peas & carrots — good) & handful of dried fruit (delicious). But pain in lumbar region has spread to left buttock & leg, impeding walking & moving about.

Am told that +/-120 cases of malarlia — nearly half our population. But not a single case among Cubans. According to table gossip, they allege malaria is an African disease — very vulgar & ignorant comment. Cub doctor, I'm told, shows no interest in what amounts to an epidemic — surely of concern to medical science — & inclines to view that many of us are malingering. If true, this attitude reflects the width of chasm between "them" and "us".

My "special platoon" is progressing. Members do most of the talking — I join in to give factual information or ask questions or dispute points of view. But some members of the group hardly participate & seem to be below average.

9/2 Friday Letter from Ray (29/1 — 2nd written on same day but only one received), UNIP, Lesotho & Guardian, 2 papers, briefings & ANC Strategy & Tactics. Note: 1st letter of 29/1 received 4/2. She acknowledged my letter of 19/1 (handed to Wolfie on 23/1). She is to receive or report receipt of letters of 29/1 (No 7 & 5/2 (8th) via Commissar.

More dried fruit — a treat. With canned peas & carrots I'm well catered for. Stomach back to normal, & lumbago is easing off.

Letter from Mainze Chona asking me to take part in 6 month teaching course at PCT College, Kabwe. Shall tell him I'll be glad to join when I return.

Also from Lesotho, asking for a chat on Krishnamurthy. Both letters replied to — & awaiting typist.

10/2 Saturday First long walk since bout of malaria. Backache almost gone — appetite excellent.

11/2 Sunday 8.30. Lumbago bad — why? Perhaps yesterday's walk was premature. Also bed sags — should look around for board.

Lying awake last night & pondering next move, I recognised that I'm not a free agent, but duty bound & must carry out orders. Organisation must decide where to place me. If it considers that my contribution is best made in military camp, I must & shall abide by decision without protest — as in the past.

12/2 Monday 12.10. Precisely 8 weeks since leaving Lusaka. Hard to realise this. On other hand, Lusaka seems far away in space & time. But I'm still below par. Much backache, poor appetite, sluggish bowels, dryness in mouth & back of throat, husky voice. I suppose these are after-effects of malaria & hope they will disappear. Very debilitating. I lack energy & just manage to work through a full 4-hour session, as I did this morning.

My mandate was to "reorientate" the "Moscow" platoon to SA. This is being done effectively, first by the Isandhlwana series, secondly by participation in the instruction of platoons, & thirdly by the course on national & class struggle.

This last, based on propositions from the Marxist texts, is more successful than I had thought likely. Only half a dozen take part — but those who discuss are obtaining a grasp of our situation, not only the theoretical concepts, but more important their actual application in our conditions, as strategy & tactics.

The programmatical aspect tends to be overlooked. Never by Lenin, however — the supreme tactician. No principle is "absolute" — except the revolution itself. That is the key to his approach.

13/2 Tuesday
Just 2 weeks since I went down with malaria (Tues 30/1). Only now feel I'm back to normal — backache mostly gone, mouth less foul, stomach working more regularly, appetite back (if food is palatable). But am still prone to spells of lassitude — want to lie down without sleeping & let my mind wander — something I don't relish.

Commander pressing for special classes for staff. I have in mind various themes. Problem is suitable literature for class to read. Will they wade through big tomes as instructors are expected to do? On other hand, one can't present elementary stuff —

they must be credited with some basic knowledge of Marxism — if not of SA.

1:45 Excellent lunch — vegs, mashed potatoes, bananas (sweet, large). This sparked off conversation about Angola's natural advantages. People talked about apples, grapes, pears, as well as bananas & pineapples, grown around Benguela. They then related experiences in USSR — kilometres of apples, vines & other fruits. USSR is a constant term of reference & index of comparison.

14/2 Wednesday Finish 1st series of classes of special group. Intend to start another round on Nations & Nationalities in SA — looking at particular "ethnic" communities. Problem is to find literature suitable for seminar & research by students.

Very hot. Rains appear to be tapering off. Sun bakes my side of barracks in afternoon. I dare not open door or window to cool night air for fear of admitting mosquitoes.

Stopped smoking — Tuesday 13/2. Second day of non-smoking — great improvement. Mouth not dry. Palate not itching, inner lining of mouth not irritated. I should stop smoking altogether, since I don't ration now (as I do when working away from home). At the moment, however, I chew sweets to counteract urge to smoke — & the sweets might not be good!

Waiting anxiously for letters from Ray — more so than ever. I think malaria has shaken me badly — morale, drive, interest in work, the lot. Certainly took the glamour (such as there was) out of Novo. It's a harsh, forbidding place exposed to elements, untamed, a pioneer camp, with few comforts. Running water (twice a day — 1 hr at a time) is dark brown & unpleasant to taste; rooms are stifling at night (sealed to keep out mosquitoes), food is often unpalatable & always monotonous, & so on. I dislike crawling under mosquito net, & dislike even more being bitten!

15/2 Thursday New series with special platoon: "How to combat enemy propaganda". Argument that political struggle, no less than military, requires us to "know the enemy". Political leader, instructor, organiser, agitator must know & explain our policy. First & most important requisite for political mobilisation. But he also needs to understand, explain, expose & demolish enemy propaganda. It is used to be mystify & brainwash people. We cannot develop political consciousness unless we "purge" the mind of enemy poison.

That is the task of political leaders, external & internal. Our classes are the practical application of our theory. Each student will debate against a text from Afrikaner copies on apartheid.

Worked with class (doing all talking) from 8 -11:15. Exhausting. I dismissed class (for genuine reason — they had to prepare material for new series: 8 days, Friday 16th to Tuesday 27th). But I welcomed break. Doubt if I could repeat 1977 effort — conducting classes 8-12, 3-5 & often 8-10pm. What stamina! And doing much the same in weekends.

I ponder this now because I feel incapable of such efforts — post-malaria depression? Other victims report similar symptoms — upset stomach, backache, foul mouth, blurred vision. But they are one third or less my age & recover more speedily.

Third day of no-smoking. Extraordinary improvements in mouth, throat & respiration. But voice remains low. I should stop smoking in toto! ...

I arranged a programme of "seminars" for staff (i.e. Commander, Chief, Dr Peter) — 2 sessions a week of 2 hours each. Topics cover 20 sessions i.e. 10 weeks. This would extend to end of April, which seems to be the likely duration of this assignment — unless, of course, I don't stay the course or am recalled back to Lusaka.

16/2 Friday. Last morning class this week. Great relief. "Special Platoon" is uneven — a few alert members, who can follow & participate. Two-thirds are dull, seldom speak & might not keep in touch. The group spent 9 months in a Moscow "school" receiving lectures from Soviet academics (professors) who no doubt set a high standard. But the students (with exceptions) were not up to the mark. We should not accept offers of this kind unless we have students qualified for the courses offered.

Letters from Ray (5th & 10th Feb) plus Nelson Richards, Ruth First, Anniversary card & Zambian Daily News & Guardian, Social Review (UCT). My letters of 29/1 & 5/2 have not reached her. No transport to Luanda notified (known) to me since 5th.

17/2 Saturday Two hour "seminar" with staff (Commander, Commissar) last night. Silent audience for most part — only Commander & Dr Peter attempted to contribute. Heavy going. I spoke on "colonialism" with a dash of Marx — but lack of response indicates that topic is strange to them — though all have had training in USSR or GDR. I suggested participation by members in "presenting" topics & undertook to prepare list.

Bad night — awake from about 1am. Right arm painful — dull ache. I attribute it to arthritis, but tablets for that condition did little to relieve pain. Now I worry — is it a condition of the blood circulation? Impending heart attack? Or what? So I lie awake in this dark, stuffy room with door & window closed, under mosquito net.

19/2 Sunday Slept fitfully — waking up at 5am, after a restless night. Arthritis (if that) in right arm a nuisance. Painkiller & anti-arthritic capsules have little effect. Prepared 14 topics for staff seminars — ranging from colonialism to SA history (wars of resistance & rise of ANC-MK). Question: Will the personnel do the "research" (reading) necessary? They might prefer to listen to me — but that process is relatively unrewarding.

Walked for about an hour (6:30-7:15). First decent walk since malaria. Vegetation still lush, but beginning to droop — seeds bursting out of pods. Prolific after heavy rains.

"Discovered" Ray's letter of 13th Feb (among packet of envelopes) acknowledging letters forwarded 16/1(5), 29/1(7) & 5/2(8) — but not 23/1 (6th — started 19/1) which went with Wolfie on 23/1. (He told Ray he had no letters from me. Why did he not say I handed him one when he was boarding the bus? Sabotage!)

Replied to Ray's letter & put mine in envelope to be given to commander tonight for dispatch to Luanda. With another letter also addressed to Ray, containing my replies to Chona & Lesotho University, also letter to Slovo, Maputo, re "traditions & customs" inquiry.

Ray letter (2) & one to Slovo handed to Commissar at night. I'm told they'll go to Luanda, perhaps today?

19/2 Monday Special group is responding poorly to series on Afrikaans propaganda. Half a dozen participate, usually the same persons in each discussion (session). Rest are indifferent or unable to comprehend. I urged them to review position critically — if they wish, I'll try another approach: different topics. I'm inclined to think that most are not up to the standard set for an advanced class. Also, only a minority benefited from the 9 months in USSR (i.e. in terms of concepts & intellectual growth. They probably gained much as "tourists" of a very privileged class!) There ought to be more care in selection. If a socialist country offers 20 places & we have only 10 suitable candidates, let us not "make up" the remaining 10 by random selection including "rejects". Not fair to them or to the hosts!

20/2 Tuesday Special group discussed my criticism amongst themselves (in my absence) & agree to continue series on condition that each member prepares outline (i.e. does research) on every topic, that chairman inspects outlines & if necessary calls on individuals to take part in discussion.

Livelier response today. Perhaps we are getting somewhere positive with group?

Fresh fried fish tonight (massbanker). I eat two — skin & all except bones, with great gusto.

Tonight (8-10) seminar with administration. Topic introduced by Commander. Brief, to the point, systematic, but limited in scope. Insufficient background information & theoretical insight. Dicussion generally mediocre — for same reasons.

22/2 Thursday Am not sure whether my presence here is rewarding — whether there is need for my services. Training of instructors, preparation of material for classes, organisation of meetings, conferences, seminars — all could be handled by existing staff. I came here under impression that "old" instructors would be moved (to GDR) long before end of January (when course begins) & that training of new instructors should begin at once — only half-employed & "running down".

As for the "special group" I suspect that the adminstration (Mzwai) does not know what to do with them, or how useful the "Moscow" training was. Actually, the best among them have been drafted into the "instructors' class", will be employed in Political Department. The class will have to be absorbed in the general student body — elsewhere?

23/2 Friday "Holiday" — in honour of Red Army Day, Anniversary of Soviet Army. Rather sweet — tribute to our ally & host (who is not represented in NC). Good thing to imprint on students the concept of int. solidarity with socialist Africa, (also, USSR & Cuba, which helps to identify us as a "Party" of socialism).

Commissar's file: (Arthur Sidweshu) Political Commissar — active, imaginative, lots of drive & devoted. Involves students in activities — which is good — Women's International Day, Freedom Radio, Luanda, visit by unknown someone.

What remains is to reduce lectures to writing. Wars of resistance, seizure of land, formation of ANC, political struggle, COP, [*Congress of the People: editor*] FC, Treason Trials, Sharpeville, ban on ANC, MK, A People's History of SA. This is what I should be working on now!

24/2 Saturday Yesterday's commemoration of Red Army Day went off well, with a display of relevant Soviet literature, introduced effectively by members of ex-Moscow "special" platoon — a baseball match (in which Cub predominated) & a football match between the "champion" Dynamos & a "picked team". At night, a culture evening — speeches by Cuban Commissar & Camp Commander (very good), followed by concert (highlight a drama, centred as usual around a shebeen — the most vividly remembered social aspect of Soweto life — coupled with crime. B/stan removals & resistance — the political element a relatively new note in "Shebeen" acts).

The concert ended at 11.35 — I managed to get back to my room in time to fix the mosquito net — but had difficulty in sleeping because of arthritis in right arm. Perhaps effect of sitting cramped at the football & again at the "culture" show?

25/2 Sunday Tea break with Commander & Commissar. Discussion on "specialisation" in Novo for specific roles inside. Mentioned were women, youth, culture (language, tradition) & "industrial" (i.e. trade unions). Agree that we should move towards the training of selected persons for these different "specialisms". Material is needed — on women, copies of VOW [*"Voice of Women": editor*] should be regularly forwarded. Youth (copies of speeches at Int. Conference). Industrial (copies of Worker's Voice). I suggested that the commissar should visit Lusaka to discuss with different departments, share some ideas & obtain material.

Letter to Ray (day 21 onwards) posted today via Thomas, who is moving to Luanda (if tomorrow, it might go to Lusaka by Monday 26/2). This is 10th in series.

19:00. This afternoon "briefing session" in development of capitalism. Pauline (Olga) "presents" one of the two parts. Good, fluent speaker — but poor researcher, who depends on memory & makes awful factual blunders — like confusing multinational states & multinational corporations, or discussing the American revolution of 1796 as a struggle over slavery (i.e. Civil War of 1865) or linking French Revolution of 1789, to Louis Bonaparte & Paris Commune of 1871 in a single broad sweep. Quite the poorest research job I've come across during present visit.

Am plagued with recurring pains in right lower abdomen — above the groin. Am disturbed — think of enlarged prostate (wrong place?) appendicitis, cancer — all because I can't remember having had such pains before. Perhaps it's wind — large amounts of peas & beans consumed.

Walked with Arthur Sidweshu. Left country 1965 on advice of Ngakane, ANC member working in Christian Council — or other such body. Previously employed as organiser of youth clubs — network operated by churches (he was Methodist but the clubs were non-denominational) — worked with SASCO, BCP, (Black Community Project) — attended conferences on churches. This aroused suspicion of Special Branch who detained him (1973 or thereabouts) with other youth organisers. On release was banned and house arrested, but allowed to work for furniture firm as sales supervisor. Had car & was able to move about — distributing church & Institute of RR material (I'm vague on this — did not want to cross-examine). Probably trained in SU — shows organising ability — & brought back as commissar. Bright & has ideas.

26/2 Monday 5:30. Awake since 3am. So after reading in bed (*Guardian*), showered & dressed. A pity. I'll get dog-tired later, when in class & shall have difficulty in keeping awake.

Ronnie (ANC K) arrived yesterday evening (with Mabaleng & Julius). Brought letters from Ray, Tanya & Mary plus 2 papers & Guardian. No briefings.

Last night's exhibition of Soweto slides proved very popular — as it should be, with so many in the audience having been participants. Unmistakable evidence of police brutality. Exhibition (by Defence & Aid) will do much to strengthen our case overseas.

Minnie *[Ray Alexander's youngest sister: editor]* died in her sleep — midnight Wednesday 14th. Tanya wants to marry Heinz, buy a house, give up law & resign from UCT. Johan is living with Mary in Sheffield (horrible place) in a purchased house & is applying for jobs & university places. But won't write to us. My feelings to all this are depressing — small wonder that I could not fall asleep after 3am.

Camp life isolates one & creates a deplorable lack of concern with family-domestic affairs. Is this why many people (also women) like the army? A world of its own with problems & worries ... but these are dealt with in a firm structure of organisation & command.

27/2 Tuesday Letter to Ray (11th) handed to Ronnie who expects to reach Luanda tomorrow (Wednesday) Ray should receive no later than Monday 5th.

State of alert following raid on Luso by Smith's mercenary thugs. A mini alarm last night & a bigger, more protracted one this morning: starting at 4am. Operation entailed evacuation of camp & taking cover some 100s of metres away. My party (HQ) & Cubans moved into a viaduct under railway bridge from 6 to 10. We were told alarm is over & went back to camp.

I'm told that exercise will be repeated till further notice, but don't see what purpose it serves except as an exercise in preparation for an actual assault — the motive for which (on part of Boers) is obscure to me. Are we such a threat that they must risk an international storm? Anyway, Smith is doing the job — i.e. of intimidating Angola (which can be the sole purpose — political & military — of the attacks on bases in adjoining territories).

28/2 Wednesday Another "alert" — breakfast at 5:30, long trek along riverbed, scrambling up ravine to reach culvert from the back. Return at 10am. Rest of morning — recuperation! No classes. I'm told this is likely to be repeated until end of week (but will Cubans give up this weekend in Lobito to participate?) I can't puzzle out logic of exercise. If SA intends to attack us, why do it this week when we are bound to be "alerted", rather than next week or later, after we've gone back to normal routine. Shouldn't a different system be devised to alert us if & when an attack is actually being planned? Can't there be a method of detecting the approach of hostile (enemy) planes in time for us to prepare?

Present arrangement strikes me as amateurish. I suggested to administration that classes be conducted in afternoon (3-5) and encountered some support from the commander, but also resistance. However, instructors are in favour — a good, positive approach.

Dr Peter Mfeleng is to attend a WHO (sub-region) conference in Luanda on March 26. Theme is Year of the Child. He wants material on effects of apartheid on infant & children's health. Wrote to Ray asking her to make inquiries about conference held in January in London on this theme. Suggested Joan Brickhill as possible source.

1/3 Thursday 10pm. Letter to Ray handed to Commissar for delivery to Aaron who leaves tomorrow early for Luanda via Benguela.

Another "alert" action this morning — dressing in dark & leaving camp at 5:30 for "stations". Disrupts normal work — but we managed to resume classes in the afternoon. Students are exhausted, but I managed to keep my end up — even to extent of preparing another round of themes for seminar on apartheid & nationalism in SA. The target is pitched high — probably above the heads of some students, but they are being "exposed" to fairly basic issues in our political situation?

2/3 Friday 3:15pm. "Alert" extended from 4:30am to 1pm — apparently because Cubans expected arrival of helicopters with a "commission" on board — to check security. Major (I guess) wanted to exhibit our "state of alert". But hunger intervened. No breakfast today. By 12:30 word came through that we had to return in "sections" for food & keep a low profile — i.e. not move around camp but remain in barracks. I can't think of any other reason for interrupting the exercise before the helicopter arrived. Actually, it came as we were returning to camp — but without the "commission". It brought 3 anti-aircraft guns to reinforce our battery.

Administration commented on reticence of Cubans who gave us no indication of what is happening. They issue instructions, don't take us into their confidence or plan with our participation.

3/3 Saturday 3:45. Up at 4 this morning — breakfasted on tea & marched off about 5, while dark enough to make walking a problem. Long uncomfortable morning until past 2pm. Purpose was to demonstrate defensive position to the visiting Commission, headed by the Cuban General in charge in Angola. Understand that innovations will be made, involving "lots of work" according to Commander.

Elias Banda, who is conducting a "survival course" in the North, arrived with a film projector. Will have our own cinema show. Brought me a letter from OR, dated Feb 24, acknowledging my letter of Jan 23. Evident that no action has yet been taken.

No letter from Ray — disappointing.

8:20pm Cuban "High Command" is perturbed at failure of frontline states to offer (put up) resistance to the "strikes" by Rhodesian planes. This weakness, they say, throws doubt on the "credibility" of the governments & the liberation forces, lowers their standing internationally & encourages more assaults. Hence the serious view taken of Novo's position — very vulnerable to attack from SA. Its planes appear to have overflown the adjoining area on the return from the Cassinga Massacre, when they circled round to the coast & flew South.

Conversation with Cesare (interpreter) suggests that Cubans are critical of lack of "spirit" & aggression among Angolans (presumably FAPLA) who, it is said, don't "defend" their revolution. This is something that Cuba cannot do for them. Angolans are untrained, have inadequate hardware & few landing strips for planes.

4/3 Sunday 8:10pm. Exhausting, big inactivity, sitting around from 4:30am to 6:45pm, waiting for "next" order. Only break came at 12:30 — 20 minutes for lunch (plus the walk to & from). Am told that this will be the schedule until the end of the year. (I doubt this — but can't get anything more definite to guide me). Meanwhile political education is "scrapped" — no effort is being made to continue classes "in the bush". (Probably rightly so).

With this prospect I suggest (to Commissar) that I be posted back to Lusaka. He tells me that this possibility was raised today. The suggestion came from Julius Mokoena (Mzwayi's deputy). Gertrude Shope arrives tomorrow with the GDR delegation (Twala?) & I'm likely to go on Thursday. With luck, I might be back Monday 12th.

Not "sorry". This tour was poorly planned, ill conceived. Administration was stuck with the ex-Moscow group & called me in as stop-gap.

Andrew came in tonight. Said the group had a feeling that I would leave & want me to prepare material (which I have done, on nationalism). They are appreciative, which is rewarding. But there's little I can do in the time left.

Suggestion is I meet the group 8-10 at night, but will they (or I) be fit for discussion at the end of this kind of brain-scrapping inactivity?

Two helicopters arrived today. Evident that top brass take the position seriously — a matter of urgency.

Another group of instructors (Ntokozo & James) arrive to discuss possibility of continuing with classes in the sections. Administration would blunder if it ignored these signals of distress.

8/3 Thursday Benguela. I arrived here Tuesday at 6:45am, having left Novo at 5:30 or earlier in Cuban land-rover with Elias Banda & "Solly" who goes to Luanda for hospitalisation. I was given my marching orders on Monday night, at 10:15 & allowed an hour to pack (I was thinking I'd be pulling out at 7am, so did not complete packing).

I learn today from Nikita that he was instructed on Sunday to book my seat (plus three others for Gertrude Shope, Oria & Solly) on Saturday 10th, which means that administration had decided to "evacuate" me at the Sunday meeting — though I was given definite orders only Monday night: at the last minute. But this is typical of army organisation.

Find things here are tedious. (My third day here & I must contain myself to sit through tomorrow with patience). Food is atrocious; there is much noise (playing of gramophone) & circulation of people. I try to get some peace for reading in the bedroom, but I share it (tonight with 2 others) & my fellow sitters wander in & out often. However, I can keep myself clean (though that was not a deficiency in Novo either).

I'm frustrated — largely because the Novo "tour" petered out & never really got going. I think the series was ill-conceived — though I helped to train new instructors, which was not part of original programme. However, I'm pleased to have been around when the state of "alertness" was proclaimed. It gave me an insight into the problems involved in preparing a camp for defence against an attack & also better understanding of Cubans' role. They took immediate, decisive action, planned the entire operation & brought in massive equipment. (Two helicopters arrived on Sunday — as previously reported). On Monday we were up at 3:30am, breakfasted at 4 & left for our positions at 4:15, when walking was difficult in the dark.

9/3 Friday Hardly slept — to bed at midnight, but my roommates (Julius & Banda) were restless & mosquito bites plagued me.

Pleasant experience at function of Angola Women's Section celebration of Women's Day. Speeches (which I had missed) were given in cinema hall before 9pm. Gathering then shifted to a former amusement park a few minutes walk from residence. I walked there with Gertrude Shope & Oria — both in MK uniform. We were admitted without question when I explained that we were from ANC(SA).

Received warm welcome, seated at table & served with Coca-Cola & (for me) beer from a long jug. Delicious, although I have been troubled by stomach upset — gastric cramps & gas — for almost a day).

Celebrations (dancing & slogan shouting) culminated in a gathering of the women which I attended from back perched on staircase. Presentation of a red rose & piece of cloth to each of about 20 leaders (evidently urban & elitist group almost all of them pale-skinned).

While watching the dancing I was grabbed by a middle-aged woman — shanty town type — who insisted on dancing. I did my best, but her pace was too fast: prancing & kicking of feet, which I had to emulate to maintain the rhythm. I pleaded exhaustion after 10 minutes & literally tore myself away — hopefully having contributed my bit. Two leaders joined our table: Leonard Seke, Provincial Secretary of UNTA (old guerrilla, who had lived in Luanda in 1968 onwards & lived with or knew the Shopes); Isabel Maria, Secretary of Education UNTA. Address of both UNTA, Benguela. The Women's Section is known as Organizacao da Muhler

Angolana (OMA) Benguela. (Leader is "Comrade Alice") I undertook to see that letters are written 1) SACTU to UNTA, 2) Women's Secretariat to OMA & a personal letter to Isabel Maria, expressing solidarity, appreciation of Angola's support & thanks for reception to women's delegation.

11/3 Sunday Luanda. Arrived yesterday — after tedious wait of four and half hours at Benguela airport — no food (other than rolls and tea at the Residence for breakfast). No money for a meal ticket in airport restaurant. Gertrude Shope was in party that accompanied me — on her way to meet the "north". Will leave on her return for Nigeria.

Ray's mail (her letter & those of Tan & Mary) awaiting me with 2 newspapers. One of the parcels could have been forwarded to NC — with Gertrude. People here don't co-ordinate — or bother to find out who is leaving for Novo. Ronnie (Kasrils) says that letter I gave him to forward from here is still lying around, though Max left last Sunday for Lusaka.

Residence is swarming — especially with girls, many of who cannot possibly be usefully employed. A case of congestion: bottlenecks. I'll be glad as always to escape! Am told that my seat is reserved on Aeroflot taking off at 7am tomorrow.

13/3 Tuesday. Back in Lusaka — by Aeroflot. Left residence Luanda at 6:45 — late & just made the plane (which took off at 8). Am told (Ray) that OR instructed my return by 25/3 — in response to UNIP request for participation in scientific socialism programme. *[Diary closed for time being]*

15/3 Thursday 10:45pm. OR called. I explained position in Novo. He showed me a letter from "Doc" reporting that SA planes bombed Novo yesterday (14th) at 7. Three dead (including one Cuban) & eight wounded. Letter added that camp has 14 anti-air guns & Strala.

Almuth reports (tonight) that SA Radio announced two SA planes "crashed" in Angola (time is uncertain) — Possible hit by our ack-ack?

New phase in our struggle. Enemy takes initiative on search & destroy operations. We need to plan strategy — possibly in conjunction with allies (SWAPO, ZAPU, Frontline States & Cubans).

19/3 Monday 10:20am. *Sunday Times of Zambia* reports that SA attacked a camp in Angola, killing 3 & wounding 14. This then referred to NC — though not specified. Reported by Pretoria last week that one plane "crashed" — two occupants died. Was plane hit by defence?

Ronnie's letter: Novo was flattened. Other reports: all buildings razed to ground. 3 deaths (one a Cuban), two S Africans – one being Chairman.

24/3 Saturday Joe Slovo passes through. Reports conversation with GDR ambassador to Angola. Constraints on supply of arms to Angola to repel SA attack: warning by USA that more SU "tricks" (like one in Angola) would mean no Salt II agreement & direct intervention by West. Cubans think we should evacuate NC.

27/3 Thursday OR's visit. Upset by death of Mfundisi in GDR plane crash at Luanda. German crew & 5 ZAPU killed with Mfundisi. Angola embargoes publicity on destruction of NC Caterpillar destroyed with other vehicles in workshop. Attack by 2 Canberras escorted by 3 others. 500 bombs dropped & machine-gun firing — in one and half minutes. Our defence ineffective. Two "Stralas" not in action — suspected that Cubans failed to man guns. We scored a hit on one of the bombers — which crashed (killing a major & a lieutenant).

Attack at 7:30am. Chairman & one other killed when running from shelter to take refuge in railway cutting. Railway lines also bombed. All buildings destroyed.

19/4 Thursday Mzwayi says that defence system at Novo was barely operated. He blames Cubans who told the gun crews to "take cover" — instead of manning & finding the attackers. Of the 6 guns, only two were fired, both by our people who defied the order to take cover. One of them hit & brought down a bomber. But the 18 Strala (heat-seeking missiles) were not fired. All were to be operated by Cubs, who had received their instruction from our men. He blames the Cubs for the failure & accuses them of cowardice. Our people have lost confidence in the Cubs — the gap between the two sides has widened. He recognises, however, that the prompt action by Cubs to evacuate the camp saved our lives.

20/4 Friday Informal meeting of "Manpower Committee" (Mzwai, Dilingo & self) from 2-3:30pm. Evident that no thought has been given to committee's functions & organisation. Discussion showed need of a survey to catalogue personnel & assess the qualifications of individuals. Someone would have to visit centres to complete register. Secondly, placing of students to further studies should be carried out with reference to present & future needs. For this purpose, the committee should direct the allocation of scholarships by the Youth & Student Dept. Thirdly, the selection of persons to train or guide persons in forward bases should be monitored by the committee, to ensure adequate political & industrial training.

I spoke about the ANC school (Morogoro) & the need of specialised building workers, but doubt whether my plea received attention. It was agreed that the committee should meet to formalise its work – but no definite date fixed.

As regards political education & preparation of textbooks, Mzwayi reported that Bunting's idea was to publish the series on Scientific Socialism in the AC (*African Communist: editor*) chapter by chapter, before publishing in pamphlet form. Since this procedure might take years to complete, Bunting was asked to return the material. I'd edit & an attempt would be made to have the printing done by the OAU plant in Dar. Meanwhile the history of the liberation movements (ANC), on the basis of the syllabus agreed to at Morogoro.

27/4/79: Sonia tells Ray that Brian retrieved manuscripts from Rusty & is editing the script himself. No information about intention to publish or modus operandi. [*The relevant section of the diary ends here: editor*]

Lectures on Marxism-Leninism
Novo Catengue 1977-1979

This section records the actual lectures that Comrade Jack used to educate the platoons and prepare the political instructors. The lecture notes have been included in full, with only minimal editing. But Comrade Jack never used these texts verbatim in the classroom. Rather, he spoke to the outline of the lecture notes. This allowed him to give freshness — new anecdotes, up-to-date examples, questions particularly suited to current learners — to material he had covered time and time again. This was vitally important to his teaching method, and is a useful tip for all educators.

Note: A number of comments have been added to each lecture of this second series: these include discussion points made by Comrade Jack himself in 1991, comments from Professor John Hoffman of Leicester University and accounts by teachers at the ANC's Somafco College in Tanzania of their experience of presenting these topics to their students. Teaching ideas are presented at the end of each lecture, and each lecture is linked to a consolidated further reading list at the end of the chapter.

Comrade Jack's comments

John Hoffman's comments

Somafco teachers' comments

Teaching suggestions

Further reading

Scientific Socialism for South Africa: Course outline

1. Science and social change
1.0 Scientific method
1.1 African technologies
1.2 Scientific revolution
1.3 Industrial revolution
1.4 Industrial revolution (S.A)
2. Dialectics of change
2.0 African philosophy
2.1 Religious theory and practice
2.2 Idealism vs materialism Dialectical and social change
3. Historical materialism
3.0 Labour; the basis of society
3.1 Forces of production
3.2 Relations of production
3.3 Economic structure
3.4 Superstructure
3.4 Uneven development
4. The Communist Manifesto
4.0 A call to revolution
4.1 Capitalist crisis
4.2 The working class
4.3 A revolutionary party
5. Social Formations
5.0 Classification of social types
5.1 Historical stages
5.2 Slavery
5.3 Serfdom
5.4 Free workers
6. African perspectives
6.0 Cradle of humanity and centre of civilisation
6.1 African civilisations
6.2 Slavery and slave trade
6.3 Socio-economic formations
6.4 Colonial rule

7. Proletarian revolutions
7.0 Our revolutionary epoch
7.1 Russia's revolution in 1905
7.3 The Social Democrats; a revolutionary party
7.4 From capitalism to socialism
8. National liberation
8.0 Social and political revolutions
8.1 Bourgeois revolution
8.2 Colonial capitalism
 • State and nation
 • National consciousness
8.5 Political revolutions
9. Theory of revolution
9.0 The art of revolution
9.1 Bourgeois revolution
9.2 Permanent revolution
9.3 Vanguard party
9.4 Revolutionary theory
9.5 Objective and subjective conditions
10. Elements of socialist construction
10.0 Emergent socialism
10.1 Birthmarks of old order
10.2 An art of creation
10.3 Permanent revolution
10.4 Dictatorship of the proletariat
10.5 The struggle for world peace
11. Socialism and nationalism
11.0 Class and nation
11.1 Socialist principles
11.2 Nation and State
11.3 Bourgeois nations
11.4 Imperialist multinationalism
11.5 Oppressors and oppressed

11.6 Proletarian internationalism
11.7 Two streams merge
12. World socialism and national sovereignty
12.0 Science in action
12.1 Conscious, planned organisation
12.2 Self-determination
12.3 Freedom of association
12.4 Lenin's principles
12.5 Civil war & armed intervention
12.6 Proletarian nations
12.7 Socialist internationalism
12.8 Equal development
12.9 World socialism
13. Imperialism and colonialism
13.0 Early colonies
13.1 Capitalist expansion
13.2 Settled colonies and chartered companies
13.3 The rape of Africa
13.4 The imperialist stage
13.5 Multinationals mean war
13.6 Imperialism means war
13.7 Crisis of capitalism
13.8 Neo-colonialism
13.9 Our allies
14. One society: one nation
14. Introduction
14.1 Our common society
14.2 A common culture
14.3 One economy
14.4 Building a nation
14.5 Afrikanerdom: an oppressor nation
14.6 Techniques of domination
14.7 An historical necessity

Lecture One: Science and Social Change

1. What is scientific method?
• The observation, classification, measurement of things and changes in things.
• The study of the causes and effects of such changes.
• The formulation of 'laws' or descriptions of regularities in the relationship between cause and effect.
• The proof of such laws by means of research and experiment.

1.1 What are the branches of science?
The physical or natural sciences, which are concerned with inorganic (non-living) matter: mathematics, astronomy, mechanics, physics, chemistry, geology. These exact (more or less accurate) sciences can largely but not entirely be described in mathematical form.

(a) **The historical sciences, which are concerned with living things**
Botany, zoology, physiology, anatomy, pathology, psychology. This is a large, complicated field of knowledge, with many branches each linked to the other, so that important advances, such as the discovery of cells, may lead to a revision of many previously held theories.

(b) **The social sciences: the study of human (and animal) groups**
(Family, tribe, nation), the interactions between people and their modes of organisation: political economy, political science, sociology (including anthropology) and social psychology.

1.2 Science is relative
Scientific knowledge (sometimes called laws) is relative not absolute. It is subject to change, rather than final and immutable. Every advance is science leads to new problems and new methods of investigation.

Friedrich Engels writes in *Anti-Duhring* (1877):
"In physics, we are dealing with the motion of molecules, in chemistry with the formation of molecules out of atoms ... As time goes on, final and ultimate truths become remarkably rare in this field.

In biology, there is such a multitude of interrelationships and causalities that not only does the solution of each question give rise to a host of other questions, but each separate problem can only be solved piecemeal, through a series of investigations which often requires centuries to complete ..."

Engels notes that the social sciences investigate:
"The conditions of human life, social relationships, forms of law and government, with their ideal superstructure, of philosophy, religion, art, etc.

In social history, the repetition of conditions is the exception and not the rule, once we pass beyond the primitive stage of man, the so-called Stone Age; and when such repetitions occur, they never arise under exactly similar condition — as for example the existence of an original common ownership of land among all civilised peoples, and the way in which this came to an end ... Therefore, knowledge is here essentially relative ..."

1.3 Practice and theory

Scientific knowledge grows out of attempts to satisfy human need — for food, clothing, shelter, health, transportation and security (in defence and aggression); to save labour, increase production, improve living conditions, cure disease, save life or destroy life.

Such activities result on the one hand in the growth of skills (technology) and on the other hand in the development of scientific laws (theory) through abstraction (drawing out) from practice knowledge. These laws create expectations among scientists that the world will behave in certain ways.

Engels (again in *Anti-Duhring*) explains:
"*Like all other sciences, mathematics arose out of the needs of man; from the measurements of land and of the contents of vessels, from the computation of time and mechanics. But, as in every department of thought, at a certain stage of development the laws abstracted from the real world become divorced to form something independent, as laws coming from outside, to which the world has to conform.*"

1.4 African technologies

Africans in traditional societies (before colonial conquests) knew much about their world: seasonal changes, the movements of the stars, soil, water, plants, animals, metals. They specialised in many crafts including the smelting of metal ores, the working of metal and the manufacture of tools, weapons, pots, cloth and ornaments.

People throughout Africa grew crops, herded cattle, hunted, fished and carried on trade, often over long distances, in grain, hoes, spears or cattle. Doctors, with special knowledge of medicinal plants, treated patients, mended broken bones, cured infections and performed operations to remove tumours or deliver infants in difficult childbirth cases.

As in most parts of the world before the European scientific revolution that began in the 15th century (1400 onwards) this practical knowledge and these skills (which contained the seeds of science) were linked to religious beliefs and the practice of magic, for both good and evil ends. People prayed to the spirits of their forefathers for protection against bad luck, enemies, crop failure and disease. There was no clear distinction between the world of nature and the world of spirits (the supernatural).

People with this world outlook believed in a unity between the dead, the living and the unborn; between humans and other life forms; between nature and the supernatural. Such ideas of continuity between different forms of matter laid a solid ideological framework for small, rural states based around clans and extended families and dependent for their livelihood on the natural world. This social system and its pattern of beliefs tended, however, to discourage research into the causes of things or the formulation of abstract scientific laws.

For these reasons and because of the resulting weakness of technology (especially in the manufacture of weapons), African states failed to combine their forces against invading colonialists with more advanced, long range weapons. The under-development of the productive forces in traditional Africa enabled the invaders to impose economic and political systems which had benefited from the scientific revolution.

1.5 The "scientific revolution" (Europe: 400 onwards)

Revolution, in a general sense, means a big, far-reaching change, a real "turning over" of the existing order. The separation of science from religious-magical beliefs was such a revolution. It gave rise in practice — though not always in theory — to materialist explanations of matter and motion: explanations based on concrete observation of the world.

Scientists with a materialist outlook ruled out the possibility of miracles or divine intervention in the workings of nature — which, they said, was self-contained. Using new research methods and instruments (the telescope, the microscope) they made great advances in astronomy, physics, chemistry and biology.

Their new discoveries and theories contradicted (went against) the teaching of the Bible which, according to the Church, was the only true source of knowledge. The Church tried to stamp out scientific materialism by persecuting progressive scientists and banning their books.

We read in the Soviet publication *Fundamentals of Marxism-Leninism* (1960) that: *"In every exploiting class society there are forces, the reactionary social classes, that stand to lose by the spread of progressive scientific views. In the past they either directly opposed science and persecuted progressive scientists and philosophers — even burning them at the stake or imprisoning them — or sought to distort scientific discoveries so as to deprive them of their progressive, materialistic meaning".*

But scientific progress could not be stopped. The rising capitalist class encouraged the advances made in physics, chemistry, biology and mathematics. Natural science was the source of technological improvements. It enabled Western European fleets to cross oceans, conquer and exploit colonies, extract great masses of wealth, and improve the forces of production, making possible bigger profit for bankers, merchants, capitalists and the landed aristocracy.

1.6 The "Industrial Revolution" (Western Europe 1750 onwards)

The scientific discoveries of the 17th and 18th centuries — advances in metallurgy, mechanics and other branches of applied science — resulted in the invention of power-driven machines and revolutionised industrial processes.

L Leontyev has written about the effects of the industrial revolution (*A Short*

Course In Political Economy, 1968, p10):
"Capitalist machine industry first emerged and developed in Britain. Within a short time (the last third of the 18th and the early 19th centuries) a great many machines appeared in Britain and changed the country's face beyond recognition. Once an agricultural country, Britain turned into an industrial power. Large industrial centres sprang into being all over the country. A numerous industrial proletariat developed. Soon large-scale machine industry spread from country to country."

Factory goods were cheaper than goods made by villagers in their cottages and workshops. Village industry could not stand up to the competition. Spinners and weavers of cloth, carpenters, ironsmiths and other small-scale producers lost their livelihood. Many were forced to leave their homes for the big manufacturing towns. There they became wage earners, working in factories on machines driven by steam engines.

In the words of the *Communist Manifesto (1848)*:
"In proportion as the bourgeoisie, that is, capital, develops, in the same proportion to the proletariat, that is, the modern working class, developed — a class of labourers, who live only so long as they find work, and who find work as long as their labour increases capital. These labourers, who must sell themselves piecemeal, are a commodity, like every other article of commerce, and are therefore exposed to all the ups and downs of competition on the market."

Industrial capitalism spread to all continents. Capitalists needed markets for their factory-made products and raw materials for their industries.

"The cheap prices of its commodities are the heavy artillery with which it batters down all walls. It compels all nations, on pain of extinction to adopt the bourgeois mode of production". (Communist Manifesto)

1.7 South Africa's industrial revolution

White settlers brought capitalism to South Africa, made war on the inhabitants, seized their land and cattle and imposed bourgeois systems of government, economy, religion and morality. Traders sold factory-made goods, which took the place of those made by village craftsmen. Africans were forced into the cash economy because of land hunger, the decay of village industries, government taxes, the pressure of labour recruiters, and a growing dependence on manufactured goods. Villagers migrated to ports, construction works, mines and manufacturing towns in search of wage employment. A large urban proletariat developed.

a) **The agrarian period (1650-1850):** White farmers and stockbreeders compete with their black counterparts for land, cattle, grazing, water and labour. Slaves were imported from the East Indies (1660-1800). Indian labourers were imported under contract for Natal (1860 onwards) to swell local labour resources. Boer "trekkers" penetrated the interior from the Cape and Natal to extend the area of white domination and agrarian capital.

b) **The mining era (1870 onwards)**: Diamond mining at Kimberley produced huge surplus capital and attracted foreign capital for investment in gold mining on the Witwatersrand. Mines employed migrant villagers housed in "compounds" without their families and paid less than subsistence wages. Pass laws were introduced to stop miners from breaking their contracts (called "desertion") to obtain higher wages elsewhere or return to their villages.

c) **The manufacturing period (1914 onwards)**: Secondary industries developed to serve the mining industry and replace imported manufacturers. An urban black population took root. Segregation (Urban Areas Act, 1923) and "influx control" were introduced to prevent the growth of a proletariat.

1.8 Colour bars

In capitalist systems based on open competition:

> *"The various interests and conditions of life within the ranks of proletariat are more and more equalised, in proportion as machinery obliterates all distinctions in labour, and nearly everywhere reduces wages to the same low level."* (Communist Manifesto)

This is not the position in South Africa. Here, colonial forms of race discrimination, introduced during the period of slave labour or in wars against independent African states, continued after the growth of the mining and manufacturing industries.

White workers demanded and received protection from African competition at higher levels of employment: in mines, factories, railways, docks, transport, construction, shops, offices, schools, hospitals, offices and research institutions.

We have, in South Africa, no black train drivers, air pilots, engineers, architects, scientists. An African cannot rise above the level of a "boss boy" in the mines, a machine operator in the factories, or a "helper" (spanner boy) to a white artisan in garages and mechanical workshops. The colour bar is built into the relations of production. It shapes education, health care, housing, social relations, recreation and culture — in fact, every facet of life.

Liberated African states have abolished race discrimination and all skilled, professional and scientific jobs are open to black people. We in South Africa are backward in comparison and will continue to lag behind until we have won our own liberation.

John Hoffmann comments

"To simply plunge into a discussion of what science is seems to me a bit abstract. It is important to sketch in first why a theory of nature and society is of relevance to a revolutionary movement; why non-scientifically-minded movements (utopian movements) have failed.

"Also, in talking about scientific knowledge as relative, it is important to stress that this does not exclude an absolute dimension. Truth is both absolute and relative ..."

How did it go in practice?

Somafco teachers commented: "Discussion was very lively, with some mild clashes of opinion."

Teaching ideas

There are four main themes in this lecture:
- what science is all about — and why science can be used to look at social change;
- how Western empirical science developed, how it differs from traditional African science, and the effect this had on colonial expansion;
- how all this applies to South African history; and
- why capitalist development in South Africa was warped by the pervasive and persistent colour bar.

All of these themes are revisited in subsequent lectures; this serves as a general introduction. It's quite complex material, particularly for learners with a limited general education. And the material which directly links to Lecture Two is the discussion of science.

One possible way to start might be by getting participants to discuss their own ideas about science, and how these relate to traditional practices such as using curative herbs for certain illnesses. The common thread — that such traditional science rests on observing the effect of plants and then generalising from that makes a good bridge into talking about how the 'hard' sciences built on and developed that methodology.

Further reading sections

A, B and C

Lecture Two: The dialectics of change

2.0 African philosophy

Africans in olden days, like many still today, believed in the unity of matter (things, nature), humans and a world of spirits occupied by gods, demons and the souls of their ancestors. As we saw in Lecture One, they had much knowledge of the material world around them (their environment), including the movement of the stars, the changes in seasons, plant and animal life. They were skilled in growing crops, breeding livestock, hunting and making tools, weapons and household goods.

In every part of their daily life, however, they showed respect for the spirits which, they believed, lived in the natural world, in trees, stones or streams. People prayed to these spirits to help women bear children, or to produce rain, provide good crops and cure sickness.

This belief in a unity between the world of nature and a world "above nature" (the supernatural) brought comfort and strength. In times of drought, flood, sickness and war, people appealed to the spirits for assistance, blamed their troubles on evildoers (witches, *umthakathi*), and turned to diviner-priests (*inyanga*) for assistance. Religion, magic and practical skills went hand in hand.

Peoples everywhere — Indians, Chinese, Europeans — had the same kinds of beliefs in religion and magic before the days of the scientific revolution. European nations passed laws against "witches" quite late in their histories, and often these laws reflected rivalries between church or government and these unofficial figures of power, rather than the growth of rationalism.

2.1 Religious theory and practice

There was no contradiction (conflict, disunity) between the beliefs (theory) and practice of religion in old Africa. People lived according to their beliefs. For example, kings were said to have great spiritual powers because their ancestors had formed the state. Only the king could obtain the blessing of these powerful spirits. He was a divine (sacred) king who had both spiritual (magical) and secular (practical) powers. Belief was one of the forces holding these societies together. Productive activities (agriculture) depended on spiritual support.

Beliefs in divine kingship remained in Europe until the age of bourgeois (capitalist) revolutions against the feudal system, as in England (1640s) and France (1789). But even before that religions had ceased to be a unifying force. Class struggles (between feudalists and capitalists) and contradictions between religious beliefs and scientific laws put and end to the old unity of beliefs and practices. People may have continued praying to their gods, but they depended on scientific laws for production and profit making.

Religion and the established church belong to what we call the superstructure: the institutions and organisations that grow up on the economic foundations of any society. They serve the interests of the ruling class. The Church teaches and upholds the moral system of that class, persuades people to obey laws, respect government, work hard and be submissive. Established churches defend slavery in a slave-owning society, private property in a capitalist society and race discrimination in a segregated society.

But as the class struggle grows fiercer, divisions arise in the ranks of priests and their followers. In South Africa, Afrikaner churches support Vorster and apartheid; certain other churches, influenced by world opinion, condemn racialism. Some African preachers, among them ordained ministers such as Rabusana, Mahabane and Calata, were leaders of the ANC. Because the ANC struggled for African rights, it won the support of Africans including members of churches.

2.3 Idealism

Religion is a philosophy of idealism. This word, when used to describe a philosophy, does not mean the "ideals" or lofty motives of, for example, a revolutionary fighting for liberation. Philosophical idealism is a way of describing certain theories about thinking or consciousness and its relation to nature and matter (the real world).

Religions teach, in one form or another, that:

• a supernatural, godlike, mind or consciousness existed before matter;
• this divine force created the universe (as is described in the Book of Genesis of the Old Testament);
• a god or gods instructed people to follow a given code of morality (e.g. the Koran or the Ten Commandments);
• the "conscience" (awareness of right and wrong) come from a "soul" which exists in the body and leaves it at death on a secret mission to an unknown destination; and
• therefore the business of a priest is to prepare souls for a life after death.

Such a philosophy is described as "idealist" because its starting point is that an idea came before and dominates matter.

These beliefs are irrelevant to science, technology and production and can be an obstacle to progress, yet they persist because of:

• the influence of early religious instruction in the home, schools and churches;
• the alliance between government and churches which teach obedience to authority and the official code of morality;
• the fear of death and the desire for immorality (life after death);
• ignorance of causes of natural disasters (drought, flood, epidemics, earthquakes, volcanic explosions) an inability prevent or control them; and
• ignorance of causes of social disasters (wars, revolutions economic crisis, unemployment, poverty) and failure to prevent them.

Engels (*Anti-Duhring*) explains that imaginary gods personify (stand for, reflect) the natural and social forces which dominate humans. Man proposes (intends, plans) but God (in fact natural and social forces) disposes (settles the outcome). Mere knowledge of causes is not enough to bring social forces under control. "What is above all necessary for this is a social act."

When people through action obtain control of economic, political systems, when they can carry out their plans, they will have no need to imagine a spiritual force that dominates physical force.

2.4 Materialism

Idealism and materialism are part of a wide range of philosophies.

The word means "love of wisdom" and in ancient societies it covered all branches of learning, both natural and social. As science advanced, each branch became a separate "discipline" with its own methods of study, laws and theories (hypotheses). Only one big problem was left to philosophy: understanding the way people think. (And now psychology is taking over that territory.)

Writing in 1886, Engels explained (in *Ludwig Feuerbach*) that:
"The great basic question of all philosophy ... is that concerning the relation of thinking and being."

Philosophers, he said, split into two great camps:
"Those who asserted the primacy of spirit to nature and, therefore, in the last instance, assumed world creation ... comprised the camp of idealism. The others, who regarded nature as primary, belonged to the various schools of materialism."

In the materialist view, thinking — or consciousness — is a function (condition) of being, of physical life; the universe was not created by the act of will of a spirit and has no limit in time or space; while humans, like other living things, are a product of evolutionary changes. Neither gods nor souls nor other kinds of spiritual essences exist.

The dispute between the two schools of thought — which became acute at the time of the scientific and industrial revolutions and has continued since — could not be settled by words alone. The answer had to come from practical experience, science and technology, which enabled humans to change nature and create new forms of matter.

Materialism made a big breakthrough when Charles Darwin published his book *The Origin of Species* in 1859. It dealt idealism a deadly blow by showing that all organic matter — plants, animals, humans — had evolved over millions of years from small single-cell organisms which themselves resulted from chemical processes.

This revolutionary approach showed that there is unity in diversity. Though living things differ greatly they have common elements or properties. Thinking and consciousness are properties of the brain and the nervous system, which is most advanced in humans but by no means peculiar to them.

2.5 Humans and social evolution

Humans are not descended from monkeys but share with them a common ancestry. The links in our evolutionary chain are slowly coming to light through the discovery of pre-human skeletal remains in South and East Africa. To explain the process of change, materialists stress the importance of body changes, tools, production and language.

Soviet scholars have summarised the materialist view in the following passage (*Fundamentals of Marxism-Leninism*, p43):
"The great English scientist, Charles Darwin, proved that man and the anthropoid apes have common ancestors. In the distant past, man's animal ancestors were marked by the high development of their forelimbs. They learned to walk erect and began to use natural objects as tools to procure food and to defend themselves. Subsequently, they proceeded to fashion tools, and this marked the gradual transformation of the animal to the human being. The use of tools enabled man to master such a natural force as fire and made it possible for him to improve his food and vary it, which in turn helped to develop his brain."

Food production, defence against enemies, reproduction and the care of children led to the formation of family and wider social groups.

> *"For collective labour, men had to associate with one another, and for this, the limited stock of sounds that had sufficed for animals was no longer adequate. In the course of labour activities, the human throat gradually developed and changed. Men learned to pronounce articulate sounds, which gradually developed into words, language. Joint labour would have been impossible without the faculty of speech."*
>
> *"Humans think in words. The growth of speech developed the brain.*
>
> *"Thus man's social labour, and later, in association with it, speech, were the decisive factors influencing the development of the brain, the development of the capacity to think."*

This outline of human evolution, though given only in wide terms, shows a many-sided interaction between the human species' environment, eating habits, production, social formation and anatomical change. Walking upright on two legs requires a suitable position and structure in the spine, neck and head. It enables the eyes to focus on a greater distance than is possible for four-legged creatures; and may allow the cranial (brain) cavity to expand, thereby making room for an increase in the size and complexity of the brain.

According to evolutionary theory, such changes take place in genetic structure and are passed on from one generation to the next. Small changes that may easily escape notice accumulate until they bring about a visible change in structure. The transition from "quantity" to "quality" is an important principle of dialectical materialism.

2.6 Dialectical change

Dialectics, in ancient Greece, meant a debate, a formal discussion, between two parties in an argument. The word was later extended to describe the thinking process, and, finally, historical and social change. As a way of describing a debate, for example, one person might state the "thesis" that South Africa belongs to the people; his opponent would put up the "antithesis" (counter proposal) that South Africa currently belongs to the capitalists. The two sides would agree on the "synthesis" (the combination of these two positions) that South Africa will belong to the people when they have overthrown capitalism.

Marx and Engels, who applied dialectical principles to the study of history and society, showed that both thinking and nature operated "dialectically".

In Engels' words (*Ludwig Feuerbach*):
"Dialectics reduced itself to the science of the general laws of motion — two sets of laws which are identical in substance, but differ in their expression. The human mind can apply them consciously, while in nature and also up to now for the most part in human history, these laws assert themselves unconsciously in the form of external necessity in the midst of an endless series of seeming accidents".

The "accidents" are only "seeming". Events appear to be accidental because of human failure to anticipate, prevent or control them. The failure may be due to negligence (motor car collisions), ignorance (insufficient understanding of explosives in the making of a bomb), inability to control (lightning, hailstorms, economic crisis of capitalism), or neglect to apply known scientific measures (to prevent diseases and epidemics).

2.7 Social change

Natural scientists carry out controlled experiments in laboratories to discover the qualities of matter (the composition of plants or minerals) and the effects of changes in temperature or pressure on matter (heating or cooling gases, metals and chemicals). To study the behaviour of a gas at different degrees of temperature, the scientist "controls" the pressure and keeps it constant. A scientist can control experiments so that all conditions are kept constant except the "variable" being studied.

A social scientist cannot easily use laboratory research methods and controlled experiments to study the behaviour of people and their interactions. The scientist depends on such research methods as direct observation (watching and talking to people), questionnaires, sample surveys and opinion polls.

So although the causes of change in both nature and society are multiple (many-sided), natural scientists are able "isolate" a single possible cause under laboratory conditions, while the causes of social change are less easy to sort out and identify.

Engels has mentioned one of the difficulties: the difference (and often contradiction) between what people intend and what they achieve:
"Men make their own history, whatever its outcome may be, in that each person follows his own consciously desired end, and it is precisely the resultant of these many wills operating in different directions and of their manifold effects upon the outer world that constitutes history. But, on the one hand, we have seen that the many individual wills active in history for the most part produce results quite other than those they intended — often quite the opposite; their motives therefore in relation to the total result are likewise only of secondary significance. On the other hand, the further question arises: what driving forces in turn stand behind these motive? What are the historical causes which transform themselves into these motives in the brains of the actors?"

What, for example, were the "historical causes" behind the Soweto uprising? Neither the students not the police expected the peaceful demonstration against Afrikaans to trigger off a countrywide revolt against white domination.

Individual actions merged into a great revolutionary stream, the outcome of which was not foreseen.

To understand the chain of events that, for example, brought militants from South Africa to distant African countries we need a theory linking our struggle to the national liberation movement in Africa. Historical materialism is such a theory. It is both a tool of analysis and a guide to action.

Second thoughts from Jack Simons

Comrade Jack is reported as saying that he doubted if the SACP's attitude to religion as "an obstacle to progress" was any different from his at the time of the lectures "when the churches in SA, with hardly any exceptions, were opposed to the liberation struggle — let alone the communists. Missionaries were agents of colonialism; the NGK a principal advocate of apartheid. Religion was, in fact, an obstacle to progress, being a source of superstition."(7/10/91)

"I personally am not anti-religious, in the sense of thinking that I should conduct a crusade against forms of religion. However, I was convinced then and still am that [superstition] is a problem that one has to cope with in Africa. Not only is this made quite clear in the literature of anthropologists, but also with common observation … So I think my main concern was to disabuse people of the belief in magic and witchcraft." (27/9/91)

John Hoffman comments

"I would drop all reference to thesis/antithesis/synthesis in an exposition of dialectics. The 'wooden triad' creates more problems for understanding dialectics than it is worth. I would not be happy, either, with the formulation of accidents as only 'seeming': accidents mould the form of events at a given time and place — all general laws necessarily express themselves in an accidental way. In general, I would say that despite some excellent material on religion and African philosophy, the exposition of dialectics is too piecemeal and bitty."

How did it go in practice?

Somafco teachers commented: "Discussion tended to be rather abstract and dry at first, but it livened up later when the focus shifted to questions of religion and how materialists should relate to religion and religious people, especially in liberation struggles. The view was expressed that the atmosphere in Somafco was such that a Christian student would not feel comfortable about expressing his/her ideas freely. It was felt that we ought to teach about Christianity, Hinduism, Islam, etc., because they were social forces of some significance in the world. Differences of opinion were expressed, but time did not allow for a deeper look at this question."

Teaching ideas

There are two main themes in this lecture, the role of religion, and the role of dialectical materialism as a tool of social analysis and for social change. The first is controversial, as Somafco teachers found: it is a pity their timetable did not allow them to draw out this debate and try out alternative approaches. It is also clear from his own comments that Comrade Jack himself shaped the content of this lecture to suit very specific historical circumstances. The current South African Constitution, and the policies of both the ANC and the

SACP, affirm openness towards religions and believers.

How might Simons do it today? He would, no doubt, have noted and incorporated the many recent developments illustrating contrasting facets of the role of religion. For example, the churches playing a role as organs of civil society working for change (liberation theology in Latin America; church people playing an active role in toppling the Banda dictatorship in Malawi, etc). On the other hand, religious fundamentalism, particularly in the USA, is increasingly providing huge backing for right-wing internal and international policies. And believers were important in toppling Communist Party governments in eastern Europe, particularly in Poland — was this because believers are inherently anti-Communist, or because of the harsh official treatment religion had received?

(We also now know much more about the evolution of Earth and other aspects of science than scientists had discovered when Comrade Jack drafted these lectures.)

As a dialectician, Comrade Jacks would undoubtedly have engaged his students in debate on the contradictions around religion: between established and independent churches; between majority and minority faiths and between religion-inspired ethical frameworks and the practices of some churches. What do they show? How can they be useful in the struggle to build fairer societies?

One teaching tactic might be to find a case study (e.g. a current news story) dealing with religion, and begin the session with discussion of this. For example, what are the rights and wrongs when a school bans a female Muslim student from wearing a headscarf, while her parents insist she cannot attend school bare-headed? Inevitably, this kind of debate finds its way towards discussion of some beliefs having a basis in material conditions, while others rest on the word of a religious teacher or holy scripture. This makes an ideal transition point into the second part of the lecture, on dialectics.

We have to sympathise with John Hoffman's point that the "wooden triangle" of thesis/antithesis/synthesis is indigestible and not necessarily helpful in explaining dialectics. It's highly abstract, and may lose the point that dialectics are a process, not a set of three positions. It might be better, again, to focus on a real historical example where the clash of two opposing forces or arguments produced a result which was different from either though it contained elements of both. The struggle against colonialism and the post-colonial (neo-colonial) settlements provide many ongoing examples.

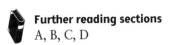 **Further reading sections**
A, B, C, D

Lecture 3: Historical materialism

3.0 Labour: the basis of society

Humans, like other creatures, must eat to live and have children for the survival of their species. They must work to eat — to produce food for themselves and their children. Production and reproduction are basic (or primary) activities. In carrying out these activities, people form groups, socialise their labour, establish families, villages, towns, and enter into relations with one another: social relations and relations of production. The links in this chain of cause and effect are the need for food and sex, production and reproduction, social relations and relations of production.

This sequence is plain enough for anyone to understand. Yet philosophers and historians through the ages overlooked the obvious. They looked down on labour. It was fit only for slaves, serfs and the poor. The fact that these people produced the means of subsistence did not make them important. Kings, priests and the rich were on top of the social scale. Only they were important.

Not, however, in the writings and thought system of Karl Marx. His heroes were the working man and woman: the makers of things, the source of wealth, the class that would do away with all classes, the builders of socialism. He spent his life teaching working people to understand their importance and to fulfil their historic mission.

Marx died on 14 March 1883 at the age of 65. Speaking at his funeral, Friedrich Engels, his lifelong friend, co-worker and fellow revolutionary, compared Marx's scientific contribution with that of Darwin. "Just as Darwin discovered the law of evolution in organic nature, so Marx discovered the law of evolution in human history." We call that law historical materialism.

Marx, said Engels, discovered a simple fact: "Mankind must first of all eat and drink, have shelter and clothing, before it can pursue politics, science, religion and art." Therefore, because of the primary importance of production, the mode of production (the way production is carried out) in any society is "the foundation upon which the state institutions, the legal conceptions, the art and even the religious ideas of the people concerned have been evolved".

What is the mode of production? How does it shape systems of government and social consciousness? What is the connection between economy and revolution? Historical materialism gives these answers.

3.1 Forces of production

Labour, tools and materials are the elements of any mode of production: they constitute the "forces of production". The simplest economy is found among hunters and food collectors. Their tools are the bow and arrow, stone axes and wooden clubs. They live on what nature provides: water, wild plants, fish, birds and animals. The Khoisan (called "bushmen") of Namaqualand and the Kalahari were clever hunters, experts in finding water and edible plants. They survived in desert-like areas where other people could not subsist. Their mode of production, however, limited the size of their social groups, division of labour and forms of government. The Boers of the North-Western Cape hunted them down and shot them like wild animals, but the Khoisan could not unite in defence against the enemy.

The mode of production determines the amount of food available and the density of population (the number of people to a square mile) that is possible. Cattle owners, like the Khoi-Khoi, have a bigger and more reliable food supply than hunters. Cultivators who grow crops and breed livestock are able to form dense settlements. The bigger the population, the more complicated becomes the system of government. Zulu, Xhosa, Sotho and other kingdoms in South Africa were governed through minor chiefs and village headmen who administered provinces, districts, wards and villages and offered loyalty upwards to the king (chief). Social differences in power, authority and living standards developed between royal families, local chiefs and villagers.

The industrial revolution, by greatly expanding the forces of production, led to the formation of huge industrial and commercial cities whose inhabitants obtained their food and other materials from agricultural producers in many countries.

Marx and Engels described this process in the *Communist Manifesto*:
"The bourgeois has subjected the country to the rule of towns. It has created enormous cities, has greatly increased the urban population as compared with the rural ... It has agglomerated population, centralised the means of production. Independent or but loosely connected provinces, with separate interests, laws, governments and systems of taxation, became lumped together into one nation, with one government, one code of laws, one national class interest, one frontier and one customs tariff."

Industrialisation — the use of power-driven machines in mines, factories, workshops, power stations, transport and agriculture — enables people to achieve high levels of production, to supply the needs of enormous populations, whose concentration in big cities gives rise to problems of housing, sanitation, medical care, education, transportation and the distribution of goods. Industrialised societies have different social structures: socialist, capitalist and state capitalist. South Africa is highly industrialised, but retains a colonial type of social order. For it is not only the forces of production that determine the social order, but also the relations of production.

3.2 Relations of production
People are related or linked to one another in many ways: by marriage or descent (kinship), through common allegiance to a state (citizenship), in societies (trade union, political party, church) or at their place of work.

The relations of production link together people taking part in the business of producing and exchanging goods or services. These relations vary according to the forces of production, on the one hand, and the positions of producers, on the other. Slave owners and slaves, employers and workers occupy different positions in the process of production and so have different relations of production.

How do productive forces influence production relations? The connection can be traced easily in a community of hunters. They possess the same kinds of tools (instruments of production), hunt collectively and share the proceeds. A huntsman may have his own weapon and personal possessions (skins, pipes) but other things are held in common, which is why this mode of production is called early or "primitive" communism.

Inequalities of rank and property appear among cultivators and stockbreeders. In many traditional African systems, although the land and its natural fruits belonged to all, every family and village had its own gardens. The bigger the family the more it could produce. Where cattle were handed over at marriage (ukulobola), a rich cattle-owner might marry several wives, thereby adding to his family's labour force.

Kings and chiefs often had many wives, big gardens and a plentiful supply of food and beer. They also collected taxes or tribute from villagers and conquered dependent peoples. Such systems are called "tributary states" and contain the beginnings of class division.

Slaves and serfs were a source of labour in many African states. If a slave consumed only a part of what he produced, the owner could retain the surplus or exchange it for goods supplied by traders and neighbouring societies. The division between owners and slaves was a class division, perhaps the first to appear.

Improvements in methods and instruments of production lead to increased outputs. The introduction of ploughs, for instance, enables cultivators who own ploughs and oxen or tractors to increase the size of their fields. Families who possess only hoes have small gardens, usually no more than a hectare in size. Many African states have nationalised the land, but its distribution is unequal between big farmers and small family farmers, between big cattle owners and villagers without cattle. This is a case of changes in the productive forces which result in new relations of production: big landowners, village farmers, landless peasants and wage workers. Colonial capitalism in Africa changed the forces of production by introducing machines and the relations of production by introducing private ownership of land, mines and factories. These changes destroyed traditional modes of production, transformed peasants into wage labourers and created an African proletariat.

In South Africa capitalism has developed an advanced industrial economy but stubbornly clings to colour bars inherited from the colonial relations of production. This dissonance between the economic structure and the social superstructure is a major reason why our revolution is necessary.

3.3 Economic structure

Productive forces and productive relations together form the economic system or structure. Marx wrote that this was "the real foundation, on which rises a legal and political superstructure" (Preface to the Critique of Political Economy, 1858).

. Before we consider this statement — a major key to the understanding of social change — something should be said about the way we use words taken from physical activities to describe social systems: basis, foundation, framework, structure, superstructure. They describe a building of stone, bricks, concrete or other materials that last, and are used only as an analogy to describe society, which consists of people who constantly change as they grow old, die and are replaced by new generations. Structure, superstructure and other such words are "mental constructs": ideas or notions employed to analyse the interactions between individuals and groups or institutions. Scientists select those interactions that they think are of special importance and in this process of generalising and developing theory, these abstract terms become useful.

Starting with the economic systems we have the following points:

• Labour is basic for human life.
• Labour, instruments and materials are forces of production.
• Interactions between persons taking part in production are the relations of production.
• Forces of production and relations of production together constitute the economic structure.
• Relations of production form part of both the structure and superstructure.

As regards the last point, Marx stated that relations of production are the same in legal terms as property relations or forms of ownership. In capitalist systems, the relations between workers and capitalist (owners of the means of production) are class relationship which dominate government, law and other aspects of the superstructure.

3.4 Superstructure

This includes all the activities and institutions that fall outside the specific forms of economic life (mode of production). Government, political parties, law and courts of law, family life, education, health services, religion, arts and philosophy all belong to the superstructure.

Social consciousness — expressed in beliefs, customs, morals, laws, ideologies — is shaped in the superstructure. Apartheid, racialism and colour bars are therefore part of the economic structure and also of the superstructure.

South Africa's forces of production are comparatively well-developed. It is the most highly industrialised state in Africa. But its government, laws, religion — the whole superstructure — conforms to an outdated colonial system of race discrimination and minority rule.

3.5 Uneven development

Unlike a machine, which has well fitted and co-ordinated parts, society functions unevenly, some sectors undergoing rapid change while others lag behind. Development is uneven when capital and labour are invested mainly in the most profitable industries while less favoured areas are neglected.

The mining industry in some African states attracted much capital and advanced at the expense of rural people, many of whom migrated to towns in search of wages. Uneven development of this kind results from the unplanned, profit-seeking system of capitalist economy. In much the same way, the productive forces can also move ahead of property relations and the superstructure.

This passage in the *Communist Manifesto* examines uneven growth in feudal society:

"... the means of production and of exchange, on whose foundation the

bourgeoisie built itself up, were generated in feudal society. At a certain stage in the development of these means of production and exchange ... the feudal relations of property became no longer compatible with the already developed productive forces; they became so many fetters. They had to be burst asunder; they were burst asunder".

The new capitalist class of factory owners, bankers, traders and lawyers attacked the feudal lords and clergy, demanded political rights, equality before the law and a free and competitive market. Liberal bourgeois ideology challenged the monarchy, the church and the privileges of the landed aristocracy.

The bourgeoisie raised the slogan of "Liberty, equality, fraternity". These were also the demands of the workers and peasants, who supported the bourgeois revolution only to find that legal equality without economic equality strengthened the power of capital.

South Africa's reactionary superstructure similarly fetters the country's already developed productive forces. Colour bars and discrimination prevent the growth of a free market, an efficient use of workers and the expansion of external trade and investment. The conflict between productive forces and property relations has brought into being a revolutionary movement and consciousness spearheaded by African nationalism and communism.

John Hoffman comments

"It is important to include under 'focus of production' science and knowledge. The compressed formulation that the forces of production determine the social order is misleading. Surely the forces of production determine the relations of production and these determine the 'social order' i.e. the super-structure."

How did it go in practice?

Somafco teachers comment: "Discussions centred on the section 'Economic Structure'. After some discussion, it was felt that the following statements were incorrect:
• Productive forces and production relations together form the economic structure.
• Forces of production and relations of production together constitute the economic structure.
• Relations of production form part of both the structure and the superstructure.
Rather, it was felt that what should be said was:
• The relations of production form the economic system of the structure.
• Relations of production constitute the economic structure."

Teaching suggestions

This lecture deals with a description of economic systems, their historical development and the terminology used to discuss them. Everybody

seems to have become a little confused around the structure/superstructure issue, but the terminology here is less important than that students understand that how wealth is created in society is a major determinant of:
• how different social groups relate to one another; and
• what ideas and institutions a society creates.

It may be simpler to begin by asking participants to discuss how a society develops its rules, and drawing out the relationship between rule-making and economic power. Then the facilitator can track backwards into the historical part of the lecture, which is straightforward, interesting and concrete.

The terminology may be better explained by using the term "base" rather than "structure". The economic base consists of the forces of production and the relations of production which these entail. These relations are reflected in — but are not part of — the superstructure of ideas, institutions, etc. which grows up on this base. Apartheid South Africa was somewhat aberrant in the way in which the colour-bar pattern over-determined both the relations of production and the elements of the superstructure, and the final section of the lecture makes this clear.

Many young South Africans don't remember the details or the horror of this. An interesting exercise might be to ask them to question their parents, grandparents and older relatives about the ways in which the colour-bar affected working life and "superstuctural" activities like the operation of the courts, recreation or religion.

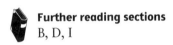 **Further reading sections**
B, D, I

Lecture 4: The Communist Manifesto

4.0 A call to revolution
The Communist League, an underground workers' party, asked Marx and Engels to write its programme. This appeared in 1848 as *The Manifesto of the Communist Party* or *The Communist Manifesto*.

It remains "the most concise and the most important single document of Marxism". It has been called the "death certificate" of capitalism and the "birth certificate" of scientific socialism. The Communist International programme of 1928 restated the *Manifesto* in a form suited to the imperialist stage of capitalism. Though it was written 130 years ago, succeeding generations of revolutionaries have found in the *Manifesto* a constant source of inspiration, a storehouse of knowledge and a guide to action.

1848 was a year of misfired bourgeois revolutions in France, Germany, Austria and Italy. The *Manifesto* appeared a few weeks before the February Revolution in France, when the workers of Paris forced the bourgeoisie to declare a democratic republic.

Marx and Engels, when writing the *Manifesto*, sensed the gathering storm. When it broke, they had no doubt *"that the great decisive struggle had broken out, that it would have to be fought out in a single, long and changeful period of revolution, but that it could only end with the final victory of the proletariat"*.

This mood of optimism, which fires all great revolutionary movements, sets the tone of the *Manifesto*. It provides a materialist explanation of the French bourgeois revolution of 1789 and applies the same analysis to the coming proletarian revolution. The conviction that the overthrow of capitalism is close at hand appears throughout, as in the following passages:

> *"The weapons with which the bourgeoisie felled feudalism to the ground are now turned against the bourgeoisie itself. But not only has the bourgeoisie forged the weapons that bring death to itself; it has also called into existence the men who are to wield these weapons — the modern working class — the proletarians.*
>
> *The development of modern industry cuts from under its feet the very foundation on which the bourgeoisie produces and appropriates products. What the bourgeoisie therefore forces, above all, are its own grave-diggers. Its fall and the victory of the proletariat are equally inevitable. They have a world to win.*
> *Working men of all countries, unite!"*

Nearly 50 years later, in 1895, Engels explained why this forecast had not been fulfilled. *"History has proved us, and all who thought like us, wrong."* Capitalism still had a long way to go before creating the conditions necessary for the proletarian revolution. Another 20 years passed. The workers and peasants of Tsarist Russia made their revolution in 1917, proclaimed the Union of Socialist Soviet Republics, and proved the correctness of the *Communist Manifesto*.

4.1 A world view

France's revolutions and wars had dominated Europe since the great bourgeois revolution of 1789. Wars of intervention against the revolution, the mobilisation of mass armies in defence of the revolution, the wars of conquest by that army under Napoleon, created a spirit of national consciousness — the first of its kind — that united the workers, peasants and bourgeoisie of France against the alliance of European states, headed by capitalist England and feudal Russia, which forced Napoleon to give up his throne in 1814.

This huge upheaval in economic, political and social systems forms the background to the *Manifesto*. It begins with the rise of capitalism within the "womb" of feudalism.

> *"From the serfs of the Middle Ages sprang the chartered burghers of the earliest towns. From these burghers the first elements of the bourgeoisie were developed."*

The age of European colonialism began. Spain and Portugal, having freed themselves from 700 years of Arab domination, sent ships across the seas to explore, trade, conquer and exploit. Other western countries — Holland, France, Britain — followed.

"The discovery of America, the rounding of the Cape, opened up fresh ground for the rising bourgeoisie."

Gold, silver and precious stones, seized from the peoples of Africa, Latin America and India, poured into Europe. This store of wealth was used to finance improvements in the means of production. Feudal industry could not satisfy the growing wants of the new markets. A manufacturing middle class took charge of production.

"Meantime the markets kept ever growing, the demand ever rising. Every manufacture now had to revolutionise industrial production."

Capitalists wanted a free market to take advantage of the improved means of production. Feudal laws and tariffs, however, put brakes on the growing of capital. To obtain economic freedom, the capitalist class seized political power *"conquered for itself, in the modern representative state, exclusive political sway"*.

Industries then as now drew their raw materials from distant countries and sold their products in every corner of the globe.

"The bourgeoisie has through its exploitation of the world market given a cosmopolitan character to production and consumption in every country ... It compels all nations, on pain of extinction, to adopt the bourgeois theme, to introduce what it calls civilisation into their midst, i.e. to become bourgeois themselves. In one word, it creates a world after its own image."

These glimpses into the growth of world capitalism cover a period of about 400 years. Marx and Engels could do no more within the limits of a short party programme than give a bare outline. Nevertheless, this outline shows a remarkable insight into the dynamic nature of the capitalist mode of production and its impact on pre-capitalist social formations. That insight, however, was only a prelude to their main objective — the abolition of capitalism.

4.2 Capitalist crisis

The capitalist mode of production burst through and shattered the property relations of feudalism. Marx and Engels concluded that "a similar movement" was taking place within capitalism. The productive forces of capitalism had become "too powerful" for its property relations.

"The conditions of bourgeois society are too narrow to contain the wealth created by them."

How can an economy be said to create "too much" wealth? The aim of capitalism is to maximise profits, for which purpose it keeps on expanding the productive system. Capitalism measures its level of progress by the amount of goods and services it produces. The higher the national income per head of population the more prosperous a country is said to be.

Yet the *Manifesto* says that "too much means of subsistence, too much industry, too much commerce" are a major, if not fatal, weakness of the system. These excesses cause economic crises "that by their periodical return put the existence of the entire bourgeois society on trial, each time more threateningly". The crisis appears in the form of over-production. To overcome it, capitalism destroys a great part of its productive forces, conquers new markets and exploits old ones more thoroughly.

Marx was the first leading economist to understand the importance of these crises, which come and go in cycles leaving behind bankrupt firms, lower share prices and large-scale unemployment. He spent many years tracing the causes and published the results of his labour in *Capital*, the first volume of which appeared in 1867. Already in 1848, however, he had linked the February Revolution of that year to the world trade crisis of 1847, which resulted in the closing of factories. The crisis passed, industrial prosperity reached a new level, and the conclusion in 1850 that: "A new revolution is only possible as a result of a new crisis. It is just as certain, however, as this."

4.3 The working class

"The object of the *Communist Manifesto*," wrote Marx and Engels in 1882, "was to proclaim the inevitable impending downfall of present-day bourgeois property" – in other words the downfall of capitalist property relations based on the private ownership of the means of production, and collective, socialised labour.

Capitalist crisis created the objective conditions for the downfall. The subjective force needed to bring it about is a mature, politically organised working class. The *Manifesto* therefore outlines the growth of the proletariat and the factors that weld it into a class in itself and for itself.

The workers grow in number to the extent that capital expands. Modern industry destroys the little workshops of traditional craftsmen, just as it destroyed the village industries of African societies. The lower ranks of the middle class — small tradesmen, handicraft workers, peasants — become wage workers. The proletariat is recruited from all sections of the population.

> *"Masses of labourers, crowded into the factories, are organised like soldiers under the command of overseers (boss boys), foremen and managers. Slaves of the capitalist, they are daily enslaved by the machine. All are instruments of labour, more or less expensive to use, according to their age and sex."*

Capital extracts surplus value, the source of profit, from the workers. The greater the degree of exploitation, the bigger the profit. Workers struggle to defend their living standards, oppose wage cuts, raise wages, reduce working hours. The struggle goes through stages as the working class matures.

> *"At first the contest is carried on by individual labourers, then by the work*

people of a factory, then by the operatives of a trade, in one locality, against the individual bourgeois who directly exploits them."

The concentration of workers in mines, factories and construction increases their strength. They feel strong and unite their forces. Trade unions are formed, first in single factories, then in whole industries. The unions insist on solidarity, refuse to allow non-union workers to take jobs, force employers to enter into collective bargaining, and call on the workers to come out on strike in support of their demands.

The workers develop a class consciousness in the course of their struggles. They learn that their interests are opposed to the bosses' interests. They become a class in themselves.

Strikes bring them into conflict with the state, its police and courts. When African miners struck work in 1946, the police shot them down and drove them down the shafts. The government blamed the Communist Party and put its executive committee on trial for sedition. Unable to convict them, the government banned the Party under the Suppression of Communism Act of 1950.

4.4 A class for themselves

Conflicts with employees and the state teach workers that the state is not a force "above" all classes. It does not "balance" the interests of different classes but acts as an instrument of the dominant class. "The executive of the modern state," says the *Manifesto*, "is but a committee for managing the common affairs of the whole bourgeoisie."

The economic struggles of workers therefore have a political content. "Every class struggle is a political struggle." To win the right to form trade unions and bargain collectively, workers in the older industrial countries had to overcome opposition from employers, the government and the laws. They went into politics and became "a class for themselves".

The introduction of capitalist democracy — votes for all — left unchanged the relations of production. These remained a system of private, capitalist ownership in the means of production. Even today, working class parties, competing with capitalist parties for office (prime minister, cabinet ministers, members of parliament) often preach socialism while practising capitalism. The most that such parties can achieve is to remove the worst anti-trade union laws and to obtain social reforms such as improved housing, education, health services, pensions and unemployment benefits.

Democracy has a very different meaning in the *Manifesto*, which declares that democracy comes into being when workers become the ruling class. They will then use their political power "to wrest, by degrees, all capital from the bourgeoisie, to centralise all instrument of production organised as the ruling class".

4.5 A revolutionary party

There can be no revolution without a revolutionary party, no socialism without a socialist party. This is the concluding message of the *Manifesto*. It discusses the part played by communists — "the most advanced and resolute section of the working class parties of every country, that section which pushes forward all others".

Communists have the same immediate aim as other workers' parties: "Formation of the proletariat into a class, overthrow of the bourgeois supremacy, conquest of political power by the proletariat." Their theory, summed up in a single phrase, is: "Abolition of private property".

But there are many brands of socialism. Some are reactionary, looking backward to feudalism; some appeal to peasants and petty manufacturers; some are cloaks for a bourgeois nationalism; some fight for reforms that leave unchanged the property relation between capital and labour; some are Utopian — they attack capitalism, call for socialism but reject the class struggle.

Communists, however, "openly declare that their ends can be attained only by the forcible overthrow of all existing social conditions". They "support every revolutionary movement against the existing social and political order of things". They bring to the front, as the leading question, the abolition of private, capitalist property.

Comments from John Hoffmann

"It is important to stress here how Marx and Engels show in the *Manifesto* that it is capitalism itself which impresses upon thinkers the need for a materialist theory of history. I would say this lecture gives a slightly negative view of what working class parties can obtain in bourgeois democracies. It rather dodges the question (as in Lecture 9) of what the role of the communist party is in a bourgeois democracy. A few sentences on some of the contemporary expressions of 'utopian, conservative, petty bourgeois etc socialism' (dealt with in Part III of the *Manifesto*) would be useful. Is 'African socialism' a candidate here?"

How did it go in practice?

Somafco teachers comment: "The discussion started off rather dry and stilted but later livened up. Most discussion tended to focus on the question of class struggle in the advanced capitalist societies, e.g. Is the working class still revolutionary in these countries? Is it possible that a revolutionary movement could develop there? How does the bourgeoisie manage to retain power in a bourgeois democratic state?"

Teaching suggestions

If contemporary politics have not entered the discussion around previous lectures, they surely must at this stage. A good starting-point for the topic might be discussion of how we use the term "revolution". What does it mean? Can we describe any revolutions we know of? What happened? Time could easily get hijacked by the question of "what went wrong" with the revolutions in Eastern Europe at this stage. This will be a recurring question throughout the course, and it is certainly one Comrade Jack would not have shied away from. A good way for the facilitator to deal with it would be as a "hanging question", recorded on a board or flip-chart and returned to whenever relevant, with participants' comments and suggestions also recorded. At the end of the course, these collected points could form the basis of an extra discussion session. The *Communist Manifesto* remains one of the simplest and most readable revolutionary texts. It might be worth looking at the original as well as this lecture's synopsis.

 Further reading sections
D, E

Lecture 5: Social Formations

5.0 Classifying societies

Humans have developed social systems (social-economic formations of many kinds during the long period — 50 000-100 000 years — of their existence as members of the human species (homo sapiens). All these societies include the same basic elements: forces of production, relations of production, economic structure and social superstructure. The elements, however, take different forms and combine in different ways. Is it possible to discover a uniform pattern behind the differences?

Scholars throughout the ages have been interested in the range of variations in human society. Many ancient writers of Egypt, India, China and Greece have left accounts of people discovered by traders and explorers between four and two thousands years before the present (AD) era. Some also tried to classify animals, plants, rocks and other forms of matter. Classifying things according to their likeness and differences is often a first step to understanding the reason for variations in form and structure.

Charles Fourier (1772-1837), a French utopian socialist and famous forerunner of Marx, divided the history of society into four stages: savagery, barbarism, patriarchy and civilisation. Subsequent students of social evolution followed his arrangement. Even Engels (*The Origins of the Family, Private Property and the State, 1884*) speaks of the "three principal stages of human development": savagery, barbarism and civilisation.

But these labels are misleading. The so-called "savages" and "barbarians" did not live in anarchy. They had definite customs and morals, an economic system and social organisation that worked well for their level of technology and conditions of life.

The categories usually adopted in studies of historical materialism are early communalism, slavery, feudalism, capitalism and socialism. Those are the main social-economic formation.

We read in *The Fundamentals of Marxism-Leninism* (p153) that:
"The development of society proceeds through the consecutive replacement, according the definite laws, of one socio-economic formation by another. Moreover, a nation living in the conditions of a more advanced formation

shows other nations their future just as the latter show that nation its past."

5.1 Historical stages

The idea that all peoples pass through the same stages is based on the history of European nations. This is not, however, a correct statement of world history. Many peoples "jump" or leave out one or more stages. It is not necessary for every people to develop capitalism in order to achieve socialism. Many traditional African states, including our own, never passed through slavery or feudalism.

There are "underdeveloped" social systems but no "underdeveloped" peoples. All humans, in every kind of social formation, have the same physical and mental make-up. All can learn to speak one another's language and master advanced technologies. Hunters like the Khoisan, cattle herders like the Khoi-Khoi, farmers and stockbreeders like our own people, moved from their customary social formations to advanced productive systems using power-driven machines.

The theory of fixed stages also leaves out the effects of interactions between peoples of different social formations through migration, conquest and settlement.

The *Communist Manifesto* is more accurate in pointing out that:
"The bourgeoisie, by the immensely facilitated means of communication, draws all, even the most barbarian, nations into civilisation."

Imperialist expansion and colonial rule imposed capitalist productive forces and property relations on millions of people in different stages of social formation. But their future lies in their own hands. They will decide to live under capitalism or to take the non-capitalist road to socialism.

5.2 Resistance to change

Not all societies move through an internal process of change to a more advanced kind of formation. Some stay rooted for centuries in a mode of life even though they are in close contact with more highly developed systems. This "marking time" is especially true of hunting people and food collectors, such as the pygmies (Twa) of the Congo rain forests, native Australians ("Aborigines") and the native Americans ("Red Indians") of North America.

Commenting on the Red Indians, Engels writes (in *The Origin of the Family* ...) that their division of labour "is purely natural; it exists only between the two sexes". Men make war, hunt and produce tools; women look after their houses, cook and make clothing from buffalo skins. The society was one of early communalism.

We should note that the introduction of domesticated horses and firearms changed Indian methods of hunting and warfare. They united in "confederations" against English and French invaders and put up strong resistance, but were defeated by soldiers with long-range rifles and other advanced weapons.

Some stockbreeders, like the Khoi-Khoi and Mongolian horsemen of North-East Asia, made no attempt to grow crops. They lived on milk products, meat, wild animals and plants.

A young Jack Simons in 1932 at the age 25 (above) and Jack on his way to England in 1964 (left).

Ray Alexander hard at work as a dedicated trade unionist in the 1950s (opposite).

Photographs: Mayibuye Centre

Cape Argus

Jack Simons and Julius Lewin outside the Cape Town Supreme Court during the case Republic vs Alan Brooks, De Keller, Kemp and Daniels

Mervyn Bennun

On the way into exile in May 1965 Comrade Jack and Ray stopped next to a baobab tree in Zambia (above) and on their arrival at Barney and Sonja Gordon's home in Lusaka (below).

Mervyn Bennun

Photographs: CDC

Typical conditions in ANC training camps in Tanzania, Zambia and Angola (opposite and above) where this artwork (below) was produced by Thami Mnyele and (right) course material used in class.

Comrade Jack at a Frelimo rally in Kabwe, Zambia in 1979 (above) and with Oliver Tambo at the ANC National Consultative Conference in 1985.

Family time at home in Lusaka, Zambia: Comrade Jack with his daughter Tanya and friend Nyosa (above) and with his grandson Jacques Barben (below) at his 70th birthday in 1987.

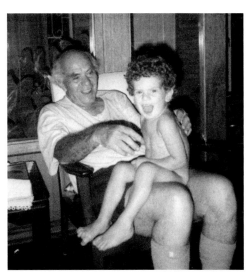

Photographs: Cedric Nunn

Leaving Lusaka for the last time in August 1990 Comrade Jack and Ray examine a map book of their destination — Cape Town (opposite top) and Jack walks out of the gates for the last time (opposite below). Ray checks the baggage at Lusaka airport before boarding the plane for home (above) and is greeted joyfully by old friend and activist Frances Baard on arrival in Cape Town (below).

Mayibuye Centre

Old comrades reunited: Comrade Jack and Ray with Nelson Mandela (above) in Windhoek, Namibia in 1990 and Comrade Jack and Raymond Mhlaba meet after many years of separation in 1990 (below).

Times of Zambia

Sue Kramer

Comrade Jack celebrates being awarded an honourary Doctor of Laws degree by the University of Cape Town on June 24 1994

Comrade Jack and Ray celebrates with Constitutional Court Judge Albie Sachs (above) and Ray with President Thabo Mbeki at a book launch function (right).

Sue Kramer

Sue Kramer

Sue Kramer

The moment
that made all
the years of hard
work and sacrifice
worthwhile:
Comrade Jack and
Ray after voting in
the first democratic
elections in 1994
(above) and at the
opening of
Parliament (left).

Sue Kramer

Comrade Jack and Ray watch the election results on television at home in Cape Town

Some became great warriors, plundered other people and formed tributary states such as the Mongol Empire of Genghis Khan in the 14th century.

5.3 Changing formations

Trade, migration, wars and conquest have often speeded up the rate of change in different formations. The main driving force, however, is a qualitative change in the instruments and forces of production. Such changes act on the property system and through it on the superstructure. Iron smelting was such a qualitative change.

The domestication of seed-bearing grasses (maize in South America, wheat in Ethiopia, barley in Europe) gave rise to agriculture. Early cultivators used digging sticks. The introduction of metallurgy led to the use of copper, bronze and iron implements and weapons.

Engels (*The Origin of the Family* ...) wrote that "iron extended agriculture to wider areas clearing more extensive stretches of forest, it provided handicraft with a tool of a hardness and cutting power that no stone or other known metal could withstand". The introduction of iron ploughshares, drawn by oxen or horses, had long range results in Egypt, Asia and Europe. To summarise some in broad terms:

• Stock owners using ploughs could cultivate bigger areas than farmers without stock.

• People without cattle would borrow or hire them for ploughing and become dependent on cattle owners, after losing their share of the land.

• Owners of big herds took over common grazing land for their use and turned arable land into their private property. Through this, a class division emerged between landowner and landless people.

• An increase in output provided a surplus for trade, encouraged a division of labour between farmers and craftsmen, separated the country people from townsmen, gave rise to specialisations of crafts and led to the growth of a merchant class.

• At different points in this development, shortages of labour resulted, giving rise to the use of slaves and serfs, the first major class division.

Changes did not take place everywhere in this order. It can be said, however, that the model gives a reliable account of the links between changes in productive forces, relations of production and the social superstructure.

5.4 Slavery: an economic category

A slave is property. His owner can sell, even kill him. But the slave is a valuable commodity and therefore not lightly destroyed.

To make profit for his owner, a slave must produce more than he consumes, enough to cover his purchase price and the cost of feeding, clothing and housing him. Since slaves reproduce themselves, the breeding of slaves for sale is a profitable business in addition to the surplus value they create through production. Slaves captured in war did not involve capital investment and were valued as an extra source of labour.

Slavery was found at different levels of development, including systems with fairly low standards of production and little trade. Slavery appeared at an early stage of iron hoe cultivation (though by no means in all societies at that level) in China, India, Greece and Rome. It continued in Europe before and during feudalism and broke new ground in the colonies of western Europe. The Arabs, Portuguese, British, Dutch and French raided Africa for slaves and transported them across the Atlantic Ocean to America and the West Indies.

Engels noted (in *The Origin of the Family* ...) that "with slavery, which in civilisation reached its complete development, came the first great cleavage of society into an exploiting and an exploited class. This cleavage lasted throughout the whole period of civilisation."

Further (in *Anti-Duhring*), he noted:
"It was slavery that first made possible the division of labour between agriculture and industry on a considerable scale ... Without slavery, no Greek state, no Greek art, science; without slavery, no Roman Empire."

Capitalism grew on the backs of African slaves.
Marx pointed this out in *The Poverty of Philosophy* (1847):
"Direct slavery is just as much the pivot of bourgeois industry as machinery and credits. Without slavery you have no cotton, without cotton you have no modern industry. It is slavery that has given the colonies their value, it is the colonies that have created world trade, and it is world trade that is the pre-condition of large-scale industry. Thus slavery is an economic category of the greatest importance. Without slavery, North America, the most progressive of countries, would be transformed into a patriarchal country ... Abolish slavery and you will have wiped America off the map of nations."

In fact, America did abolish slavery in 1865, after a bitter civil war between the industrial North and the slave-owning South. One of the big questions to be settled was whether slave labour or free labour would be used to develop new territories, such as Texas and California. The defeat of the Southern States opened the way for the expansion of industrial capitalism. Instead of falling back into a patriarchal, agrarian economy, the United States moved on to become the big giant of industrial capitalism. Slave owners had to carry the expense of feeding, clothing and housing their slaves, however poorly. Industrial capitalists needed to do nothing but exploit their free workers.

5.5 Serfdom: Backbone of feudalism
Colonial capitalism, which injected new life into slavery, did much to bring about the downfall of feudalism. Although feudalism was found in many forms — in China, Ethiopia, East Africa, Latin America — here, we discuss only European feudalism.

The word comes from the Latin "feudum", meaning land granted by the king to lords and knights under a "fief" which carried with it a duty to pay taxes and provide soldiers for the king's armies. Large pieces of land (estates) went to the nobility and the church. They in turn made land grants to their followers, also under fiefs obliging them to give military service to their lords.

Some peasants owned their farms. But most were serfs, bonded to their lord, tied to the land, and not allowed to move from one estate to another. Under some systems, they worked part of the week on their plots and the rest of the week (three or four days) on the fields or their lord. Under others, the serf paid rent in the form of grain and cattle for the right to cultivate his plot. Serfs could also be called upon for military service as foot soldiers armed with bows and spears.

Serfdom was close to slavery in old Russia. Landlords sold serfs, lost them at cards, exchanged them for horses. Even under such conditions, however, the serf, unlike the slave, worked some time for himself on his own piece of land.

The growth of trade, linked to improvements in farming and manufacturing, encouraged the formation of towns and a commercial sector. As the money economy spread, the lords, ever hungry for cash, made serfs pay rent, thereby forcing them to sell produce on the market. Some grew rich, but most fell into poverty and lost their land. They became wage workers.

Marx, writing about the decline of feudalism (*Capital*, Vol 1, Ch 27) records that: *"In England, serfdom had practically disappeared in the last part of the 14th century ... The wage-labourers of agriculture consisted partly of peasants, who utilised their spare time by working on the large estates, partly of an independent special class of wage labourers, few in numbers."*

Serfdom lasted longer in most of continental Europe. Peasants often revolted against the feudal lords but the main resistance to the continuation of feudal rule came from manufacturers, bankers and merchants of the towns. They overthrew the feudal nobility with the mass support of peasants, but left intact the system of feudal tenure in many European countries. Big landowners owned much of the land and continued to exploit peasant cultivators and craftsmen. In Russia only the October Revolution put an end to the last remains of feudalism.

Serfdom was a complex system which included some obligations by the landowners towards their serfs (although these were often neglected) as well as the massive obligations of serfs to landowners. The capitalist system is bound by no such obligations.

5.6 Free workers

Capitalism needs and creates an army of free workers — free in the double sense of having no means of production of their own and being free to sell their labour power on the market to the highest bidder.

"The capitalist system presupposes the complete separation of the labourers from all property in the means by which they can realise their labour".
(Capital, Vol 1, Ch 26)

The formation of a propertyless working class is also a process of converting communal and peasant land into the private property of capitalist owners. South African colonialists expropriated, taking by force the land of hunters and stockbreeders and forcing them to work for wages in the farms, mines and factories of the capitalist class.

"The expropriation of the agricultural producer, of the peasant from the soil, is the basis of the whole process by which great masses of men are suddenly and forcibly torn from their means of subsistence, and hurled as free and 'unattached' proletarians on the labour market."

South Africa's population in the reserves — reservoirs of African labour — have experienced this process to become migrant workers in capitalist enterprises.

John Hoffman comments

"Linkage between this and earlier chapters would be helpful. And in the first section, more emphasis is needed that the theory of fixed stages has nothing to do with historical materialism."

How did it go in practice?

Somafco teachers comment: "The major focus of the discussion was on two quite different questions:
• How did the transition from pre-class to class societies happen?
• Which social system is South Africa in now, and which one will it be in after the revolution?"

Teaching suggestions

A good way to start this discussion would be to use the example of a very basic social organisation, such as the society of San hunter-gatherers. Using material written on the San, and photographs, participants could be asked to describe the differences between San economic structure and social organisation and that of a modern industrial state. That provides an entry point for discussing the two contrasting theories of how societies change:
• the mechanical notion of inevitable progress through stages; and
• the dialectical notion that different social formations are appropriate for different levels of technology and economic capacity (rather than better or "worse").

There are many opportunities here for talking about the effects of contact between societies with very different economic and social formations, including questions about superstructural aspects, such as cultural integrity and dislocation. And, of course, the Somafco students' second question about South Africa remains highly relevant.

Further reading sections
D, F, H, I

Lecture 6: African Perspectives

6.0 Cradle of humanity

Biologists (specialists in comparative anatomy, physiology and genetics) agree on the unitary origin of humans. All peoples have descended from the same stock. Physical differences (skin colour, shape of nose and eye, hair form) have a use value in the climates and environments in which they evolved.

Dark skins, for example, are caused by melanin, a chemical under the epidermis or outer skin layer. Melanin is a protection against strong sunlight in the tropics. Dark-skinned people suffer far less frequently from the sunburn, sunstroke or skin cancers which affect pale-skinned people in sunny climates.

According to evolutionary theory, such differences arose through genetic mutation, small, inherited changes in individuals that multiplied over thousands of years after people had migrated, probably before the Ice Age, from a central region. Inbreeding within isolated communities produced special strains or physical types within the human race.

Many scientists think that the central region was located in Africa. The evidence comes from the study of early human skeletons, the remains of people who lived perhaps 50 000 years ago. It suggests that Africa is the cradle of humanity.

6.1 Centre of civilisation

Africa is also home of one of the first civilisations. It arose in Egypt where agriculture advanced at an early stage along the Nile. Some specialists think that civilisation spread from Egypt and Mesopotamia into India, China and South America. Others take the view that these civilisations arose independently along great rivers (the Indus in India, the Yangtse in China). There is no doubt, however, about Egypt having produced one of the earliest great civilisations.

What is civilisation? The word is used to describe not one but many kinds of social formations that rose and fell during thousands of years and resulted in socialism, which alone among societies is designed to be free from exploitation.

Early civilisations are marked by the division of labour and by trade between farmers and craftsmen, between country and town; the exchange of food for manufactured goods, the use of metal coins as a medium of exchange; the private ownership of land, slave labour, and the rise of a merchant class; written records kept by officials, a priesthood and the formation of a state.

Engels (*Origins of the Family ...*) notes:
"The combining link of civilised society is the state, which in all typical periods without exception is the state of the ruling class, and in all cases continues to be in essence a machine for holding down the oppressed and exploited class."

6.2 African civilisations

These arose in West Africa along the coast and in the interior on the great rivers such as the Niger. Divisions of labour had reached a high level by the year 1200. Skilled craftsmen, working in metals (gold, bronze, iron), wood, ivory and natural fibres produced goods of outstanding quality like the famous Benin bronzes. Large feudal estates, worked by slaves, serfs and individual villagers, produced food and raw materials for the nobility, merchants and craftsmen of the towns.

Trading caravans transported gold, ivory, cloth, oil products and other agricultural commodities across the Sahara to North Africa. With the spread of Islam after 800AD, its converts, speaking and writing Arabic, carried on most of the long distance trade.

Rest houses and markets along the routes of the caravans grew into commercial towns with mosques and priests, who instructed pupils in Arabic and the Koran and settled disputes under Islamic law. Though many people whom the Arabs called caffres (originally meaning unbelievers — the origin of the derogatory term "kaffir"), clung to their traditional customs and religions, Islamic culture was spread by traders and missionaries over wide areas of the sub-Saharan region.

Commercial capitalism, which arose within these feudal structures, expanded until the 1500s, when Portuguese traders, followed by the Dutch, French and British, changed the course of development. They built trading stations, called forts, along the coast, and organised an enormous trade in slaves captured in the interior. The slavers robbed Africa of about 25 million slaves in the next centuries. Only about eight million, however, survived the slave raids, the journey to the coast and the voyage in ships packed with shackled slaves across the Atlantic to America, the West Indies and the Caribbean.

6.3 Slavery and the slave trade

Africa's loss was Europe's gain. The forcible seizure of people and their transfer to colonies deprived Africa of its human resources, undermined its flourishing civilisations and laid the foundations of bourgeois industry. Slavery, wrote Marx, gave colonies their value; the colonies created world trade; and world trade is necessary for large-scale industry.

> Marx traced the links in *Capital* (Vol 1, Ch 31):
> *"The discovery of gold and silver in America, the killing enslavement and entombment in mines of the aboriginal Indians, the beginning of the conquest and looting of the East Indies, the turning of Africa into a warren for the commercial hunting of black skins, signalised the rosy dawn of the era of capitalist production."*

Brute force, as in the colonies, was the source of capital accumulation which hastened the change from feudal modes of production to the capitalist mode of production.

> *"Force is the midwife of every old society pregnant with a new one. It is in itself an economic power."*

Holland, the leading capitalist nation in the 1600s had a colonial record of extreme "treachery, bribery, massacre and meanness". To get slaves for Java, the Dutch trained man-stealers. "The thief, the interpreter and the seller were the chief agents in this trade, native princes the chief sellers." Jan van Riebeeck, a Dutch agent and thief, went to the Cape in 1652 to found a half-way feeding station for the Dutch East India Company's wars against the Javanese.

The slaves used for this enterprise, referred to as Malays or Muslims, are among the ancestors of the people classified "coloured" in South Africa. Slavery at the Cape gave rise to the colour discrimination that spread and hardened into apartheid during 300 years of colonial wars, conquest, forced labour and exploitation.

6.4 Socio-economic formations

Farmers and stock breeders lived in Eastern, Central and Southern Africa long before the arrival of Arabs and Europeans. The Tonga, believed to be the first to settle in Zambia, came there not later than 600. At about this time, people were mining and smelting iron ore in the Northern Transvaal.

Portuguese shipwrecked sailors reported the presence in the 1500s of Xhosa and Zulu-speaking people along the Eastern coast, in regions they still occupy. It is probable they settled there by or before the year 1000. Meanwhile, the Sotho-Tswana were established on the high plateau south of the Limpopo River and spreading westwards from the Drakensberg to the semi-arid regions of Kalahari and Namibia. Both the main stockbreeding communities absorbed some and pushed others southward or towards the Kalahari.

The remains of stone-built houses, pottery and iron goods suggest that the mode of production changed little in the next few hundred years. Apart from the Basarwa, descendants of Khoi and Tswana, who were serfs of the Bakgalagadi in Botswana, there is no evidence of persistent slavery. Prisoners of war became dependents but were absorbed as full members of the community through intermarriage and continued residence.

The household or village was the basic unit of production and consumption. There was division of labour between men and women and a number of specialists (metalworkers, potter, weavers, carpenters and herbalists) but even they usually also farmed with land and cattle.

Some people, like Bemba, Tonga and Chewa, traced descent through the maternal line, whereas some other groups, such as those in South Africa and Zimbabwe, were patrilineal: children belonged to the father's clan (*isiduko, isibongo*) and inherited from him, instead of from the mother's brother (*malume*) as in matrilineal society. These kinship and marriage differences had little effect, however, on modes of production.

The land belonged to the state. The king administered it, appointed heads of provinces and districts (*indunas*), regulated the times of ploughing and harvesting, and carried out religious ceremonies to bring good rains and harvests.

Every member of the state had a right to build and cultivate land, and to a share of water, plants and animals. Cattle belonged to households (*imizi*), under the control of their heads. When the head died, the stock and other property were divided among the houses of the various wives and went to the eldest son in every house.

6.5 Government and law

Systems of government differed somewhat, even among peoples with the same mode of production. Some, like those in southern Africa, had centralised states, under hereditary rulers, assisted by members of the royal family and outstanding commoners, leaders in the army and councils of state. Many agrarian societies, combining farming with stock raising, had no central rulers, but were governed by village elders, or heads of kingship groups (clans) or senior members of age sets. The Masai and other cattle owners of East Africa initiated their young men into age sets which went through various stages as warriors, heads of families and finally elders, when they took charge of government and the enforcement of law.

In the absence of social classes, based on differences between propertied and propertyless people, systems of government remained stable even though there were many wars of rivalry. A ruler might be ousted but another member of the royal family nearly always took his place. There were factions, but no revolutions in the political order.

Class divisions did result, however, through conquest and domination, usually by stockbreeders over cultivators. The Bahima cattle owners imposed their rule on the Bahira in Buganda, took tribute from them in garden produce and refused to let them own cattle or marry Himan women. The rift between Hutu and Tutsi in Rwanda and Burundi began as a class distinction between cattle-owners (Tutsi) and tribute-payers (Hutu) which was later aggravated by the Belgian colonialists.

Slavery, the main source of class divisions at an early stage of social development, existed among some people, such as the Bemba or Lozi of Zambia. Slaves were gradually taken into the families to which they belonged, but slavery was a major source of labour, especially in Bulozi, where they were used to build the canals that drained and irrigated the great plains along the Zambezi River.

Political changes of a different kind followed the Tshaka wars at the beginning of the 19th century. They consolidated the Zulu ruling class against white invaders and gave rise to new states: Lesotho under Moeshoeshoe, Swaziland under Dhlamini, Ndebele under Mzilikazi and the Ngoni kingdom in Eastern Zambia. Some of the new states might have grown into bigger empires were it not for the white colonialists who infiltrated through southern and central Africa during the 19th century.

6.6 Colonial rule

Colonialism came to Africa at different times and with different amounts of economic power. The Portuguese were the first and in many ways the worst. Their chief business for over 200 years was to supply slaves for Brazil and other colonies. When slavery was replaced by industrial capitalism, Africans were taken to Portugal as a source of cheap labour. Lisbon seized the surplus value created in the colonies and stopped the growth of industries that could have competed with Portugal's domestic economy.

In South Africa, at the other end of the colonial scale, foreign capital made huge profits from gold and diamond mines. Some of the profits were ploughed back into engineering plants and workshops serving the mines. Industries expanded during this century to make South Africa the leading industrial country in Africa. The expansion took place through super-exploitation of black workers and the complete neglect of their agriculture. Village communities in the reserves were neglected and underdeveloped sources of labour for mines and factories.

This story has been repeated throughout Africa. Big mineral deposits, such as copper in Zambia and Zaire, have been exploited to provide raw materials for industries in Europe and America. Workers for the mines were drawn from rural areas, which suffered heavily from the loss of labour power and the decline of the viable economy.

Countries that depend heavily on agriculture, such as most of West Africa, Uganda and Malawi, produce coffee, cotton, groundnuts, vegetable oils, cotton and other tropical products for the world industry. In return they import factory-made goods. Industries in Africa are neglected. The gap in the wealth and living standards between Africa and the rich capitalist countries grows wider.

Colonial capitalism stopped the natural evolution of Africa, destroyed its civilisations, undermined its culture and turned it into an appendage of Western capitalism.

Nowhere has this process been carried out with the same ferocity, cruelty and thoroughness as in South Africa. Nowhere else have colonialists stolen so much of the people's land. Nowhere else have such great masses of dispossessed, landless peasants been hurled on to the labour market. The course of events that Marx described in his chapters on "primitive accumulation" in Europe have an exact parallel in South Africa.

"The transformation of the individualised and scattered means of production into socially concentrated ones, of the pygmy property of the many into the huge property of the few, the expropriation of the great mass of people from the soil, form the means of subsistence, from and from the means of labour, this fearful and painful expropriation of the mass of the people forms the prelude to the history of capital ... The expropriation of the immediate producers was accomplished with merciless vandalism, and under the stimulus of passions the most infamous, the most sordid, the pettiest, the most meanly odious."
(Capital, Vol 1 Ch 32)

John Hoffman's comments

"There is some excellent material here. The reference to the 'absence of social classes' in the context of systems of government needs careful clarification — perhaps the distinction between 'government' and 'state' could be explored here?"

How did it go in practice?

Somafco teachers comment: "The discussion focussed mainly on two questions.

• The large size of the peasantry in most African countries and whether or not this posed a problem for economic and social development. One feeling expressed is that a large peasantry is a symptom of underdevelopment and not a cause of underdevelopment; the peasantry will decrease as agriculture becomes more efficient and the industrial sector expands.

• The basis for African unity. Although everyone agreed that there was a need for the OAU and that this need would continue even after the liberation of Namibia and South Africa, there was disagreement over whether there was any basis for real unity — e.g. is there a basis for unity among countries with such different social systems and levels of development. Some people thought there was such a basis (in anti-imperialism) while others disagreed.

Teaching suggestions

An obvious starting point for this session is the recent archaeological discoveries at Sterkfontein Caves and Mapungubwe, which underline the points about Africa as both the birthplace of humanity and as a continent possessing early and sophisticated civilisations. There is some good photographic material from newspapers and magazines, which could form a starting point for such a discussion. It's also worth discussing the way the ideologists of apartheid quite literally hid this history, and the psychological impact this had on many African communities denied their own history. We have experienced much more of the impact of neo-colonialism (and some new aspects like globalisation and the impact of World Bank/ IMF debt conditionalities) since 1977. It could be relevant to introduce some of this information here, particularly in terms of the impact on African industry and agriculture. And the ideas around "African Renaissance" are especially relevant to this lecture and worth discussing — with a similar spin to those Somafco students' questions: what is the basis for it?

Further reading sections
C, F, G, (section africa)

Lecture 7: Proletarian Revolutions

7.0 Our revolutionary epoch

The 20th century will go down in history as an age of great revolutions in science, technology, economic structures and socio-political systems.

Transport and communications on land, sea and air have taken a tremendous leap forward from ox-wagons to space rockets. Internal combustion engines, jet-propelled planes, television, electronics are marvels of our age. Computers, linked to machines, open up possibilities of industrial automation that could release workers, the machine-minders and operatives of today, for creative labour.

Men have landed on the moon and will travel further through space to more distant planets and even galaxies. The splitting of the atom provides new sources of energy, both for destroying and preserving life. Advances in biological sciences make possible great increases in food supplies and speeds up our progress in preventing and curing diseases.

Science, if used in the interests of humanity, provides the means to do away with poverty and ignorance, prolong life and free humans from the physical and mental constraints that held up the progress of the mass of people — workers and peasants — throughout the ages.

To harness science to the service of humanity we need a social order that is free of class divisions and exploitation, a system that will liberate people from all forms of oppression.

South Africa, in the present century, is an intolerable anachronism, a sordid hangover from the colonial past, a medieval relic in the age of space travel, atomic energy and automation. South Africa's superstructure is a burden to our people and an insult to the whole of humanity. It is our historic task to liberate our people, the whole of South Africa, from the crushing load of poverty, discrimination and oppression that the racist bourgeoisie imposes to maintain exploitation for the sake of super profits and capital gain.

7.1 Revolutionary streams

Our revolution will succeed. Of this there is absolutely no doubt. Success is guaranteed by the political, economic and social transformation of the world in the present epoch. Two great revolutionary waves have made our revolution both possible and inevitable.

One is the great Russian Revolution of November 1917 — 60 years ago. It opened a new era: the era of socialism under the rule of working people, workers by hand and by brain. The other stream is the movement for national liberation. It has emancipated millions of people from direct imperialist domination and colonial rule.

The two streams of revolution are interlocked and intertwined. The Soviet Revolution of 1917 changed the balance of world power and created conditions favourable to the struggle against foreign domination and colonial rule. Communist parties taught Marxist socialism, organised trade unions and supported national movements against colonialism.

Socialism spread after the war of 1939-45 to embrace one-third of the world's population. The struggle for liberation reached a new height. Imperialism, suffering severe defeats, withdrew only to continue its exploitation in new, indirect forms.

South Africa's white racist rule opposed both revolutionary streams. Both have combined against apartheid. But the overthrow of Baaskap is the task of the revolutionary vanguard.

7.2 Russia's revolution of 1905

The revolutionary movement against Tsarism began in 1825. From there up to the assassination of Alexander II in 1881, middle-class intellectuals led the movement. Their heroic sacrifices contributed to growth of political consciousness, but only a working class party could call forth a popular revolution.

A strike wave swept through Russia in 1905 after the severe defeats inflicted by the Japanese in the imperialist Russo-Japanese war. Nearly three million factory workers struck work during 1905, peasants in one-third of the country set fire to the mansions of big landowners, looted stores and killed police. Sailors and soldiers mutinied.

The revolution began on "Bloody Sunday" January 22, outside the Tsar's Winter Palace in Leningrad (then called St Petersburg) where Cossacks fired on unarmed people who had gathered to petition the Tsar for democratic rights. They received bullets instead of votes and gained a big political lesson, but at the price of more than 1 000 killed and 2 000 wounded.

"The unenlightened workers of pre-revolutionary Russia ... did not know that the Tsar was the head of the ruling class of large land-owners, who by a thousand tiers were already bound up with a big bourgeoisie ready to defend their monopoly, privileges and profits by every violent means" (Lenin, 1917)

The workers used the weapon of political strikes, a proletarian weapon, to achieve a bourgeois democratic system of government.

The Tsar offered concessions: an elected assembly (Duma) with advisory powers only, and a small number of votes. Law-making would remain in the hands of the Tsar: an absolute monarch who "alone promulgates laws, nominates officials and controls them" (Lenin, *Our Programme*, 1899).

The revolutionary Social-Democrats rejected the "advisory Duma" and forced the Tsar to increase the number of voters, to give the Duma legislative powers.

7.3 Social-Democrats: a revolutionary party

A number of Social-Democrat and Marxist groups merged in 1898 to form the Russian Social-Democratic Labour Party (RSDLP). Its practical tasks were to organise and lead the workers' class struggle for socialism and against capitalism and for democracy and against Tsarist absolutism. The two tasks were inseparably linked — just as our own revolution struggles against both capitalist exploitation and racist dictatorship.

In *The Tasks of the RSDLP*, 1897, Lenin explained that:
"Both economic and political agitation are equally necessary to develop the class consciousness of the proletariat ... because every class struggle is a political struggle."

The Russian worker was bound by a double yoke: capitalists robbed him, police persecuted him.

"Any strike against a capitalist results in the military and police being let loose on the workers. Every economic fight of necessity turns into a political fight, and social-democracy must indissolubly combine the economic with the political fight into a united class struggle of the proletariat." (Our Programme)

To perform its tasks and carry them to a successful conclusion the RSDLP turned itself into a "party of a new type" with:
- theoretical unity based on scientific (Marxist) socialism;
- organisational unity under a single high command (the central committee);
- one programme, with minimum and maximum demands;
- a membership of activists, committed to the party's theory, organisation and programme, belonging to a unit of the party, paying a subscription, and carrying out assignments; and
- a party newspaper, carrying out the functions of a collective propagandist, agitator and organiser.

Divisions over the party's theory, programme and conditions of membership split the party into two camps: the Bolsheviks (majority) and Mensheviks (minority). The programme, adopted in 1903, set a minimum target of establishing a democratic republic and the maximum target of a socialist revolution under a proletarian dictatorship. The 8th Congress, held in March 1919, after the seizure of state power, changed the name to the Russian Communist Party (*Bolsheviks*), and decided to reject imperialism and form a Soviet Republic.

7.4 February to October

The Bolsheviks worked legally (in trade unions and the Duma) and illegally (forming underground party groups in the factories and secret societies). They called for opposition to the imperialist war of 1914-18. Many activists were jailed, exiled or drafted into the Tsarist armed forces. Though few in number, the Bolsheviks formed a network of party cells, held illegal meetings, distributed banned papers and leaflets, and prepared for the coming revolution.

It broke out in 1917 after heavy defeats inflicted on the Tsarist armies, the near collapse of the economy, a sharp fall in living standards, a country-wide political strike and revolts of soldiers and sailors. Workers and soldiers formed Soviets: representative councils in which Bolsheviks provided leadership.

A revolutionary crisis broke out. Representatives of the capitalist landowning class deposed the Tsar, set up a Provisional Government and continued the imperialist war.

Workers and peasants were now able to take part in open political struggles. Revolutionaries released from prison and returning from exile threw themselves into the battle. The Bolsheviks, emerging from underground, resumed publication of Pravda, the party newspaper, and revived party branches. They called on the Soviets to mobilise the people against the bourgeois government, to demand peace, bread and freedom.

"The revolution is a bourgeois revolution," wrote Lenin from exile in March. "It cannot give peace, bread and freedom. To win these, to complete the revolution, to achieve socialism, the workers must take power into their own hands, smash the bourgeois state machinery and arm the people."
(*Letter from Afar*, March 1917)

Lenin urged that the situation was ripe for revolution: "*Armed uprising is inevitable and has fully matured.*"

In his *Ten Theses* (*The Tasks of the Proletarian Revolution, April 1917*) he wrote that the situation was:
"*a transition from the first stage of the revolution, which, because of the inadequate organisation and insufficient class-consciousness of the proletariat, led to the assumption of power by the bourgeoisie — to its second stage which is to place power in the hands of the proletariat and the poorest sections of the peasantry*".

The bourgeois government launched a counter-revolutionary attack, resumed the wholesale arrests of Bolsheviks, issued and order for Lenin's arrest — but failed to stop the growth of the Party. It formed new cells, worked widely in the Soviets, trade unions and army, and spread the slogans: "All power to the Soviets, Land to the Peasants, Bread to the Hungry, Peace to the Nations."

The workers and soldiers of Petrograd overthrew the Provisional Government on November 7, 1917. Thus began the Great October Socialist Revolution, the first proletarian revolution. It opened a new era in history.

7.5 Capitalism and socialism

The critical choice before the Bolsheviks was either to accept bourgeois democracy, their minimum programme, or to strike out at once for the maximum, a socialist republic under the proletarian dictatorship. It was a difficult decision. A premature call for socialism might find the masses unprepared, thereby exposing the Party to ruthless oppression. On the other hand, if the Bolsheviks misjudged the situation, if they allowed the revolutionary wave to reach its peak without moving into action, they might lose an opportunity which would not easily recur. There were leading Bolsheviks who wanted to postpone the proletarian revolution.

Stalin, reporting in August 1917 for the Central Committee to the 6th Party Congress, said:
"*Several comrades argue that since capitalism is only feeble developed here, it is utopian to raise the question of a socialist revolution. They would be right if it were not for the war, if it were not for the devastation, if the foundations of national economy had not been shaken...Under these circumstances it was impossible for the worker to refrain from interfering in economic life. This is the real reason why the question of the socialist revolution could arise here in Russia*".

Lenin analysed the situation at the end of September. Revolution, he said, was an art, a creative act, the result of a deliberate, thought-out strategy. It took note of the position of the ruling class and its government, the mood of the people, the strength of the revolutionary forces. An uprising in July, when the bourgeois government launched its counter-revolutionary offensive, would have been a mistake: neither the workers and soldiers nor the Bolsheviks were prepared. Now, at the beginning of October, "We have before us all the objective requirements for a successful uprising", at "the crucial point ... when the activity of the vanguard of the people is at its height".

But the Central Committee of the Bolshevik Party was divided and uncertain. A majority decided in favour of an uprising, yet delayed action, ignoring Lenin's arguments. He thereupon handed in his resignation from the Committee so as to press his views freely "in the lower ranks of the party and at the Party Congress". This threat jerked the Committee into taking a stand for immediate revolution. Lenin wrote on the evening of November 6: *(This lecture is incomplete — no complete version exists — Ed)*

Further thoughts from Jack Simons

"Bolshevik and Menshevik are Russian for majority and minority. They came into use in the early days (1903) of the formation of the RSDLP when Lenin claimed to have a majority in the party. The difference was important, not merely verbal. The Bolsheviks wanted a revolutionary party of 'a new type' consisting of full-time members; the Mensheviks preferred the western social-democratic party model, loosely-knit and taking part in elections to a legislature.

"Concepts of 'scientific socialism' introduced by Marx and Engels had fallen into disuse after their death, being overrun by 'revisionism'. Lenin revived the doctrine during the First World War, for example in State and Revolution, and this notion was embodied in the Communist International. The SACP today prefers to define its aim as 'democratic socialism', rather than 'socialist democracy', the label attached to Labour Parties in South Africa before World War II and to the British Labour Party. However, both democratic socialism and socialist democracy are versions of the orthodox Marxism which emerged from the traditions of early Russian and international Marxism." (7/10/91)

Commenting on the phrase about the "inevitable success of our revolution" in 1991, Comrade Jack noted: "The decision of the SACP to keep its name and adopt a programme aimed at public ownership of the means of production reflects an abiding confidence in the moral values and structural aims of the founders of communist theory. It is rooted in the history of human societies, ranging from those of the hunters and food gatherers (like South Africa's Bushmen/San) to advanced capitalism, which exhausts and destroys natural resources for the sake of private property. In contrast 'bourgeois society must always come up against an ... obstacle for its starting point, and its goals are always ... an apologia for the existing order of things or at least the proof of their immutability'." (R Gottlieb (Ed) An Anthology of Western Marxism OUP 1989 P56)

Comrade Jack wrote an essay in Lusaka in 1987 to commemorate the 70th anniversary of the Russian revolution. This paper, in his words, "drew attention to the pressure applied by Lenin on members of the of the Communist Party's

Central Committee to agree with his proposal for an immediate insurrection. He threatened to resign from the Central Committee and campaign among the rank and file of the party if the Bolsheviks failed to follow his lead. The insurrection thereupon took place, but the one-party rule that they established was far removed from the the Marxist notion of the dictatorship of the working class. 'Russia,' remarked Lenin, 'had the most advanced political system in the world.' Yet it failed to lay even the foundations of a national economy: the socio-economic base necessary for the realisation of the Soviet Union's attempt to create a model society. This proved to be a fatal weakness that led to the downfall of Communist systems in the Soviet Union, Eastern Europe and most countries in all parts of the globe." (7/10/91)

John Hoffman's comments

"I'm not sure it is correct to say that the choice for the Bolsheviks was whether to accept bourgeois democracy or fight for the socialist republic. Surely, in the very momentum of events, bourgeois democracy was being shattered by a move to counter-revolution. It was not a 'choice' as the Mensheviks thought."

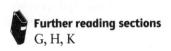 How did it go in practice?

Somafco teachers comment: "Discussion focused on the distinction between bourgeois democratic, national democratic and socialist revolutions. There was a discussion on the necessary conditions for the existence of a revolutionary situation and to what extent these conditions existed in the advanced capitalist countries and in South Africa."

Teaching suggestions

It's important to point out that this lecture was written in 1977. There's a very optimistic view of the possibilities in politics, science and technology. Perhaps this is the place to discuss what has happened since, including the collapse of Communist governments, and the way global capitalism has held back the potential of new discoveries? Comrade Jack's own comments point towards both positive and negative developments. It is also worth discussing the notion of "taming" the environment for human benefit. Many attempt to do this — large dams, new, genetically-modified crops — have proved to have drawbacks (and, indeed, to be environmentally destructive) in ways which were not foreseen in 1977. The issue of the conditions for revolution which the Somafco students raised is still relevant.

Further reading sections

G, H, K

Lecture 8: National Liberation

8.0 Social and political revolutions

A social revolution such as the Great October Revolution of 1917 changed both the structure and superstructure of the old formation, and created a new socio-economic formation.

The revolution is in the first place political: it puts political power, the control of the state machinery, in the hands of the revolutionary classes. Secondly, the revolution is economic: it changes the relations of production, which are property relations. Thirdly, the revolution is social: it changes the system of government, including army and police, law, education and ideology.

A revolution which transfers power from one socio-economic group of people to another, but which does not change the structure, is a political revolution. The old forces of production and relations of production remain, in essence, the same under the new government. Divisions between classes — employers and workers, property owners and the propertyless — persist, and may even grow stronger and more pronounced, under the new regime.

In summary — a social revolution changes the whole society: a political revolution changes only the superstructure, or part of the superstructure.

8.1 Bourgeois revolutions

To decide whether a revolution is social or political, we need to examine its history, component parts, aims and results. In particular, whether it has changed the class system, property relations and ideology.

For example, bourgeois revolutions were in the first place political. They transferred political power from the nobility and church to a capitalist class of manufacturers, merchants and bankers. For this reason Marx and Engels stated in *The Communist Manifesto* that "the executive of the modern state is but a committee for managing the common affairs of the whole bourgeoisie".

The bourgeois state, however, retained the property relations, based on private ownership of the means of production, that had developed within the "bowels" of feudalism, largely as a result of colonial trade. In the words of the *Manifesto,* "The guild-masters were pushed aside by the manufacturing middle class; division of labour between the different corporate guilds vanished in the face of division of labour in each single workshop."

Industrial capitalism introduced power-driven machines, increased the size and output of production units and, during this process, created a huge proletariat. But the relations between workers and employers, between labour and capital, remained much the same as in the early days of modern capitalism.

According to our definition, therefore, the bourgeois revolution was a political and not a social revolution.

8.2 Colonial capitalism

Colonial officials, traders, settlers, mine owners, missionaries and their agents imposed the capitalist mode of production on communal societies and those with feudal and semi-feudal systems.

Marx and Engels summarised the effects in *The Communist Manifesto*:
The bourgeoisie "compels all nations, on pain of extinction, to adopt the bourgeois mode of production; it compels them to introduce what it called civilisation into their midst, i.e. to become bourgeois themselves. In one word, it created a world after its own image".

The colonial masters introduced new forces of production: wage labour, machines, minerals and agricultural products. They introduced capitalist relations of production: private ownership of the means of production and divisions between the owners of capital and propertyless workers. They imposed their system of government, law, education, religion and ideology on traditional rulers and their peoples. Colonial capitalism, coming from outside as an external, dominant force, therefore started a social revolution which changed the structure and superstructure of ancient societies.

Marx has given us an early insight into the colonial impact in a series of articles written between 1852 and 1859 on British rule in India. His main theme was that while the British greed for plunder and profit brought misery to India, it pushed the people out of a superstitious feudal society into the stream of modern life. England, "in causing a social revolution in Hindustan, was actuated only by the vilest interests ... but, whatever may have been the crimes of England, she was the unconscious tool of history in bringing about that revolution".

Among other crimes, Britain:
• neglected to keep up public water-works and irrigation canals on which much of agriculture depended;
• imported cheap factory-made cotton goods which destroyed the village industries of spinning and weaving;
• allowed agriculture to deteriorate;
• shattered the economic base and dissolved village communities of farmers and craft workers; and
• extorted great fortunes by exploiting India and plundering its accumulated wealth.

Britain "modernised" India by building railways to transport raw materials for British factories and manufactured goods imported from Britain. But Indians would not reap the fruits of modernisation until they had thrown off the English yoke. Wherever colonialism took root it started a social revolution with effects similar to those of British rule in India.

8.3 Social categories

The grave-diggers of industrial capitalism are the working class. Who digs graves for the colonialists?

There is no single answer because of big differences in the structures of traditional societies, the policies of colonial powers, their degrees of economic development, and ideologies.

The starting point for an inquiry into the nature of colonial social formations is the class system. A class, in the strict sense, is a group of people occupying a special and common position in relation to the means of production. The two great classes in capitalism are the owners of the means of production and the workers, whose only property is their labour-power or capacity to work.

Typically, in a colonial situation, the capitalists belong to the dominant, foreign group of colonisers. The workers are members of the colonised group (the "natives") but many may have property: land rights and livestock in the villages from which they migrate. Class distinctions are sharper in colonies with a feudalistic structure, as in the Emirates of Northern Nigeria, or the monarchies of Buganda and Bulozi. For the purpose of generalisation, however, it is advisable to specify categories rather than classes.

The categories commonly found in a colonial state are:
• traditional rulers incorporated into the colonial administration as its agents (for example, under British "Indirect Rule");
• officials, clerks, interpreters, teachers, nurses, professionals, the educated, "white collar" salaried employees of government and capitalist firms;
• petty bourgeoisie — shopkeepers, marketeers, small-scale manufacturers, owners of "service" undertakings (garages, beauty parlours, undertakers), commercial farmers;
• wage workers — a small but growing urban proletariat and migrant peasant-workers; and
• villagers and peasant farmers — between 60% and 80% of the total population.

8.4 State and nation

The members of these socio-economic categories make up the population of an individual state system. The categories are organised around a common economic structure and superstructure.

The colonialists drew the boundaries of each state during the period of imperialist rivalries that led to the so-called "partitioning" of Africa. They fixed these boundaries to suit the interests of one or another imperialist power and without taking note of the traditional rights and claims of the independent states that had existed before colonial conquests.

Different ethnic communities, each with its own language, customs and government, were grouped together in the new colonial states. Their boundaries cut across ethnic communities, distributing people of the same clan, tribe or nation between two or more states — as between Namibia and Angola, Angola and Zaire, Zambia and Malawi, Malawi and Mozambique and the Transvaal and Botswana.

Colonial powers created new states to further their aims of domination and to exploit resources, control labour supplies, monopolise investments and markets, and strengthen themselves for imperialist war. Colonial violence and force turned independent nations into subjects of the new states. Resistance to colonial conquest continued as resistance to colonial rule. New nations arose in the course of the struggle. "The nation", wrote Lenin (*The Teachings of Karl Marx*, 1914) "is a necessary product, an inevitable form, in the bourgeois epoch of social development." So it was in the colonies. Change, imposed from above on traditional social formations, created objective conditions for the emergence of nations. Among other things, colonialism:

• deposed rulers or kept them as minor agents of its administration;
• imposed a central government and uniform laws throughout the colony;
• developed a national economy, based on the production and exchange of a common market;
• introduced new forces of production, giving rise to mining and manufacturing towns, which were also centres of commerce and administration;
• turned villagers into wage workers, employed on farms and plantations, mines, works, railways and factories;
• built schools for training the clerks and officials required to man the lower levels of administration, industry and commerce;
• converted people to the Christian religion, thereby laying the basis for a common ideology and organisation; and
• made its language — English, French, Afrikaans, Portuguese, German — the official language in government, courts, schools, commerce and industry.

8.5 National consciousness

Colonialists did not want to unite their subjects into a nation. Instead, governments divided the population. They propped up ethnic (tribal) systems in peasant communities; placed them under chiefs and headmen who were servants of the colonial state; upheld the customs law of marriage, family and inheritance but enforced colonial law to protect property and injustice. The protests came from different sections of the population,

• traditional rulers in the early days who defended their state and people against the invaders;
• workers, who first took individual action by deserting employment (breaking their contracts) and later acted collectively in strikes and through trade unions;
• ministers of religion, especially the independent churches, who protested against the failure to practice Christian morality;
• small businessmen, struggling against colonialist monopolies and discrimination under licensing and land laws;
• teachers, clerks and professional people, who were most in contact with the colonial bureaucracy (officials) and recognised its dependence on the colonised population.

The educated, usually trained, section was also often the first to understand and express the need for unity between chiefs and commoners, workers and peasants, educated and uneducated, tribes and nations for the overthrow of colonial rule. They formed early societies for the protection of people's rights. Out of these came national parties and movements, such as the African National Congress, forerunner of similar organisations in many other countries.

All national parties, though formed at different times and under varying conditions, had the same aim and demanded the same rights of self-determination and secession from the imperial state. Conditions were favourable to their struggle after the Second World War which saw the demise of some imperialist powers, the remarkable spread of socialism and an upsurge in national liberation movements in Asia and Africa, which eventually led to the collapse of colonialism.

8.6 Political revolution

National democratic revolutions were political revolutions. They took control of the state machinery, did away with all legal and conventional forms of race discrimination, expanded the system of education at all levels, gave votes to the people, introduced elected lawmaking assemblies and allowed opposition parties to compete for office within a parliamentary system.

In a few states, where the people seized power through armed struggle, they created their own constitution. In most cases, however, the new states began with constitutions drawn up by the imperial power after the consultation and agreement. National democratic governments therefore seldom destroyed the old machinery of the state. More often, they took over the imperialist-colonial institutions, parliamentary procedures, multiparty systems, the courts and the body of laws, army and police organisations, and the bureaucratic administration. They appointed their own nationals as soon as possible to the positions formerly held by expatriates from the colonising state: permanent secretaries, assistant secretaries, clerks, judges, magistrates, army and police chiefs took over the offices, privileges and functions of the colonial bureaucracy.

Many states, after ten years or so of independence, introduced their own constitutions, providing for one-party governments, creating military regimes or various kinds of autocracy. The general effect was to narrow the popular basis of government and reduce the amount of participation by workers and peasants.

8.7 Capitalism remains

It is possible for political revolutions to change the superstructure but retain the economic structure and property relations of the previous social formation.

This principle operated in most national democratic government states. Few national democratic governments did away with the capitalist relations of production which the colonialists had introduced.

The forces of nationalism, however, penetrated the capitalist relations of production in two important ways. Firstly, the state extended its control over the economy by acquiring some shares in the private enterprises owned by foreign capital. Secondly, nationals were encouraged and assisted to establish their own private, profit-making enterprises, either on their own or in partnership with foreign capital. These interactions between public and private capital produced forms of state capitalism, whose dominant aim is to make profits rather than to serve the people's interests.

State capitalism can develop along a "non-capitalist" road into socialism. But whether it does this or reverts to wholesale capitalism will depend on the nature of the class forces, the political strength and maturity of working people, the ideology of the ruling party, and the relations between the people and the world socialist forces.

John Hoffman comments

"I'm not happy with the argument here that bourgeois revolutions are simply political revolutions. Surely they are also socio-economic? And although it is true that the bourgeoisie develop some of their economic muscle under feudalism, they still need a political revolution to further their social-economic advance. Likewise, is it correct to characterise the national democratic revolution as a purely political revolution? Even if 'capitalism remains' in the independent state, a different kind of economic structure emerges as the colonial-type economy is transformed into a more developed bourgeois economy."

How did it go in practice?

Somafco teachers comment: "According to the lecture, bourgeois revolutions are not social revolutions. It was felt that it is a historical fact that in the transition from feudalism to capitalism, political power changed hands from the feudal lords to the capitalists, and property relations were also altered. The capitalists became the owners of the means of production and the producers of wealth; the peasants were converted into landless workers. The capitalists also introduced their own ideology and laws. The whole social sytem was changed, and therefore a social revolution occurred.

"On whether the national-democratic revolution in South Africa will bring about a social or a political revolution, it was felt that the question should not be posed as either/or. Social and political revolutions should be seen as two extreme poles of a scale. Revolution in South Africa will definitely be political, but with a substantial social factor: on the "scale" it will definitely gravitate towards the social revolution end. But another view was put: that although the national democratic revolution will not usher in a new socio-economic formation, the whole apartheid system will be overhauled and the new system will differ markedly form the apartheid system. And this dramatic change from the apartheid system to a democratic system like that envisaged by the Freedom Charter is a social revolution"

Teaching suggestions

This material is hugely generalised. To make it real for students, it might be useful to begin by discussing the history of a neighbouring African state before and after independence. Zimbabwe — which provides 20 years of history and a number of interesting changes in policy — might be a good example. To conclude the session, students might be asked to discuss the predictions of the Somafco students about the nature of the revolution in South Africa. How close did they get to what has actually happened?

Further reading sections

G, H, I, K

Lecture 9: The Theory of Revolution

9.0 The art of revolution

War — the "human slaughter industry", Marx called it — has its own forces and relations of production. As in other economic structures, the means of production decide the organisation of labour (the armed forces). The more advanced the weapons are, the more detailed is the division of the army, and the more specialised are its branches; infantry, artillery, tanks, mine-laying, demolition, communications, air force, navy and submarines.

Scientific discoveries and technological improvement impact on methods of warfare, while wars in turn speed up scientific, technological and social changes. Wars often give great impetus to economic development.

Warfare makes use of science but it is not a science. It is an art. Politicians and generals make war, adopt planned strategies, but cannot foresee or control all the many factors that result. The outcome of a war is uncertain, as the Americans discovered in Vietnam.

A revolution is like a war — it is an art. Engels, commenting on the defeat of the bourgeois revolution of 1848 in Germany, remarked that "insurrection is an art quite as much as war or any other, and subject to rules of proceeding, which, neglected, will produce the ruin of the party neglecting them".

Lenin reminded the Menshevik opposition in November 1917 that "it was Marx who called uprising nothing but an art, who said that uprising must be treated as an art".

The rules of revolution are both general and particular. The general rules hold true for all revolutions. The particular rules apply only to one or other kind of revolution: bourgeois, proletarian, national democratic or guerilla war. Stress will be placed in this discussion on the rules of proletarian revolution, but something needs to be said about bourgeois revolution.

9.1 Bourgeois revolution

A bourgeois revolution is typically a rising of the capitalist class for the seizure of political power from a feudal autocracy. The democratic bourgeois aim only at reforming the superstructure to give them a majority in parliament and to make life more profitable for them. When in control of the state, they use its machinery to bring the revolution to a close and to suppress the revolutionary workers' party.

The workers support the struggle for democratic rights and make common cause with the middle-class democrats but can never be satisfied with the achievement of bourgeois reforms. Marx told the Communist League in 1850 that "it is our interest and our task to make the revolution permanent, to keep it going until all the ruling and possessing classes are deprived of power...until the more important forces of production are concentrated in the hands of the proletariat".

Marx laid down several rules, based on his political experience and study of bourgeois revolutions. The workers' party should:
• refuse to merge with bourgeois parties; operate both an underground movement

and a legal organisation; mobilise workers for intensive, even "excessive" activity; present their independent demands and form revolutionary workers' councils;
• arm the proletariat with rifles, guns and ammunition, resist any attempt at disarming them, organise a workers' militia with its general staff under the workers' revolutionary authority; and
• strengthen their organisation under a central committee as the new government is in power, put up its members as working class candidates in all forms of federalism and other measures which enable reactionary groups to sabotage progressive changes.

9.2 Permanent revolution

The situation Marx had in mind is likely to arise when a middle class revolution succeeds with the mass support of workers and peasants. He warns the workers' party to remain independent, arm the people and prepare to defend themselves against treachery on the part of the new government. Fight legally and illegally, he advises, but at all times and everywhere, fight for the workers' independent line. Keep the revolution going, "make it permanent", develop the middle-class democratic revolution into the proletariat revolution.

A workers' party has to maintain its independence during and after a middle class revolution both to save itself and to defend the revolution against the bourgeois. This lesson was taught in the French Revolution of February 1848. The workers made the revolution, put the middle class in power and were forced, by the new government's repressive measures, to rise in armed revolt on June 22 in the streets of Paris. They suffered defeat after five days of heroic battle against the government's troops. The bourgeoisie took its revenge by slaughtering over 3 000 defenceless prisoners.

The lesson was repeated at a more advanced level in the Franco-Prussian War of 1870-71. The French government accepted defeat by Prussia, agreed to surrender Paris and with it the whole of France to Bismarck's armies. But the workers of Paris refused to lay down arms. They formed a National Guard of working men, seized governmental power, and proclaimed the Paris Commune on March 18, 1871.

The Commune abolished the standing army and police; opened schools to all the people; withdrew state grants to the established church; placed factories under workers' control and began the construction of a socialist order. The French bourgeoisie, who had laid down their arms before the Prussians, turned their guns on their compatriots, the French working men, women and children. The Commune was overthrown after eight days of bloody civil war in May 1871. There followed a repetition of what happened in 1848: the wholesale slaughter of insurgents, the torture of prisoners, a merciless hunt for concealed leaders and the persecution of political enemies.

9.3 A new state

The last fighters of the Commune yielded to superior forces on May 28, 1871. Two days later, Marx read to the General Council of the Working Men's International an address on the Civil War in France. It remains, down to our own time, a major source of revolutionary theory. Of special importance is his discussion of the transfer of power. The Commune proved, he pointed out, that "the working class cannot simply lay hold of the ready-made state machinery and wield it for its own purposes". The reasons are:

• as modern industry expands and conflicts between capital and labour increase, the state power more and more becomes the power of capital over labour, a public force for social enslavement, an engine of class dictatorship;
• the state becomes even more repressive, more of an instrument of class oppression, after every advance in the class struggle;
• all past revolutions retained the old state, built on it, added more officials, increased the police and armed forces, improved the state's coercive power;
• all past revolutions strengthened the private ownership of the means of production, added to the economic power and wealth of the propertied class, used the state machinery to protect and expand private ownership; and
• a workers' party, which aims at the abolition of private property, which builds socialism, must do away with the old repressive machinery, shatter the bourgeois state and replace it with a new workers' state.

> "Between capitalist and communist society lies the period of the revolutionary transformation of the one into the other. There corresponds to this also a political transition period in which the state can be nothing but the revolutionary dictatorship of the proletariat". (Marx, *Critique of the Gotha Programme*, 1875)

9.4 Vanguard party

To seize power, there must be a revolutionary party. To build socialism there must be a socialist party.

The *Communist Manifesto* declared that "The Communists do not form a separate party opposed to other working class parties". It was an historic mission of Lenin, however, to form precisely such a separate party. He wrote in 1902 (*What is to be Done?*) that "Without a revolutionary theory there can be no revolutionary movement ... The role of vanguard fighter can be fulfilled only by a party that is guided by an advanced theory."

To be the vanguard, a party must have a revolutionary theory, programme, organisation and strategy.

9.5 Revolutionary theory

The theory of revolutionary workers' party is Marxist: "the first [theory] to transform socialism from a utopia into a science" (Lenin, Our Programme, 1899). Revolutionary theory helps us to know and understand:

• the origins and forms of class exploitation, national oppression, and race discrimination;
• the relations between industrial capitalism and feudal-colonial superstructure;
• the contradictions between economic development and socio-political stagnation;
• the impact of world socialism, and imperialism on our struggles;

- the objective conditions of our struggle, such as:
- the effects of industrial colour bars on labour-organisation.
- labour migration, a special type of labour-organisation.
- the pauperisation of peasants and farm workers;
- the growth of problems of the middle class of oppressed nations;
- the role of 'tribal nations' in Bantustans and their effects on national unity against white domination;
- capitalist crisis and unemployment;
- the repressive character of the state machinery; and
- the relationship between national struggle and class struggle.

9.6 Period of illegality

Just as the productive forces determine the organisation of labour, so the conditions of political struggle determine political organisation. A socialist party that operates legally under bourgeois democracy will labour under difficulties. The capitalist class controls the state, press and other official means of communication; it spreads its ideology among working people, incites national and racial divisions; bribes a privileged section of workers and provides social welfare benefits for the unemployed and poor.

On the other hand, socialists can own their own press, hold public meetings, form and lead unions, teach socialism, agitate against the system, appeal to courts against ill-treatment by police. All this is allowed for as long as these socialists do not become a serious threat to private property and the bourgeois state.

Such socialist parties take part in elections, appeal to voters for support, and are unsuited for revolutionary struggle. They are election organisations not militant vanguard parties leading the workers to seize power.

Our movement is banned; our societies and papers are banned; our meetings and demonstrations are banned; our leaders are imprisoned — many for life. Our legal organisations — trade unions, friendly societies and debating clubs — are penetrated by informers and the leaders are detained or banned.

The fascist-police regime has forced us into illegality; this compels us to organise underground, to educate our people for revolutionary struggle, to establish links with the socialist world, independent African states and the progressive bourgeoisie and workers of capitalist countries.

9.7 Objective and subjective condition

In a period of legality, the political organisation is a "movement", loosely formed into branches and regional committees. It has no clearly defined membership, draws no clear distinction between activists and supporters. It concentrates on cultural work, meets in annual conferences, demands reforms within the existing system of authoritarian government, presses for the removal of unjust laws, campaigns for an extension of the parliamentary vote to the majority.

In the present period of fascist-police dictatorship, the trickles of protest have merged into a mighty torrent. Thousands of people who are not members of our organisation have joined in the struggle. They demonstrate against the regime, defy the police, agitate for revolutionary change, risk death, detention and imprisonment.

The people show, in militant action, their utter disregard for the "law and order" of the fascist police. Their spirit is one of extreme defiance of the bourgeois racist state. Militant students, teachers, professionals and the advanced section of the proletariat have decolonised their minds. They reject bourgeois morality and law.

This rising sea of revolution results from the contradictions between:
• a huge propertyless proletariat, whose labour has been socialised in mines, factories and workshops and the exploitative nature of capitalist ownership of these means of production;
• foreign migrant workers from independent states and the rejection of apartheid by those states;
• the interests of migrant workers generally and the interest of the permanent urban proletariat;
• industrial colour bars and the efficient organisation of the labour force;
• the vital role of the working class in production and their complete exclusion from all forms of political power;
• the poverty of peasants in the reserves and the fraud of tribal nationalists in the bantustans;
• the growth of a petty bourgeoisie of shopkeepers and manufacturers among the oppressed nations and the monopoly of the big bourgeoisie over the means of production and exchange;
• the search of capitalism for markets and fields of investment in Africa and the rejection of apartheid by independent African states;
• politically mature people demanding national liberation from a system of national oppression;
• the wave of liberation that is sweeping through Africa, and Africa's opposition to apartheid.

These are some of the objective conditions that favour our revolution. They show themselves in the political awakening of our people. A period of intense struggle has opened. Only a revolutionary vanguard party can provide the subjective forces needed to turn the tide of revolution into an irresistible flood that will sweep aside the dictatorship of the feudal-colonial state.

9.8 Political organisation

A vanguard party in a period of revolutionary upsurge has the following characteristics:
• an organised membership of cadres who accept the party's programme and rules, belong to a specific party unit, take part actively in its work, and contribute to party funds;
• a central committee of members experienced in the party's practical work and having a thorough understanding of the party's theory and aims;
• decentralisation of responsibilities for specific tasks allocated to units with specialised functions;

• democratic centralism, decisions taken after discussion by units are binding on members and lower organs of the party;

• reliable feedback of information on activities and experiences of individual members and units to the centre; and

• control and direction of discipline by the centre over all units and members, strict observance of rules, effective execution of tasks and subordination of lower units to higher units.

The emancipation of the nation must be the act of the nation itself. Its real emancipation requires a social revolution. Only a vanguard party can lead the revolution to victory over the colonial-fascist dictatorship.

John Hoffman comments

"This lecture is on the theory of revolution. Should it not be placed after Lecture 7 — or even before that? Is it correct to say that revolution is an art and not a science, rather than saying it is both? It is not clear whether the reference to socialist parties operating in conditions of legality also applies to communist parties. Surely it is possible — and necessary — to have a vanguard party under conditions of legality?"

How did it go in practice?

Somafco teachers comment: "The following points were discussed: The relationship between class exploitation, national oppression and racial discrimination. The point was made that not all blacks are exploited as a class, and it is the black working class that is doubly oppressed — as members of an oppressed nation and as a class. Also, it was pointed out that African working women are oppressed three times — as women, as women workers and as members of an oppressed nation. The relationship between national oppression and racial discrimination was not clearly defined. It was agreed that there is no black bourgeoisie. There is only a black petty-bourgeoisie which is supported and abetted by government and the big monopolies. But, small and oppressed as it is, we were warned to work very hard to win it to our side and create a 'buffer zone' for the national liberation movement.

"Also discussed was the question of whether the ANC is a vanguard party. It was agreed that it satisfies some of the characteristics of such a party, but there was no unanimity about whether or not it was fully a vanguard party. An observation was made that the South African situation is a unique one, comparable only to Russia before the 1917 Revolution. Therefore it was felt that the categories and concepts of classical Marxism cannot be applied to the South African situation with precision. In our analysis, we should move away from simplistic declarations that the ANC either is or is not a vanguard party; the South African revolution either is social or political.

We found unclear the paragraph which states "The emancipation of a nation must be the act of the nation itself ..." This seems to suggest the ANC should convert itself to a vanguard party, but no conclusion was reached on this."

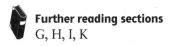

Teaching suggestions
When it was written, this lecture was about strategy. Now, it is about history. This would be a wonderful opportunity to invite an older comrade who has taken part in these events to participate in a question-and-answer session with students, which could deal both with what happened and with whether the strategic decisions were appropriate.

Further reading sections
G, H, I, K

Lecture 10: Elements of Socialist Construction

10.0 Emergent socialism

The transition from one social formation to another is a process. It involves decay and growth: the decline of old formations and the emergence of new social relations. Capitalist productive forces and property relations reached an advanced stage within the feudal structure. In the same way the preconditions for socialism are generated within capitalist society.

New growth within an existing formation causes uneven development, disharmonies, antagonistic contradictions between changing productive forces under stagnant property relations, between the economic structure and the superstructure. The recognition of this antagonism and the analysis of the resulting class struggle is one of Marx's major contributions to the science of social change.

Writing in 1854 (*Preface to a Critique of Political Economy*) he summarised the basic ideas that guided him in his studies of political economy. The key elements in his theory are firstly, the links between forces of production and relations of production within the economic structure, and secondly, the inter-action between economic structure and social superstructure — that is, government, law, culture and consciousness.

> "At a certain stage of their development, the material forces of production in society come into conflict with the existing relations of production, or — what is but legal expression for the same thing — with the property relations within which they have been at work before. From forms of development of the forces of production these relations turn into their fetters. Then begins an epoch of social revolution. With the change of the economic foundation, the entire immense superstructure is more or less rapidly transformed."

Marx arrived at this scientific theory of change by combining the principles of dialectics with a materialist outlook. He used dialectical materialism to explain in the *Communist Manifesto* how bourgeois society emerged. It "sprouted from the ruins of feudal society" and "it itself the product of a long course of development, of a series of revolutions in the mode of production and of exchange".

Capitalism, in turn, prepares the ground for socialism by creating the army of wage workers, socialising their labour in factories and mines, and developing the productive forces to a point where capitalist property relations fetter their further expansion.

10.1 Birthmarks of the old order

A pregnancy is said to be normal when it follows a regular course within a more or less fixed period between conception and birth. Is the creation of socialism also subject to definite laws of development?

Engels dealt with this question in a debate on the prospects for socialism in Tsarist Russia (*On Social Conditions in Russia, 1875*). To build socialism, he pointed out, needed both a proletariat and a bourgeoisie "in whose hands the social productive forces have so far developed as to allow of the final destruction of class differences".

A country without proletariat and bourgeoisie, he said, could not advance to socialism for the following reasons:
"Only at a certain level of development of the social productive forces, even at a very high level for our modern conditions, will it be possible to raise production to such an extent that the abolition of class differences can be a real and lasting process without causing stagnation or even decline in the mode of social production. But the productive forces have reached this level of development only in the hands of the bourgeoisie. The bourgeoisie, therefore, in this respect also is just as necessary a pre-condition of the socialist revolution as the proletariat itself."

This is not a problem for us. South Africa has a huge proletariat, a mature bourgeoisie and a highly developed and industrial economy. We are in the position that Marx describes, of being unable to expand to the productive forces until we revolutionise the system of property and the entire superstructure. The point at issue is, however, relevant to our condition for another reason, contained in a comment by Marx (*Critique of the Gotha Programme, 1875*) on the emergence of a socialist society (the first stage of communism).

"What we have to deal with here is a communist society, not as it has developed on its own foundation, but, on the contrary, as it emerges from capitalist society: which is, in every respect, economically, morally and intellectually, still stamped with the birth-marks of the old society from whose womb it emerges."

Our revolutionary society will likewise be "stamped" at birth with the marks of the old order: the foul laws of apartheid and repression, the pass system, "compound migrant labour", segregated housing, education and the rest of the racist rubbish that has to be swept into the dustbin of feudal-colonial relics. To decolonise minds and social relations involves both pulling down and building up. It is a process that cannot be carried through overnight. The seizure of political power is the first and most important stage of our revolution. To accomplish that task and build our new society we need theory, programmes, policies and strategies.

10.2 An act of creation

A socialist revolution is a social, that is to say, a total revolution. It transforms both the economic structure and social superstructure.

Whereas all previous political revolutions changed the superstructure but retained the system of private property, socialist revolution does away with private ownership of the means of production and turns them into public social property.

The seizure of power by the working people, like all political revolutions, is a deliberate, intentional act, the pre-conditions for which emerge in the course of capitalist development. But the building of a socialist society is an act of creation, not a "natural" spontaneous growth arising from interactions between individuals each seeking their own interest. Socialism comes into being through the conscious, organised struggle of working people under the direction of a vanguard socialist party.

10.3 A permanent social revolution

The bourgeoisie cannot make a revolution on their own. They need workers and peasants to provide the fighting force. To obtain their support, the middle class claims to be a "friend of the people", promises votes for all, higher wages, better living conditions, recognition of trade unions, freedom of movement and association. Workers support the middle class because it is in their interests to defeat the ruling class. The alliance between workers and the middle class is unstable. When the bourgeoisie have won their demands, they turn their guns on those workers who continue their struggle. As Engels noted (*Germany: Revolution and Counter-revolution*, 1851) they do this "as soon as the class below ... the proletarians, attempt an independent movement".

Engels was describing here the failure of the German petty bourgeoisie of shopkeepers to compete their democratic revolution of 1848-49 for fear of a workers' uprising. Marx, talking to the Communist League on the same subject in 1850, made a major contribution to revolutionary theory. He called for a "permanent revolution".

> *"While the democratic petty bourgeoisie wish to bring the revolution to a conclusion as quickly as possible and with the achievement of the above demands [that is, for a democratic state constitution], it is our interest and our task to make the revolution permanent, until all the more or less possessing classes have been displaced from domination, until the proletariat has conquered state power."*

The aims of workers differ from the aims of capitalists. "For us, the issue cannot be the alteration of private property but only its abolition ... not the improvement of existing society but the foundation of a new one."

The permanent revolution means that the socialist revolution comes to an end only when it has transformed every remnant of the old capitalist system, until it has gained the final objective — a communist society.

Will our revolution be permanent? Or will it stop at the seizure of state power? Will it be a political revolution or a social revolution? Is our political power sufficient for the task of national liberation? Or must our revolution also advance to the seizure of economic power?

These are problems that face a revolutionary national movement during the struggle to build a national democratic republic.

10.4 Dictatorship of the proletariat

A dictatorship of working people is necessary for the building of socialism and during its transition to communism. This is a basic principle of scientific, Marxist, socialism. Marx wrote in 1852: "The class struggle necessarily leads to the dictatorship of the proletarian", which "itself only constitutes the transition to the abolition of all classes and to a classless society".

Though called a "dictatorship" the workers' state is actually the most democratic of all states for the following reasons:

• all people in a mature socialist system are workers by hand or brain, possess political power and exercise it by taking part in day-to-day affairs of the party and government;

• they also own, collectively, the means of production, and therefore possess economic power which formerly, since the days of slavery, has belonged to a small minority — the dominant economic class, whether of slave owners, feudal lords or capitalists;

• the diffusion or spread of political and economic power throughout the whole population creates conditions favourable to the disappearance of class which Marx, in the passage quoted above, thought would result in the disappearance ("withering away") of state power; because

• when all people exercise political and economic power; when there are no antagonistic classes, there will be no need of a coercive, public force of army, police, prisons and courts; and the state withers away.

The withering away of the state will take place in the higher stage of socialism: communism.

Engels has offered a preview of the process in a famous passage
(*Anti-Duhring*, 1877):

"*The proletariat seizes the state power, and transforms the means of production in the first instance into state property. But in doing this, it puts an end to itself as the proletariat, it puts an end also to the state ... The first act in which the state really comes forward as the representative of society as a whole — the taking possession of the means of production in the name of society — is at the same time its last independent act as the state. The interference of the state power in social relations becomes superfluous in one sphere after another, and then ceases of itself. The government of persons is replaced by the administration of things and the direction of the process of production. The state is not 'abolished', it withers away.*"

The state cannot wither away, however, in a single socialist system while it is enriched by capitalist imperialism which prepares for global war and plants its agents within the workers' state. A stable, enduring world peace is therefore a necessary condition for the evolution of socialism into communism.

10.5 The struggle for world peace

Capitalism finds new markets and fields of investment by means of trade and wars of conquest. The two methods have been linked together throughout the history of capitalism, first in its commercial phase, when it turned independent nations into colonies, and in the phase of industrial capitalism, which led to imperialism, "the monopoly stage of capitalism".

The biggest capitalist powers had completed the territorial division of the world by the end of the last century. They then fought the first imperialist world war of 1914-18.

Planned production and distribution is a basic law of socialist economy. It is possible because the means of production belong to society. However, private ownership under capitalism leads to anarchy.

Every capitalist tries to maximise his profits by raising or reducing his output according to the state of the market. If he cannot sell at a profit, he cuts back on production, dismisses some workers, makes the rest work harder and waits for prices to rise. However, socialism maximises production, guarantees full employment, constantly improves the forces of production, gives workers technical training, encourages them to improve efficiency, and at all times seeks to raise living standards for the entire population.

Capitalism develops unevenly. Industries that are most profitable, for example armaments, jewellery, or drugs, are given preference over the production of food, clothing, housing and education for the working class. South African capitalism has neglected agriculture in the reserves, first to safeguard capitalist farmers against competition, secondly to compel peasants to leave their land for labour on farms or in mines and factories.

Socialist planning, on the other hand, aims at equal or 'proportionate' development between different sectors: agriculture, mining, manufacturing, food and clothing health services, education and housing. The proportions between different economic departments are planned according to social need, availability of labour, the level of productivity, and the standard of technology. Less developed industries, communities or regions receive special attention to raise them to the general level of efficiency and well-being.

Social ownership, planned production and maximum production enables socialist societies to advance towards the stage of abundance. When there is enough for everyone, it will be possible to do away with commodity production and the wages system. Socialism will then evolve into communism. The division of labour between workers by hand and workers by brain will wither away. The principle of communism will apply: from each according to his ability, to each according his need.

John Hoffman comments

"There is valuable material here, but the fact that section 10.0 covers material dealt with before highlights the problems of arranging material systematically in a primer."

How did it go in practice?

Somafco teachers comment: "The following points were discussed. Engels' statement on the impossibility of a country advancing to socialism without the existence of the proletariat and the capitalist class provided the comment that the existence of the world socialist system makes it possible for underdeveloped countries to by-pass the stage of capitalism. Countries on the non-capitalist path of development need material and technological assistance to lay the material basis for socialism and this assistance can only be obtained from the socialist countries. Self-reliance for these countries is a pipe-dream.

"Doubts were also expressed about the validity of Engels' statement on the inevitability of socialist revolutions, because seemingly there is no country that was industrially developed where there has been a socialist revolution. Russia was said to have been feudal when the revolution took place. But a different view was argued and accepted: that Russia was an advanced capitalist country in 1917. The short period between the bourgeois revolution and the socialist revolution is explained by the fact that the mode of production had been capitalist for a long time while the superstructure had remained feudal.

"The political consciousness of workers in advanced capitalist countries was discussed. It was agreed that the power of the bourgeoisie is immense. The mass media is effectively used and the bourgeoisie exercises all its power, material and coercive, to sustain its rule.

"Nevertheless, the political consciousness of the workers is advancing. The bourgeoisie is in a very precarious situation in that the systems of colonialism have collapsed and it is these systems that had enabled the capitalists to buy time. Meanwhile, the socialist world system is getting stronger. The escape routes of imperialism are being closed."

Teaching suggestions

Again, history has overtaken this material. This may be the ideal session to return to the question of why the communist governments of Eastern Europe collapsed, and also to look at how developments like the new modes of colonialism and the globalisation of capital have allowed imperialism to buy yet more time. But what are the weaknesses of the new system?

Further reading sections

K, L

Lecture 11: Socialism and Nationalism

11.0 Class and nation

Class struggles are tightly bound up with national struggles at every stage in the growth of capitalism, from the early days of merchant capital to the "last stage", which is imperialism. Socialists have therefore found it necessary to define their attitudes to the "nation" in a number of different social formations and under varying historical conditions. Questions around nations and nationality arise in different ways, including:

• bourgeois democratic revolutions against feudal autocracies in the period of commercial capital;

• the expansion of industrial capital in its search for markets, resulting in the seizure of colonies;

• wars between imperialist states for domination and the re-division of the world;

• the overthrow of tsarist feudal-capitalism, the achievement of the socialist revolution, and the emergence of a workers' and peasants' state and nation in the Soviet Union;

• wars fought by small nations and their struggle for national liberation;

• relations between socialist nation-states;

• relations between the socialist world, imperialism, and emerging nations of liberated countries.

11.1 Socialist principles

Socialists have worked out a set of general principles to guide them in dealings with nations and national movements. The most important of these principles are:

• no nation shall have privileges at the expense of another nation or language community within the state;

• no nation shall oppress another nation or refuse to grant it fair and equal treatment;

• every nation shall have the rights of self-determination and secession;

• workers of an oppressor nation must oppose its policy of national oppression and demand the rights of self-determination and secession for the oppressed nation;

• in applying these general principles to specific situations, socialists must take into account all relevant factors, including historical background, class and national divisions, political and economic systems and the interests of the revolution; and

• a revolutionary party or movement must in all cases adopt a national policy that will strengthen the revolution.

In arriving at these principles, socialists have discussed at great length questions and issues that are important to our revolution, as will be seen from the following items:

• What is a nation?

• How can equality between nations be achieved?

• What is the difference between nation-states and multi-national states?

• What is the difference between bourgeois nations and proletarian nations?

• How can the contradiction between "love of fatherland" and proletarian class

consciousness be resolved?
• When is it correct to demand self-determination and secession?

11.2 The nation state

A nation is made up of people with a common culture and consciousness. They develop their culture and feeling of nationhood slowly and over a long period of time. Every nation has a tradition of origin and struggle, between factions or classes within itself or against external enemies. The nation is therefore a product of history; it emerges under specific social conditions. Outstanding examples of nation-building are the Zulu, Sotho and Swazi nations.

A note on the word "tribes"

This is a colonial word, like "native", and has no scientific basis. The word suggests inferiority in comparison with European "nations" and will not be used in this series of lectures. The chief objection is that what are called "tribes" in South Africa have all the characteristics of nations as generally understood. These are:
• a common territory, occupied by members of the nation, who call it their "father" or "mother" land, love it, and defend it against their enemies;
• a single government, in many smaller African states centred in an hereditary ruler, the king, whose office, authority and right to rule are acknowledged by the nation, even though there may be revolts and coups against the individual holder of office;
• a common body of laws and customs, observed by members of the nation and enforced by the king, his officials, courts and people through regional chiefs and headmen;
• a community of language, the main medium of communication, socialisation and national identity, which distinguishes the nation from other language communities;
• a single economy, under the administration of the ruler, who collects taxes or tribute, supports his officials and staff at his palace, and feeds people whose crops have failed;
• an armed force, consisting of able-bodied men of military age, who are organised to fight in wars of defence or aggression and to protect the ruler against subversion.

What the colonialists dubbed "tribes" were states with a coercive machinery, consisting of the ruler, advisers, courts of law, police (messengers of the court) and a people's militia. The existence of a state organisation shows that the nation had within it the seeds of class divisions: between royals and commoners, the founders of the nation and conquered peoples. However, the common ownership of land, the right of all nationals to use the land, and the absence of wage-labour prevented the formation of sharp class antagonisms.

11.3 Bourgeois nations

Capitalist nation-states took shape in revolutionary struggles against feudal autocracies. Sometimes, each nation within a multi-national state, such as the Austro-Hungarian Empire, demanded the right of self-determination. Alternatively, the bourgeoisie of small, separate feudal states with a common culture fought to unite them into a single state under a bourgeois democratic government, as in Germany.

In each case, the capitalist class mobilised other classes — the petty bourgeoisie, workers and peasants — into a mass movement behind the demands for national liberation, supremacy of the national language, legal equality and democracy for members of the nation. There developed a national consciousness shared by all classes of the oppressed nation.

"The bourgeois nation's economic basis is its home market. Capitalism requires the free, unobstructed flow of commodities and conquers the home market for commodity production, for which purpose it puts an end to obstructions from feudal lords: tariffs, levies, taxes and dues. That is the material purpose of the revolution against feudal superstructure."

Lenin drew attention to the importance of the internal domestic market for the capitalist mode of production and of a national language for the growth of the market.

He wrote (in *The Right of Nations to Self-determination* 1914):
"Throughout the world, the period of the final victory of capitalism over feudalism has been linked up with national movements. For the complete victory of commodity production, the bourgeoisie must capture the home market, and there must be politically united territories whose population speak a single language, with all obstacles to the development of that language and to its consolidation in literature eliminated. Therein is the economic foundation of national movements."

Language is also the primary instrument for developing an ideology, creating a national consciousness, unifying members of different classes into a nation. Language has a great emotional appeal. Those who speak it bitterly resent interference by an oppressor nation.

But language also has an economic basis which Lenin described:
"Language is the most important means of human intercourse. Unity, and unimpeded development of language are the most important conditions for genuinely free and extensive commerce on a scale commensurate with modern capitalism; for a free and broad grouping of the population in all its various classes; and lastly, for the establishment of a close connection between the market and each and every proprietor, big or little, and between buyer and seller."

Conflicts over language rights within a single state are conflicts between rival sections of the bourgeoisie. Afrikaner nationalists resisted domination by the English language community, demanding full equality between the two "official" languages, and using Afrikaans to consolidate an Afrikaner nation, penetrate all fields of employment, and capture the domestic commodity market. Attempts to force

Afrikaans on the so-called "homelands" serve the economic and political interests of the Afrikaner bourgeoisie in their struggle for supremacy over the more powerful English capital.

11.4 Imperialist multinationalism

The growth of capitalist productive forces in the machine age outstrips the capacity of the home market. Big powers compete fiercely for new markets, raw materials, and outlets for capital investment. Competition in the period of imperialist expansion took the form of colonial wars, the seizure of territories, the suppression of the independence of independent nation-states and the final division of the world. Imperialism, Lenin wrote, "means that capital has outgrown the framework of national states; it means that national oppression has been extended and heightened on a new historical foundation" (*The Revolutionary and the Rights of Nations to Self-determination*, 1915)

. The capitalist class, once the champion of national self-determination, become in turn oppressors of nations. Three stages in this process can be distinguished:
• the collapse of feudal absolutism, the formation of the bourgeois democratic state involving mass national movements of all classes;
• industrial capitalist states with democratic constitutions mature, a conscious working class develops, and markets are found through the conquest of oppressed nations in colonial countries; and, finally
• imperialist wars for the re-division of the world are fought, socialist revolutions under the dictatorship of the proletariat and national revolutions for the liberation of colonial peoples occur.

Socialists follow their general principles in each stage, while always taking into account the historical and social conditions of a particular situation. The main guiding line is to support an oppressed nation against its oppressor nation and to safeguard the interests of the proletarian revolution.

11.5 Oppressors and oppressed

Socialists support progressive movements and wars for national liberation. Although, in the words of *The Communist Manifesto*, "they fight with the bourgeoisie whenever it acts in a revolutionary way, against the absolute monarchy, the feudal squirearchy (landed gentry), and the petty bourgeoisie", this alliance does not last. When the capitalist class takes power, it uses the state machinery to strengthen private property, expand its markets, seize colonial territories and oppress small nations.

Revolutionary workers of oppressor nations have a duty to reject such policies of capitalist plunder and aggression.

The International Congress of Socialist Workers and Trade Unions stated their objections in 1896:
"This Congress declares that it stands for the full right of all nations to self-determination and expresses its sympathy for the workers of every country now suffering under the yoke of military, national or any kind of absolute rule."

A show of sympathy is not enough to meet socialist requirements, which call for active, militant struggle through workers' parties and trade unions against racism, national oppression, apartheid and for national liberation.

Lenin wrote (*The Question of Peace*, 1915):
"We stand for a revolutionary struggle against imperialism, (i.e. capitalism). Imperialism consists in the striving of nations which oppress ... other nations to extend and increase that oppression and to re-partition the colonies. That is why the question of self-determination of nations today hinges on the conduct of socialists of the oppressor nations. A socialist of any of the oppressor nations (Britain, France, Germany, Japan, Russia, the United States of America, etc.) who does not recognise and does not struggle for the right of oppressed nations to self-determination (i.e. the right to secession) is in reality a chauvinist".

Lenin wrote these words during the first world imperialist war. The war brought to the surface and sharpened the contradictions between national sentiment and international socialism.

11.6 Workers of the oppressor nation

The Bolsheviks of tsarist Russia and the South African International Socialist League, forerunner of the SA Communist Party, were among the few working class parties to oppose the First World War and call for the defeat of their governments. The great majority of social-democratic parties gave "loyal" support to their "fatherland" in its war against the "fatherland" of fellow workers speaking a different language.

A "chauvinist" is a person who shouts: "my country, my nation, right or wrong"; who throws all principles aside except one, which is to "follow the flag" — to carry out the orders of his bourgeois government. With honourable exceptions, members of the oppressor Afrikaner and English nations in South Africa are chauvinists who refuse to condemn national oppression in our country or elsewhere.

Revolutionary socialists in a war between imperialist powers will work for the defeat of their own government on both sides in the war.

"Present-day democracy will remain true to itself only if it says neither one nor the other imperialist bourgeoisie, only if it says the two sides are equally bad, and if it wishes the defeat of the imperialist bourgeoisie in every country."
(Lenin, *Under a False Flag*, 1915)

At all times, in peace or in war, workers of an oppressor nation who do not fight for the liberation of oppressed nations are incapable of emancipating themselves. "A people which enslaves another people forges its own chains", wrote Marx in a resolution prepared in 1869 on the Irish struggle for independence.

The International Workingmen's Association (the First International), which adopted the resolution, declared that the separation of Ireland from Britain was "the essential preliminary conditions of the emancipation of the English working class".

This statement is true also for South African white workers. To emancipate themselves, they must join our revolutionary struggle for national liberation. For, so long as they support apartheid, follow the policies of bourgeois parties, actively take part in our oppression, they are incapable of waging a struggle for working-class power.

11.7 Proletarian internationalism

Imperialism creates privileged sections of workers who benefit from the profits of monopoly capital and colonial exploitation. Engels commented on this tendency as early as 1858 in a letter to Marx: "The English proletariat is actually becoming more and more bourgeois." He wrote in 1882 that "the workers gaily share the feast of England's monopoly of the world market and the colonies".

Revolutionary socialists counteract national chauvinism by supporting the cause of national liberation. "The most difficult and most important task in this", Lenin wrote, "is to unite the class struggle of the workers of the oppressor nations with that of the workers of the oppressed nations" (*The Socialist Revolution and the Right of Nations to Self-Determination*, 1916).

The October Revolution of 1917, the establishment of the first socialist state, the formation of the Communist International in March 1919, the spread of Communist Parties in both oppressor and oppressed nations, the split between the Third (Communist) International and the Second (Socialist) International — all these events laid a firm basis for a revolutionary policy of national liberation.

The Third International's Programme of 1928 set out the guidelines. Communist Parties were instructed to:
• maintain close co-operation between workers of the oppressor and oppressed countries;
• support every movement in the colonies against imperialist violence;
• expose all forms of chauvinism and imperialist oppression;
• give systematic, material aid to revolutionary liberation movements, and recognise the right of oppressed nations to rebellion and revolutionary war;
• lead the people in a revolutionary situation in a direct attack on the bourgeois state;
• organise workers and peasants independently in trade unions, peasant leagues and Communist Parties;
• form alliances with the national bourgeoisie for a genuine struggle against imperialism; and
• campaign for the withdrawal of armed imperialist troops, conduct propaganda in the armed forces for support of oppressed nations fighting for liberation, call on workers to refuse to transport troops and munitions for use against freedom fighters.

The Soviet Union and Communist Parties have followed these guidelines for more than half a century. The alliance between proletarian internationalism and national liberation is a major cause of the setbacks suffered by imperialism and colonialism. Our revolution will continue to benefit from that alliance in all phases of our struggle.

11.8 Two streams merge

International capitalism is the common enemy of both socialist revolution and national democratic revolution. Each strengthens the other in their common struggle. Lenin drew attention to this basis of united action in November 1919, when addressing the Second All-Russia Congress of Communist Organisations of the Peoples of the East (in *Documents on The National Liberation Movement in the East* 1952, p250).

> *"Hence, the socialist revolution will not be solely, or chiefly, a struggle of the revolutionary proletarians in each country against their bourgeoisie — no. It will be a struggle of all the imperialist-oppressed colonies and countries, of all dependent countries, against international imperialism ... the civil war of the working people against the imperialists and exploiters in all the advanced countries is beginning to be combined with national wars against international imperialism."*

Lenin's confidence has been fully justified. One-third of mankind has taken the socialist road; colonial oppression is making its last desperate stand in southern Africa. Imperialism, which once reigned supreme, is on the defensive. Anti-imperialist forces now determine the main content and trend of social development. Although divided on many issues, the socialist and liberated countries present a united front against apartheid and its imperialist supporters.

For such reasons, Leonid Ilyich Brezhnev correctly speaks of a "merging" of two revolutionary streams:
"A major feature of the 50-year period since the October Revolution is the merging of the national liberation movement and the struggle of the working class into one revolutionary torrent. The 1 500 million people living in the former colonies and semi-colonies have gained independence and emerged as an active force on the political scene. This has extended the bounds of the world revolutionary movement and accelerated social progress"
(*The CPSU in the Struggle for the Unity of all Revolutionary and Peace Forces*, 1975, p47)

The merger of the two streams is a dynamic, progressive process based on principles of mutual respect for national sovereignty, fraternal co-operation in social and economic development, and unity in the defence of peace against the divisive, militaristic character of monopoly capitalism.

Of primary importance for the growth of unity is the advance of peasant societies with a relatively small working class to a socialist order along the road of non-capitalist development.

Non-capitalism means that liberated countries which are at an early stage of industrialisation can bypass capitalism. That possibility did not exist before the October Revolution. Now, in alliance with a socialist world, such countries can advance from National Liberation to Socialist Liberation.

John Hoffman comments

"Would this be the place to put in something more extensive on the question of 'non-capitalist' development?"

[Somafco] How did it go in practice?

SOMAFCO teachers comment: "Discussion centred around the concepts of 'tribe', 'nation', 'native' and 'Bantu' in South Africa. It was agreed that the terms 'Bantu', 'tribe' and 'native' have become derogatory, and should be discarded, although originally they were non-emotive and scientific. The terms 'nationality' and 'ethnic group' were also preferred because some ethnic groups had become stable and centralised communities, e.g. the Sotho and Zulu. Opinion was divided and agreement could not be reached on whether these nationalities had become nations before colonialism arrived.

"The question of culture was also discussed: do we have one national culture or numerous cultures? It was agreed that a national culture is still in the process of formation, but agreement could not be reached on the precise status of the cultures of different language groups.

"In this context, we spent much time discussing various policy statements and what they meant. The Freedom Charter says: 'The doors of learning shall be opened! The government shall discover, develop and encourage national talent for the enhancement of our cultural life.' The Road to SA Freedom states that the state should 'encourage the development of national cultures, art and literature'. Does this mean that the democratic government of the future South Africa will develop the cultures of different nationalities, and if so, might this not undermine the development of one national culture?

"Agreement could also not be reached on the question of languages. Are we going to have one national language and what does it mean to have an official language? The Road to SA Freedom says there shall be an equality of languages, but some people had doubts about this."

Teaching suggestions

This is a very long lecture, which ranges over many topics, including:
• the definition of a nation;
• the historical development of nations;
• the policy of Communist governments towards nations and nationalities;
• some aspects of anti-colonial struggle in the 1960s and 1970s. To provide adequate time for discussion, it may require two sessions. One good starting point might be through discussion of the South African Constitution, and the way it deals with issues of language and culture.

There's some interesting and relevant history in the story of the international anti apartheid movement, and the support shown for the struggle by left-wing and workers' organisations throughout the world, as well as by socialist and communist governments.

And still relevant is discussion of the issue of patriotism — "my country, right or wrong". It would be tempting to spend time here on how the former Soviet Union — despite its principles — apparently did not deal with national issues in a satisfactory way in practice.

But Lecture 12 goes more deeply into these questions, and might be a better place to hold this discussion.

 **Further reading sections**
I, L, M

Lecture 12 World Socialism: National Sovereignty

12.0 Science in action
Socialist states are the growth points of a new world order. They are a testing-ground for the application of the theories that the founders of scientific socialism presented more than a century ago.

Lenin, the architect of proletarian revolution, closely studied the theories and put them into practice, while insisting that the principles are a guide to action and not a dogma.

Socialism is an expanding order, spreading under widely different conditions of revolutionary change. Socialist countries are at different stages of development, related to their individual historical background and national institutions. They have, however, a similar economic structure which conforms to shared basic principles: social ownership of the means of production, social planning for maximum production, equal development of people and regions, proletarian dictatorship and a vanguard party.

People who practice socialism escape from the anarchy of the capitalist mode of production to a higher stage of human development. They are taking a great step forward towards the freedom that inspired Marx and Engels. And just as natural science enables humans to understand and utilise the forces of nature, so creatively applying the principles of scientific socialism (the science of society) enables humans to understand and shape the forces of society.

12.1 Conscious, planned organisation
Engels made this comparison, nearly 100 years ago, in a passage that has stood the test of time and practice. (*Socialism: Utopian and Scientific*, 1882):

> *"The forces operating in society work exactly like the forces operating in nature: blindly, violently, destructively so long as we do not understand them and fail to take them into account. But when once we have recognised them and understand how they work, their direction and their effects, the gradual subjection of them to our will and the use of them for attainment of our aims depends entirely upon ourselves."*

However, social practice is necessary for understanding. "In practice man must prove the truth ... The philosophers have interpreted the world in various ways: the point however is to change it" (Marx, *Theses on Feuerbach*, 1845).

When the working class understands the nature of the productive forces and takes possession of them, it transforms them into willing servants.

Engels observed:
"This is the difference between the destructive forces of electricity in the lightning of a thunderstorm and tamed electricity in the telegraph and the arc-light ... Such treatment opens the way to the replacement of the anarchy of social production by a socially planned regulation of production in accordance with the needs both of society as a whole and of each individual."

The forces of production have reached a level at which capitalist relations of production and capitalist superstructure have become a hindrance to social development. By seizing the means of production, society will put an end to commodity production and therefore to the domination of the product over the producer.

Engels continues:
"Anarchy in social production is replaced by conscious organisation on a planned basis. The struggle for individual existence comes to an end ... The objective, external forces which have hitherto dominated history, will then pass under the control of men themselves. It is only from this point that men, with full consciousness, will fashion their own history ... It is humanity's leap from the realm of necessity into the realm of freedom."

Engels had in mind a world-wide socialism in which people everywhere would free themselves from the burdens of all previous social formations: class oppression, ignorance, poverty and war. This world order is now being built, but is threatened by the anarchy and enmity of world imperialism. Peace and friendship between the socialist nations is necessary for socialist construction and is guaranteed by firm adherence to basic socialist principles.

12.2 Self-determination

Two major principles apply: firstly, complete equality of rights between nations and, secondly, a unity of working people of all nations.

In discussing the first principle, Lenin wrote:
"For different nations to live together in peace and freedom, to separate and form different states (if that is more convenient for them), a full democracy, upheld by the working class, is essential. No privileges for any nation or any one language. Not even the slightest degree of oppression or the slightest injustice in respect of a national minority — such are the principles of working-class democracy."
(The Working Class and the National Question, 1913)

Our revolution also aims at the elimination of national inequalities imposed on us by privileged white nations which oppress our nations. But we reject attempts by any South African national language community to separate and form a different state. It is our intention to constitute the people of all languages into a single nation. Does this programme mean that we reject the principle of nations' right to self-determination?

The principle operates when a nation within a multi-national state wishes to separate politically and form an independent nation-state. It "would be wrong", Lenin argued, "to interpret the right to self-determination as meaning anything but the right to existence to existence as a separate state" (*The Right of Nations to Self-determination*, 1914).

Colonial peoples, who are in fact nations, demand this right in their struggle for national liberation. Socialists, while supporting that struggle, call on the working people of all nations to unite and merge their nations. "We ourselves," Lenin wrote in 1916, "are sure to implement this right, and grant this freedom (to secede), as soon as we capture power." (*A Caricature of Marxism and Imperialist Economism*, 1916).

12.3 Freedom of association

The position under discussion is that of a socialist government which has seized power from an oppressor nation. The revolutionary government on the one hand grants a free right of secession to the oppressed nations and on the other hand recommends against secession, calling on them to associate or merge with the new socialist state.

There is no contradiction between these two acts, as Lenin explained, "We favour their merger, but now there can be no transition from forcible merger and annexation to voluntary merger unless they (the oppressed nations) have freedom of secession." Freedom to separate is a necessary condition for a free association or merger.

Proletarian internationalism is aimed at an alliance between workers of all nations. The ultimate goal is therefore a merger between nations. Self-determination is not the ideal condition, but a means to the end. If granted, the right to secede must be given unconditionally, "without strings". In some cases, however, a socialist government will not concede the right.

12.4 Lenin's principles

Lenin, in the following passages, stressed the relative nature of the right and the conditions under which it might not be conceded.

• A Marxist party by no means "rejects an independent appraisal of the advisability of the state secession of any nation in every separate case. Self-determination may take the form of autonomy within a given state rather than of secession (*Theses on the National Question*, 1913).

• "The demand for a 'yes' or 'no' reply to the question of secession in the case of every nation may seem a very 'practical' one. In reality it is absurd; it is metaphysical in theory, while in practice it leads to subordination of the proletariat to the bourgeoisie's policy. The bourgeoisie always places its national demands in the forefront, and does so in categorical fashion. With the proletariat, however, these demands are subordinated to the interests of the class struggle ... That is why the proletariat confines itself, so to speak, to the negative demand for recognition of the right to self-determination, without giving guarantees to any nation, and without undertaking to give anything at the expense of another nation" *(The Right of Nations to Self-determination, 1914)*.

• The right to self-determination arises under specific historical conditions and must be assessed from a class standpoint. The right "is not an absolute, but only a small part of the general-democratic (now: general-socialist) world movement. In individual concrete cases, the part may contradict the whole; is so, it must be rejected" *(The Discussion on National Self-determination Summed Up, 1916)*.

Applying these principles to our situation, we conclude that the fiction of "self-determination" imposed from above by the oppressor nation on any race, or language community:

• serves the interest of the oppressor nation;
• contradicts our "general-democratic" movement;
• takes place at the expense of our nation;
• conflicts with the aims of our revolution for national unity and equality; and
• must therefore be rejected.

12.5 Civil war and armed intervention

The Soviet government applied its policy of national self-determination under tremendous difficulties resulting from the civil war and armed intervention that swept through most of the country between the middle of 1918 and the end of 1920 and continued in the Far East against Japanese troops into 1922.

The national bourgeoisie of the "rimlands" — Ukraine, Byelorrusia, Transcaucasia, Armenia, Turkestan — demanded self-determination, proclaimed independence, and organised a counter-revolutionary war in alliance with the feudalists and capitalists of central Russia and with the imperialists.

VS Shevstov observes:

"The separatist trends among the nationalist bourgeoisie of the borderlands of Russia became clearly defined on the eve of the October Revolution, and they even intensified after the Revolution ... The Russian bourgeoisie and the nationalist bourgeoisie of the fringe areas had the same class aim of disuniting the proletariat and the masses of various national communities, and suppressing the revolutionary national liberation movement." (National Sovereignty and the Soviet Union, 1974)

Self-determination is progressive when used against feudalism, colonialism and oppressor nations of all kinds; it becomes a counter-revolutionary demand when used to weaken the struggle for proletarian unity and socialism. The workers and peasants of the border nations, under the leadership of the Russian Communist Party (Bolsheviks), defeated the counter-revolutionary armies of the national bourgeoisie in a heroic war to defend Soviet power and socialism.

In his address to the Second All Russia Congress on Communist Organisations of the Peoples of the East, on November 22, 1919, Lenin pointed out that: *"Only due to our Civil War being waged by workers and peasants who have emancipated themselves...were people to be found in such a backward country as Russia, worn out as she was by four years of imperialist war, who were strong-willed enough to carry on that war during two years of incredible and unparalleled hardship and difficulty."* (Lenin, *The National Liberation Movement in the East,* 1952, p243).

The Red Army stopped the advance of German troops against Petrograd on February 23 1918, since celebrated as Red Army Day. Deposed feudalists and capitalists formed large armies, the so-called White Guards, with the assistance of troops, ammunitions and finance supplied by 14 imperialist countries. The bourgeoisie of national "homelands" took the opportunity to proclaim "independence", and entered the counter-revolutionary war.

Their aim was to drive out Soviet power, restore the rule of landlords and industrial capitalists, undermine the people's state, and bring the "fringe areas" under the umbrella of international imperialism. We may expect similar policies from the national bourgeoisie of the "Bantustan" fringe during our revolution.

12.6 Proletarian nations

The Soviet Republic remained a unitary state, comprising all the territories included in the Russian Empire, but only for a few weeks after the October Revolution. As early as November 15, 1917 the government issued a Declaration of Rights, proclaiming the equality and sovereignty of nations, their free development, and the abolition of national privileges.

Independence was granted to Finland, which seceded to become a separate state, the Ukraine and Turkish Armenia in December 1917. Similar independence decrees were issued in 1918-1919. At the height of the civil war, there were five independent Soviet Republics on the territory of the former Russian Empire.

Capitalism, aided by imperialist armies, regained control of Lithuania, Latvia and Estonia. These became separate, independent bourgeois states. Led by the Communist Party, the workers and peasants of other national border lands — Ukraine, Byelorussia, Transcaucasia, and the smaller nations such as Tatars, Bashkirs and Yakuts — defeated the national bourgeoisie, expelled the foreign invaders, and formed Soviet Socialist Republics, autonomous republics or autonomous regions.

A federal constitution was proposed as the best means of reconciling national sovereignty and proletarian unity. Lenin, who had earlier opposed federation, revised his opinions shortly before — and particularly after — the October Revolution. A Soviet federation, he wrote in 1918, was a step towards democratic centralism. The Third All-Russia Congress of Soviets in January 1918 adopted a Declaration of Rights establishing the Russian Soviet Republics "on the principle of free union of free nations, as a federation of Soviet national republics" (Shevtsov, p49).

Military and economic treaties between the republics formed a basis for closer co-operation. Lenin urged them to form a union to strengthen the fight against imperialism, establish a single planned socialist economy, and develop resources for the benefit of all Soviet peoples.

Delegates from all national communities decided at the First All-Union Congress of Soviets in 1922 to unite into a single union. The Union of Soviet Socialist Republic (USSR) was born as a voluntary union of equal nations. The Second All-Union Congress of January 1924 approved a constitution which stressed the need for a central authority in matters of defence, foreign relations and external trade; introduced new guarantees of equality and sovereign rights of the republics and insisted on the voluntary nature of their union.

12.7 Socialist internationalism

Soviet power, the dictatorship of the proletariat, a socialist economy and socialist planning are cornerstones of unity between nations and language communities. The peoples of the USSR have shown that self-determination is the proper basis for union between nations within a socialist state.

The USSR now (1977) consists of 15 Soviet Socialist Republics, 20 Autonomous Republics, 8 Autonomous Regions, and 10 National Areas — a total of 53 territorial entities, accommodating 131 nations, national minorities and language communities. All are represented in the central and regional organs of government.

The Soviet Republics have equal representation in the Soviet of Nationalities, regardless of their size of territory and population. This chamber consists of delegates from the various republics, autonomous regions and outlying national areas, The Supreme Soviet, which is the main legislative organ, has representatives of 58 different national communities. The town chambers meet at the same time and have equal rights and responsibilities.

All nation states and communities retain their traditional superstructure of language, literature, music, traditions, lifestyles — that is to say, their own culture. At the same time they build their societies on a common foundation: socialist ownership, socialist planning, workers' participation in government and economy and the proletarian dictatorship.

The Constitution provides for a single Union citizenship. The Union republics have their own citizenship, but all citizens of the republics are at the same time citizens of the Soviet Union. All have equal legal status.

South Africa's policy is the direct opposite. It is based on national oppression, inequality and separate citizenship for peoples of Bantustans. These continue to be backward, underdeveloped reserves of labour, economic dependencies of the more advanced region, in which whites hold 87% of the country's land surface and almost all the modern forces of production.

12.8 Equal development

The Soviet Union's policy of 'national in form, socialist in content' guarantees the levelling up of development of all nations and national communities in the USSR. Small nations — Buryats, Yakuts, Koryaks, Chukchis, Khantis and others — made a leap from early communalism to large-scale production. All autonomous republics and regions are now highly industrialised.

Small factories and cottage industries predominated in Central Asia and Transcaucasia before the October Revolution. Today they have large metallurgical, chemical, electrical, engineering and other industries. Kazakhstan, formerly the home of nomadic horsemen, exports over 300 kinds of machinery, chemicals, pharmaceuticals, metals and other industrial products. Its output of electric power per head of population outstrips that of France, Belgium, Turkey and Iran. Turkmenia, which had only a few handicraft industries, now contains more than 300 large industrial plants.

The principle of distribution according to needs applies in the allocation of funds, technology and science between nation states. A greater share of the Union budget goes to the less developed regions in terms of population than to the industrialised regions of Central Russia and the Ukraine, which also train many thousands of skilled workers and specialists for production in their own national communities. Socialist emulation and the exchange of skilled persons and specialists between national regions contribute much to the process of raising all to the same high level of economic, and cultural progress.

Education has advanced by leaps and bounds in all national regions. Most have achieved total literacy in their national language while 42 million non-Russians, at the time of the 1970 census, knew Russian or some other language apart from their mother tongue. The former backward areas, such as Kirghizia, Kazakhstan, Tajikistan and Turkmenia, have between two and three times as many students per 10 000 of population as Italy, Britain and West Germany. Uzbekistan, which had 29 000 primary and secondary pupils before the Revolution, now has over 9 000 general education schools with three million pupils, two universities, 36 institutes and 156 technical schools with 370 000 students.

The development of national languages stimulates the growth of a national literature, art and science in all their forms. At the same time, the spread of Russian as the universal Soviet language, and the mingling of peoples of different nations in every national regions promotes the growth of an international Soviet culture, shared by all citizens irrespective of nationality, race or language. Unity on the basis of diversity is an important aspect of proletarian internationalism, the most important precondition of which is socialist ownership in the process of administration.

12.9 World Socialism

Countries become socialist at different times and in different circumstances. They are not at the same level of socio-economic development. Some have a more advanced production system than those with a predominantly peasant population.

Differences of this kind may give rise to contradictions between socialist states, as between the Soviet Union and China. Where the contradictions appear in the form of sharp political conflict, one or other socialist country has departed from the basic principles of socialism.

For example, China supports PAC and other movements in opposition to the

ANC. China has also supported forces opposed to the MPLA in the Angolan Revolution. These actions are dictated by China's hostility to the USSR and not by the realities of the revolution or the interest of the peoples engaged in revolutionary struggle.

On the other hand, relations between socialist countries with similar economic and political systems conform to the principles of state sovereignty, self-determination, co-operation and equal development. The progress made by the socialist world to higher levels of economic and social well-being brings humanity closer to the goal of a universal culture, international in form and socialist in content.

Second thoughts from Jack Simons

"The collapse of communism forces one to re-examine Marxist-Leninist theories and practices to obtain an understanding of the issues involved. [For South Africa] I accept the SACP approach of an 'emerging' South African nation and the need to promote it in the interests of unity, peace and democracy."

John Hoffman comments

"There is a very interesting section here on how the ANC/SACP interprets Lenin's views on national self-determination in their context."

How did it go in practice?

Somafco teachers comment: "Discussion focused on the meaning of 'the right of nations to self-determination'. When this right is applied to the oppressed and colonised peoples, there is no doubt of its universality. But self-determination after a socialist revolution seems contradictory, because in the long run there will be a community of united socialist countries. The relation of the Russian socialist revolution with those countries colonised by tsarism was cited. It was emphasised, however, that the question must always be considered according to the interests of the national and international working class, and needed to be looked at within the current context of the class struggle.

"The discussion also touched on the differences between nation, ethnic group and nationality. It was pointed out that before colonisation, the process of nation-building had begun, especially among Zulu- and Sotho-speakers. The process was interrupted and undermined by colonialism, which placed all the peoples of South Africa on a single economic base. What we now have in South Africa are different nationalities which can be grouped into oppressor and oppressed groups. There was, however, a feeling that South Africa is one nation.

"When looking at world socialism, it was concluded that those socialist nations with wrong domestic policies — e.g. China, Rumania — were the ones which ended up with wrong foreign policies."

Further reading sections

G, I, M, N

Lecture 13: Imperialism and Colonialism

13.0 Early colonies

We think of colonies as dependent territories, situated in tropical lands, separated by sea from the imperial state that "owns" them, and inhabited by peoples different in culture and appearance from the colonisers who rule and oppress them. This description is a correct account of most colonies seized during the capitalist era, but not of earlier kinds of colonies.

The words "imperialism" and "colony" come from Latin and remind us of Imperial Rome, before and after the Christian era (BC /AD). Rome was divided into three classes: the rich patricians, the propertyless plebeians (workers) and slaves, most of whom were Europeans from Greece, Germany, England and Eastern Europe — the home of the Slavs, from whose name comes the word 'slave' (*slaaf, sklav*).

Rome planted colonists (colonii) in conquered lands in Western Europe, including England and took tribute from the oppressed nations within the Empire. After its collapse (about 300 AD) Rome withdrew its armies. Feudal multi-national states arose in the West, while Islamic culture spread into Southern Europe (Spain and Portugal) during the period of Arab domination (between 700 and 1400 AD)

England is an example of this process of colonisation. The Norman French, having won the battle of Hastings (1066) introduced a feudal system, made French the official language, and turned the English peasantry into serfs. In the following centuries, England conquered Wales and Scotland and began a long struggle to colonise Ireland.

Engels wrote in 1870 (*The History of Ireland*, in Marx-Engels: *On Colonialism*, 1959, p.261) that:

"The collapse of Britain's Empire and the weakness of Britain's economy, have revived the spirit of nationalism in Wales and Scotland, where nationalists demand the right of self-determination and secession. Irish nationalists in Northern Ireland have taken up arms against Britain in support of their claim to unite with Eire, the Republic of Ireland. Similar struggles of the Basques in Spain and the Bretons in France show that some small nations keep alive a feeling of separate identity even after centuries of domination by a bigger nation."

13.1 Capitalist expansion

Capitalism developed within the structure of feudalism, expanded internally to conquer the home market for commodity production, and spread overseas from the 1400s onwards in search of gold, jewels, markets and raw materials.

This plunder and the enslavement of Africans, Marx noted:
"Signalled the rosy dawn of the era of capitalist production ... The different momenta (impulses, drives) of primitive accumulation distribute themselves now, more or less in order of time, particularly over Spain, Portugal, Holland, France and England...These methods depend in part on brute force, e.g. the

colonial system...Force is the midwife of every old society pregnant with a new one. It is itself an economic power." (Capital, Vol 1, Ch 31)

Capitalism used two kinds of force: one, against millions of colonised people in America, India the East Indies, and Africa; the other against the feudalists in the birthplace of capital. The two streams of violence flowed along parallel courses with many connecting tributaries.

Colonial plunder provided capital for the development of the steam engine and other advances in the forces of production. Commodities from factories were sold on the home market and in the colonies. The colonies in turn supplied raw materials for capitalists industries.

Capital created home markets in struggle against the feudalists and a world market in struggle against the colonised peoples.

13.2 Settled colonies and chartered companies

European colonists settled permanently in countries with sparse populations and temperate climates, killed the local inhabitants or drove them off fertile lands, and formed "colonies of white settlement". These expanded until they covered whole continents.

The British colonies of North America liberated themselves from Britain in the war of 1776, but continued to oppress Red Indians (Native Americans) and slaves from Africa. Canada, first settled by the French, was seized by Britain in the Seven Year War of 1756-63. The Cape, a Dutch colony, was transferred to Britain in 1806, during the wars against revolutionary France. The South American colonies liberated themselves from Spain and Portugal during the 19th century. Australia, New Zealand, Canada and South Africa became self-governing dominions within the British Empire. In all these countries, the colonists stole the land, plundered resources and oppressed the original owners.

Another strategy was used in tropical lands with big populations. Great commercial companies were formed, first in the Dutch East Indies, then in British India, and, during the last century, in West, East and Southern Africa. The trading companies received "charters" from their governments, giving them a monopoly of trade, powers to govern, and the right to enter into treaties, make wars, impose taxes, issue land grants, and rob without interference from the imperial state.

The British South Africa Company was such a chartered company. It had the powers and authority of a government. Acting under the charter, the company made war on the peoples of Zimbabwe, Zambia and Malawi; turned their countries into colonies or protectorates; sold land to white settlers; and laid the foundations of colonial capitalism. Britain's colonial policy, operating through the company, was the primary cause of the guerrilla war fought for the liberation of Zimbabwe.

13.3 The rape of Africa

Capitalism develops unevenly. Spain and Portugal, at one time the "great powers" of Europe, dropped long ago to the bottom of the league table. Holland, the leading capitalist nation in the 1600s, retired after 1800 from the top league. Britain, once the "workshop of the world", now lags behind the giant industrial states of West Germany, Japan and USA. Because of this rise and fall of capitalist states, the distribution of colonies did not match the distribution of power. Weak capitalisms, like those of Portugal, Holland and Belgium, had enormous colonial possessions, whereas Germany, Italy and Japan, though they were important countries, had few colonies.

A new round of struggles, headed by Germany, began in the last quarter of the 19th Century. Competition for colonies became a scramble. Britain and France, being old hands at the game of stealing territory, made the biggest gains between 1860 and 1900. Britain's colonial possessions increased in this period from 2.5 to 9.3 million square miles and France's from 0.2 to 3.7 million. Germany, which had no colonies before 1880, acquired one million square miles, while "tiny" Belgium grabbed 900 000 square miles with 30 million inhabitants.

Almost the whole of Africa was turned into colonies between 1876 and 1900. Whereas only 10.8% of the continent had belonged to European states in 1876, they had seized no less than 90.4% by the end of the century.

The period of monopoly capitalism began in the 1870.

Lenin wrote:

"We now see that it is precisely after that period that the tremendous 'boom' in colonial conquests begins, and that the struggle for the territorial division of the world becomes extraordinary sharp. It is beyond doubt to monopoly capitalism, to finance capital, is connected the intensification of the struggle for the partitioning of the world." (Imperialism, the Highest Stage of Capitalism, 1916)

Colonialism was a major factor at every stage in the growth of capitalism. First, in the period of commercial capitalism, gold, silver, and slaves stolen in the colonies provided capital for the development of power-driven machines. Then, the rise of industrial capitalism plundered the colonies for raw materials and used them as markets for factory-made commodities. Lastly, came the stage of capitalist imperialism.

13.4 The imperialist stage

Imperialism is "the monopoly stage of capitalism". Lenin specified its five main features:
• The concentration of production and capital in the hands of great monopolistic companies;
• The formation of multinational firms which operate across state boundaries and dominate national economies;
• The merging of bank capital with industrial capital into finance capital;
• The export of capital becomes as important or more important than the export of commodities; and
• The complete division of the world's territories among the big capitalist powers.

To summarise.

"Imperialism is capitalism at that stage of development at which the dominance of monopolies and finance capital is established; in which the export of capital has acquired pronounced importance; in which the divisions of the world among the international trusts has begun; in which division of all territories of the globe among the biggest capitalist powers has been completed."

Though written a year before the Great October Revolution, Lenin's analysis remains a true and accurate account of imperialism today. The colonies have liberated themselves; the rise of world socialism confronts world capitalism with growing challenges; capitalist expansion has been forced to take indirect, disguised forms, resulting in "neo-imperialism". But the dominance of finance capital, the spread of multinational trusts, and the struggle between rival capitalisms continue to shape the policies of capitalist states.

13.5 Multinationals in South Africa

Monopoly grows out of capitalist competition on "open" markets. Big firms swallow small firms or drive them into bankruptcy. Small businessmen in African townships cannot easily compete with the large department stores and supermarkets in the main shopping centres. Monopolies limit the growth of African capitalism. Monopolies compete fiercely among themselves, using every possible means, including bribery, corruption and sabotage, to get an advantage over their rivals. The recent Lockheed "scandals", in which the manufacturers of aeroplanes bribed prime ministers, princes and government officials in many countries to obtain contracts, are an example of such competition by dirty means.

"Thus, competition gives birth to monopoly, but monopoly does not eliminate competition. Monopolies exist above competition and side by side with it. They do not eliminate the anarchic and chaotic nature of capitalist production."
(*Fundamentals of Marxism-Leninism*, 1960, p298)

Big firms become multinational, controlling banks, mines, factories and business in many countries. Anglo-American, Rembrandt, ICI, IBM, ITT, International Harvesters and various oil companies and car manufacturers are among the multinationals that dominate the South African economy. They interlock with the local bourgeoisie in the exploitation of low-paid black workers and extract high rates of profit.

The fascist-colonial autocracy guarantees high profits and "security" to foreign firms, presses them to increase their investments, offers concessions and favourable conditions of trade. In return, the big capitalist countries — USA, Britain, France, West Germany, Japan — are expected to protect their investments by opposing the international campaign for sanctions against apartheid.

Vorster's clique claims to be a fortress of Western "civilisation" in the struggle against international "communism". The government offers to make naval stations and strategic bases available to NATO's navies and air force. Our revolution is therefore a part of the world struggle against imperialism.

13.6 Imperialism means war

The two world wars of our century, fought in 1914-18 and 1939-45, were imperialist wars for the re-division of the world and, in the second of these wars, for the destruction of the first socialist state, the enslavement of the Soviet people, and the exploitation of their vast resources by world capitalism.

In general terms, the capitalists who had led progressive revolutions against feudalism for the formation of nation-states, found these states too small, too cramped to absorb the huge output of commodities and surplus capital. They therefore intensified competition for colonies, divided the territories which had not already been seized, entered the monopoly stage, and embarked on another, fiercer round of wars.

Lenin described the process during the first imperialist world war :
"From the liberator of nations, which it was in the struggle against feudalism, capitalism in its imperialist stage has turned into the greatest oppressor of nations. Formerly progressive, capitalism has become reactionary; it has developed the forces of production to such a degree that mankind is faced with the alternative of adopting socialism or of experiencing years and even decades of armed struggle between the 'Great' Powers for the artificial preservation of capitalism by means of colonies, monopolies, privileges and national oppression of every kind." (Socialism and War, 1915)

Germany, the chief aggressor in both imperialist world wars, overtook its rivals, Britain and France, and challenged their dominant control of colonies and markets.

Lenin wrote:
"Both sides in the 1914-18 war were carrying on the policies of robbery and oppression that led to the war. German capitalists said to their enemies: We are stronger, therefore we have the same 'sacred' right to plunder.' That is what the real history of British and German finance capital in the course of several decades preceding the war amounts to ... There you have the clue to an understanding of what the war is about." (War and Revolution, 1917)

13.7 Crisis and capitalism

Germany suffered defeat. It returned to the attack in 1939-45, in alliance with Italy and Japan. The result of the war was a second major blow to imperialism. A new crisis of capitalism developed around four primary factors:
• the transformation of socialism into a world system;
• further disintegration of colonialism and the growth of new contradictions between the newly independent states and imperialist powers;
• contradictions within the imperialist camp between United States, Japan and the West European block of capitalist nations; and

• the growing strength of the labour movement and class antagonisms within the capitalist states.

Underlying these elements of crisis is the permanent cause of capitalist instability: the contradiction between private ownership and social labour. This contradiction has grown sharper with the growth of monopoly capitalism.

LI Brezhnev explained:
"State-monopoly capitalism, by massively socialising production and centralising of the bourgeois system, sharpens the contradiction between the social nature of production and the private mode of appropriation. Production complexes, some of which serve more than one country, remain the private property of a handful of millionaires and billionaires. The contrasts in that situation are becoming increasingly evident. The need to replace capitalist by socialist relations of production is becoming ever more pressing." (The CPSU in the Struggle for Unity for All Revolutionary and Peace Forces, 1975, p56-57)

Imperialism camouflages itself to conceal its true nature. It adopts new strategies and takes on a new look, which is what is meant by "neo-imperialism". Unable to employ old methods of open warfare, conquest of territories, and foreign rule, the new imperialism works in roundabout ways. It carries on exploitation by other means. Non-imperialism gives birth to neo-colonialism.

13.8 Neo-colonialism

Liberation brings freedom of choice. Sovereign, independent states can choose either to build on capitalist structures taken over from the old colonial masters or to advance along a non-capitalist road to socialism. Neo-colonialism is the imperialist strategy of inducing new states to take the capitalist road. The modern imperialists:
• support counter-revolutionaries against pro-socialist governments, as in Cuba, Chile, Angola and Ethiopia;
• obtain concessions from debtor states, as in the case of Zaire's surrender of most of Shaba province to West Germany for rocket-testing, in return for an annual rental of 25 million dollars;
• sell manufactured commodities at high prices, or expensive industrial plants for which spare parts and technologies must be imported;
• buy raw materials at reduced prices, thereby keeping ex-colonies in a condition of economic dependence; and
• strengthen the capitalist sector by entering into partnership with local capitalists.

More than 80% of Africa's exports consist of "primary" products which go to advanced capitalist countries where value is added through processing. The prices for these products falls while the prices of manufactured goods rise.

Multinational monopolies control most of the minerals extracted from poor countries, and take from them profits and interest at high rates. For such reasons, the workers and peasants of most African states have made little progress since independence. They are in the same position as the worker-peasants of Bantustans, the "new colonies" of South African "neo-imperialism". They remain underdeveloped reservoirs of low-paid workers.

Our revolution will liberate South Africa from the burdens of neo-imperialism and neo-colonialism, wipe out inequalities between peoples and regions and raise the living standards of backward rural areas to the levels of the more advanced regions.

13.9 Our allies

The socialist world has demonstrated the spirit of proletarian internationalism in its generous support of liberation movements in China, Korea, Cuba, Vietnam and Africa.

Our own revolutionary movement received recognition, encouragement and material aid from the Soviet Union at a time when its people were grappling with the difficulties of building a socialist system after eight years (1914-1922) of imperialist war, civil war and armed intervention. The Soviet Union has been our loyal ally and chief supporter for 60 years.

Other socialist countries, as they took shape, have in turn carried out their international duty towards liberation movements with unfailing readiness. Their active support has enabled our movement to put into practice its policy of armed struggle, train an army on African soil and combine, in our organisation, the forces that oppose and will eventually overcome imperialism.

Our allies are world socialism, national liberation and the revolutionary proletariat, the mainsprings of the great social process that has transformed the world.

As LI Brezhnev remarks:

"... the three streams of revolutionary process have been gathering momentum and making a growing contribution to the struggle against imperialism. Experience provides convincing proof that success in this common struggle is achieved only when all the revolutionary streams co-ordinate their actions and merge to form a united anti-imperialist front. (World Marxist Review, No 8, 1969)

We ourselves bear witness to the strength of the united action of liberated African nations, socialist states and militant working people against South Africa's colonial-fascism, and for freedom from national oppression, race discrimination and class exploitation. Our victory is certain.

Teaching suggestions

Three questions could update this lecture, which is an accurate but incomplete description of the operation of modern imperialism; incomplete, because of the changes in the international organisation of capitalism which have taken place since the 1970s.

• Given that almost all colonies are now nominally independent, is there still a need for national liberation? Where? In what respects?

• What new methods is international capital using to maintain its grip?

• If there is now no "world socialist movement" with an institutional base in the Soviet Union, how can alliances be forged to bring about the liberation still needed?

Lenin's *Imperialism* in its discussion of cartelisation does anticipate the kind of globalisation which is currently happening. It is a short enough text to be used alongside these lectures. Discussion could be opened by reference to the huge anti-debt demonstrations at World Bank meetings in Seattle and Washington in 1999 and 2000; the reasons for this groundswell of opposition and the kinds of forces involved in building it.

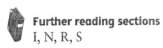 **Further reading sections**
I, N, R, S

Lecture 14: One Society, One Nation

14.0 Introduction

We begin with the premise that all South Africans form a single, common society. It is the product of more than 300 years of armed struggle, white domination, economic inter-dependence, social integration and inter-racial sex.

Dutch settlers and British imperialists made war on free southern African states, invaded their territories, robbed them of their land, destroyed their village industries and integrated them by force into British colonies and Boer republics.

Capitalism developed on the expropriated lands and the ruins of village communities. Peasants were turned into proletarians. The growth of mining and manufacturing laid the foundations of an advanced industrial capitalism.

British imperialism and Afrikaner nationalism were antagonistic partners in this process of expansion and racial domination. They joined their forces against black people but fought each other for overall supremacy.

Britain defeated the Republics in 1899-1902. The Anglo-Boer war removed the last political barriers that stood in the way of a single commodity market under a central government. Having gained their main objective, which was to eliminate Afrikanerdom as a rival power in Southern Africa, the British granted self-rule to the comprador bourgeoisie (those bourgeois who profited by economic relations with the imperial power).

The Act of Union established in 1910 an all-white government responsible to an all-white parliament. The constitution and the numerical superiority of Afrikaners in the white population enabled them to obtain control of the state apparatus.

The emergence of African nationalism under the leadership of the ANC presented Afrikanerdom with its most serious challenge. Successive Afrikaner governments since 1924 attempted to resist this threat by means of oppressive segregation laws which isolated the whites and divided the black peoples into separate racial and "tribal" categories.

White workers fought fierce class struggles during the first quarter of the century. Their resistance to exploitation reached its peak in the Rand Revolt of 1922. But they too, like the Boer Republics, accepted defeat rather than enter into an alliance with Africans against capitalist imperialism. White workers, sheltered by colour bars, became a labour aristocracy, an appendage of the bourgeoisie.

Imperialism and its offshoots — fascism, colonialism and racism — suffered a tremendous defeat in the Second World War (1939-45), when the Soviet peoples routed and expelled the Nazi invaders. The spread of socialism after the war changed the international balance of power in favour of the forces opposed to imperialism. A wave of national liberation swept through Asia and Africa.

In South Africa, however, Afrikanerdom consolidated its position by winning the general elections of 1948. The National Party came to power behind the slogan of apartheid and opened a bitter attack on the working class by banning the Communist Party in 1950.

Apartheid is the "final solution" of Afrikanerdom: its last, desperate attempt to save itself from an approaching, unavoidable defeat. The ideological aim is to reverse the historical process, destroy the common society that has grown up, recreate "tribal states" in 13% of the country's territory, and reduce millions of Africans to the position of stateless migrant labourers.

Afrikanerdom has chosen to be an oppressor nation, a bulwark of reaction and the defender of an obsolete colonial order which has degenerated into a vicious system of racial fascism. It is the most bitter and dangerous enemy of national liberation; the greatest obstacle to the cultural development of the entire people.

For these reasons the immediate aim of our revolution is to overthrow the Afrikaner autocracy and replace it by a people's democracy.

14.1 Our common society

Ours is a society of unequals, with three dimensions of inequality: race discrimination, class exploitation and national oppression.

Equality is not, however, a necessary condition for a common society. All capitalist societies are divided into classes which are unequal in terms of property, income living standards, opportunities, political power and control of economic resources. Yet capitalism everywhere creates conditions favourable to the growth of a common market and a common society. South Africa is no exception, as will be seen from what follows.

South Africa is a sovereign, independent state with a defined territory and recognised boundaries. It has a single centralised government that controls the state apparatus.

As in all capitalist systems, the state is an instrument of class rule, an organisation for the oppression of the working people. The South African state has the additional quality of being an instrument for the oppression of the black majority, regardless of class. The state is used to perpetuate white minority rule and, in particular, to maintain Afrikaner hegemony.

We deny the legitimacy of white minority rule and fight to overthrow the autocracy of Afrikanerdom, destroy the existing state apparatus and replace it by democratic institutions. But the state itself is a fundamental part of the common society and will remain, to be used in our hands against enemies of the revolution.

The legal system, which expresses the aims of the Afrikaner government and the interests it represents, is likewise discriminatory and repressive. There are different laws for racial groups; one set of laws for blacks, another for whites. But there is also a common law for all South Africans and criminal laws that apply to all. Statutes such as the Riotous Assemblies Act, Public Safety Act, Terrorism Act, Mixed Marriages and Immorality Acts are used to oppress all who oppose apartheid, both black and white.

There are black and white prisoners — freedom fighters and common "convicts" — in the prisons. There are black and white prison wardens and policemen. Members of all racial groups form part of the state's machinery. The truth is that Afrikanerdom cannot enforce its autocratic despotism without the active participation of some blacks. Even the system of oppression unites our people in a common society. — both for and against oppression!

The common society is the widest social group to which South Africans of all races belong. They interact more closely with one another than with members of any other society. And they share a common culture while retaining many elements of their traditional cultures.

14.2 A common culture

All schools teach the same kind of subjects. "Bantu" education is inferior to "white" education, but African, coloured, Indian and white pupils prepare for the same examinations. There are no separate "racial" examinations for doctors, nurses, lawyers, teachers, accountants, engineers, electricians and other professions or trades.

English and Afrikaans are "official" languages for all South Africans. A great majority speak at least one other language, usually their mother tongue, but the official languages are the media of communication in commerce, industry and administration. The Afrikaner government does not "segregate" languages although it seeks to substitute Afrikaans for English as the chief language.

Religion is another area of shared values and ideologies. Christianity is the official religion. All population groups, except the minorities of Hindus, Muslims and Jews, profess to be Christians. More than 60% of Africans claim membership of one or other Christian sects. No other African country has as large a proportion of Christians. Afrikaner missionaries compete with English language churches and encourage blacks to join the Dutch Reformed Mission Church.

Marriage customs and family systems are closely linked to religion. Members of Christian churches are not allowed by their religion to have more than one wife. Such monogamous marriages are also gaining ground for economic reasons among Africans at the expense of customary polygamous marriages. The number of Africans who enter into monogamous marriages is greater than the number of white marriages. A strong tendency therefore exists towards uniformity of family organisation on the principle of one husband, one wife.

Our art, music, drama and literature have characteristic South African themes and approaches. Artists and writers come from all sections of the population, despite the unequal access to cultural resources. Radio and television programmes are segregated by language, but this cannot in practice prevent audiences from more than the target racial group.

Similarly with sport and games. South Africans of every group play or watch football, rugby, cricket, tennis, netball, boxing and horse-racing. The international ban on racial segregation in sport is forcing whites to consider relaxing the colour bar, even to the extent of promising that a non-racial Springbok team may represent South Africa in rugby matches between countries.

A common culture encourages biological assimilation. Members of a stable common society tend to interbreed (miscegenate) in spite of the artificial barriers created by class differences or bans on sex between racial, religious and national communities. The process of miscegenation, when continued for a long time, gives rise to new population groups.

The coloured community is one example. The descendants of relationships between whites, Khoi-Khoi, Asians and Africans, its numbers are officially estimated at 2,5 million. The real number is probably closer to five million, if allowance is made for persons of mixed descent who "pass" as white or African.

14.3 One economy

The common society reaches its peak of development in towns and cities, which are "melting pots" of peoples and cultures. A majority of urban dwellers are Africans, coloured and Indians. They are the "black" people whom Afrikanerdom refuses to recognise as citizens.

Though segregated and racially or tribally divided by law, all townsmen share a common social environment, buy in the same shops, wear the same kind of clothes, enjoy eating the same foodstuffs and adopt an urban way of life.

Men and women of different language groups and races work together in factories, mines, shops and farms. They learn skills and co-operate in the process of production and exchange. Urbanisation and social labour break down barriers between working people. For this reason, Afrikanerdom forces black, brown and white workers to live in separate areas.

Segregated trade unions and job reservation serve the same purpose: dividing the working class. White, coloured and Indian workers may form registered unions under the Industrial Conciliation Act of 1956, whereas Africans are denied the right of collective bargaining. These racial barriers cannot, however, entirely obstruct the growth of production. Economic pressures, such as the scarcity of skilled workers, forces Afrikanerdom to relax and, in some industries, scrap the system of reserving certain kinds of work for whites alone.

All sections of the population participate in the economy as workers, independent producers or capitalists. There is one currency, the rand, which passes through black, brown and white hands. Commodities produced in factories or on farms are sold in all areas, including the remote rural districts and traditional homelands of the peasantry.

Migrant labour systems have linked the "reserves" to the industrial centres for more than a hundred years. Many migrants became proletarians. Those who live in the reserves lead a double life as both peasants and wage workers. The bourgeoisie have broken down barriers between town and country in the manner described by Marx.

> *"The expropriation of part of the countryfolk, and the hunting of them off the land, does not merely 'set free' the workers for the uses of industrial capital, together with their means of subsistence and the materials of their labour; in addition it creates the home market ... And nothing but the destruction of rural domestic industry can provide for the home market of a country the extension and the stability requisite for the capitalist method of production."*
> (*Capital*, Vol 1, Ch 30)

This passage is an exact account of what has happened in South Africa. The bourgeoisie bulldozed traditional communal societies, stole their land, turned farmers into proletarians and put together the capitalist system, piece by piece: the structure and relations of production, according to the principles of private ownership and maximisation of profits.

14.4 Building the nation

The bourgeoisie created the capitalist order but did not intend to form a common society. It developed in spite of their efforts to make whites a Master Race and limit intercourse with blacks to elementary economic relations. The common society grew out of the common market in accordance with the law formulated by Marx.

> *"In the social production of their means of existence men enter into definite, necessary relations which are independent of their will; productive relationships which correspond to a definite stage of development of their material productive forces ... The mode of production of the material means of existence conditions the whole process of social, political and intellectual life."*
> (*Preface to The Critique of Political Economy*, 1859)

The common society, which came into being independently of the will of the bourgeoisie, is the foundation on which to build a nation. The nation cannot exist without a common society. The common society, when fully developed, constitutes the nation.

Lenin has traced the link between society and nation:
> *"For the complete victory of commodity production, the bourgeoisie must capture the home market, and there must be politically united territories whose population speak a single language, with all obstacles to the development of that language and to its consolidation in literature eliminated. Therein is the economic foundation of the nation."* (*The Right of Nations to Self-determination*, 1914)

South Africa possesses all the ingredients of a nation except one. It has a common territory, economy, language, culture and traditions. The missing element is a national identity, a general awareness of belonging to a single nation, the identification of each and every South African with that nation.

Among themselves, when at home, people identify themselves by reference to a language-culture (Zulu, Xhosa, Venda, Tsonga, Tswana, Afrikaner and so forth), or to a racial type (coloured), or a religion (Hindu, Muslim). Only non-Afrikaner whites refer to themselves as South African, and this only if they have been thoroughly assimilated into South African society. Of all our population groups, only Afrikaners are likely to claim that they constitute a "nation".

The absence of a single national identity reflects the immaturity of a national ideology; and occurs widely in Africa. Colonialism created objective conditions for national unity. Liberation movements provided the subjective element and created a national consciousness in the course of their struggles for independence. But the conscious, deliberate construction of a nation could be undertaken only after liberation from foreign rule. The slogan "One Zambia, One Nation!" presents such an appeal for the merging of regional and language communities into a single nation.

14.5 Afrikanerdom, an oppressor nation

It is the historic mission of the African National Congress to realise the common society, develop it to a higher stage, and complete the process of welding peoples of all languages, cultures and races into a single, all-embracing nation. In emancipating ourselves, we emancipate all South Africans from the tyranny of Afrikaner autocracy, racial inequality and national oppression.

Afrikaners, who allied themselves with British imperialism in wars that destroyed free southern African states, now deny the existence of a common society. They have chosen to wage a ruthless, violent struggle to dismember the common society, crush all who defend it and entrench their dominant position as the majority nation within the white race.

Afrikaner nationalists embarked on a systematic campaign after World War One, using secret societies (the *Broederbond*) and a wide range of cultural organisations (*Federasie van Afrikaanse Kultuurverenigings; Reddingsdaad; Helpmekaar; Ossewa-Brandwag; Voortrekkerjeug*) and the Dutch Reformed Churches. Their first objective was to isolate Afrikaners from English-speaking whites.

The main instrument was the Afrikaans language. It had a strong emotional appeal and was used to find jobs and promotion for Afrikaners in public administration, the teaching profession, commerce and industry. A parallel attack was launched on the trade unions to separate Afrikaner workers under the National Party leadership in the *Blankewerkersbeskermingsbond*.

A second strategy was to segregate all whites behind a barrier of colour bars at places of work, in residential areas, and in other public places. By giving them a monopoly of power privileges, they bribed non-Afrikaner whites to abandon their opposition to Afrikaner domination and race discrimination.

Segregation failed to stop the growth of the common society. The capitalist drive to increase production and capture the commodity market overcame racial barriers, strengthened the black proletariat and speeded up the growth of the common society. The laws of capitalist economy were stronger than the laws of feudal colonialism.

Therefore, when Afrikanerdom obtained control of the State in 1948, it adopted the new strategy of apartheid. The National Party government erected new racial barriers and used the state apparatus to isolate whites from contact with blacks outside places of production and exchange.

The government also outlawed the ANC and the Communist Party, who are the vanguard of the revolution against Afrikaner autocracy. There followed a violent, ruthless repression of all opponents of apartheid.

14.6 Techniques of domination

At the same time, Afrikanerdom put its master plan into effect. These descendants of colonists who had waged war on our people in every corner of the country, decided to turn the clock back and reverse the process that gave birth to the common society.

They had left us with only 13% of the country, while keeping for themselves the remaining 87%, with the accumulated wealth extracted from the labour power of our people. Not content with robbing us of the land, they proceeded to partition even this 13% into eight or nine petty black states.

The Bantustan strategy serves many purposes:
• It means legitimate Afrikanerdom's claim to final and absolute mastery over the 87%. Our people are to be deprived of South African citizenship. Instead of "passes" we are to be given Bantustan "passports".
• The partitioning will weaken the common society, place the majority of the population under separate, so-called independent states and turn urban Africans into migrant labourers.
• Partitioning is a divisive tactic, calculated to split our forces and foster tribalism among the people.
• Bantustans are "rimlands" to be used as a buffer against our revolutionary armies.
• Afrikanerdom labels its policy the granting of "self-determination" to confuse the people and disarm international opponents of the system.
• The move to form separate "tribal nations" contradicts our objective of creating one nation.

Bantustan constitutions are an obstacle and must be dismantled by the people themselves, those who live there or who belong to the same language group. They will recognise that Afrikanerdom never grants rights to our people, that its sole aim is to remain in power against the will of the majority. Our future lies, not in the Bantustans, but in creating a common society under a democratic government that will utilise the country's wealth for the benefit of all the people.

14.7 An historical necessity

The overthrow of Afrikaner autocracy is necessary to preserve the common society and complete the process of building a single nation. Only a revolution can break the fetters that bind our people and free their energies for creative construction. Only a revolution can put an end to the civil war that has been forced on us and to the enormous waste of resources on a gigantic armaments programme.

Afrikanerdom, having converted the state into its personal property, uses the state machinery to impose its will on all aspects of social life. The state has become a racial totalitarianism. It invades the privacy of the family; dictates to people whom they may and may not marry; prohibits believers of one religion from worshipping together; segregates students of different races and language groups in separate schools and universities; imposes colour bars on sportsmen; and controls the economy in the interests of Afrikaner domination.

The Afrikaner state, like the feudal state, converts elements of social life, such as the family, religion, culture, property and types of occupation, into elements of political life in the form of racial categories. A person's rights and obligations are determined not by his achievements, but by laws that regulate his racial group. Racial inequalities obscure the realities of class exploitation, which is the essence of capitalism. Relations between employers and workers appear as relations between white and black.

Our revolution will carry out the tasks that the bourgeoisie failed to accomplish. We will:
• sweep away the garbage of feudal-colonial racism;
• liberate the economy from the political controls that hamper the growth of production forces;
• overcome the boycotts, sanctions and isolation imposed by the international community on the Afrikaner regime;
• open up doors to our people and trade in Africa and elsewhere;
• improve living standards for all in town and country; and
• make South Africa a decent, civilised home for all who live in it.

Our struggle and situation are similar to those described by Marx in an analysis of the bourgeois revolution against feudalism:
"For a popular revolution and the emancipation of a particular class of civil society to represent the whole of society to coincide, for one class to represent the whole of society, another class must concentrate in itself all the evils of society, a particular class must embody and represent a general obstacle and limitation. A particular social sphere must be regarded as the notorious crime of the whole society, so that emancipation from this sphere appears as a general emancipation. For one class to be the liberating class par excellence, it is necessary that another class should be openly the oppressing class."
(*The Critique of Hegel's Philosophy of Right*, 1844)

This passage fits our situation for the following reasons:
• Our liberation movement is a class movement, representing workers, peasants and intellectuals.
• We represent the whole society, including whites who do not follow the National Party and reject racism.
• Afrikanerdom concentrates in itself all the evils of our society; it is the main obstacle to stability and progress.
• Race discrimination is a recognised crime against humanity and is condemned by the United Nations, Organisation of African Unity, world socialism, churches and other broad organisations.

• Afrikanerdom is unmistakably the oppressing nation.
• It is necessary to overthrow Afrikaner autocracy in the interests of the common society.

We demand, on behalf of all South Africans, the right to determine our national identity. Our movement represents the aims and interests of the common society, of which we have become "the social head and heart". The development of productive forces and the national consciousness of the people have reached a stage at which revolution is historically necessary.

Teaching suggestions

This lecture has two main elements:
• an analysis of how first colonialism and them apartheid tried but failed to prevent the development of a common South African society; and
• a strategic outline of how the struggle will proceed and what it hopes to achieve once victorious.

The history can again be approached through finding "living history": older comrades who experienced various aspects of apartheid's divisive tactics and can describe and discuss them.

The questions arise:
• Have we achieved the goals outlined in the lecture? Are we on the path to achieving them.
• Have we realised the "common society" whose seeds clearly existed even under apartheid? If not, what are the obstacles and how can they be overcome?

Further reading sections
S

Appendix to Novo Catengue Lectures

In 1977 examinations were held in Novo Catengue. The members of the political department assessed the exam results and the course itself.

Comrade Jack reflected on the exam process as follows:
"The Cubans who monitored Novo Catengue wanted an evaluation of performance of MK cadres to complete their reports to the Central Command. I decided to set as written examination with measures to enable students unable to write English or their own African language. Those who 'passed' might have had an advantage, but political education took up only 60 hours of instruction out of a total of 200 hours per term of three months and probably had only a slight affect on the final rating. I adopted the practice used in the University of Zambia, Lusaka (where I headed the Department of Social Science and Social Welfare) of giving candidates an idea in advance of the examination questions. Multiple choice questions were for brief essays." (October 10 1991)

The African National Congress of South Africa

Department of Political Education: Novo Catengue Training
Quarterly Examination Test, August, 1977

To all candidates:
Section one and two deal with the South African politics, from 1652, the year in which Jan van Riebeeck landed at the Cape, to the formation of "Umkhonto weSizwe", in 1961.

Candidates will be expected to answer five questions from sections one and two, and five questions from sections three and four. From section one, candidates will be expected to answer two questions not necessarily in writing. And from section two, candidates will be expected to answer three questions, all in writing.

In sections three and four, candidates will be expected to answer all five questions in writing.

Section 1

1. Who was Jan van Riebeeck, and when did he land at the Cape? (5)
2. When Van Riebeeck landed at the Cape, he met some South Africans there.
(a) Who were they?
(b) What kind of reception did they give him?
(c) How did van Riebeeck return their kindness to him? (15)
3. It is said in the school history books that these people, that is, the people who met Van Riebeeck and his crew, stole cattle from Van Riebeeck. What is your comment? (10)
4. Between 1659 and 1660, Van Riebeeck launched a war of dispossession against the Khoi-Khoi. What was the cause of the War? (10)
5. From 1779 to 1879, the Xhosa-speaking South Africans fought bitter wars against the white invaders. What are these wars called, and which of them can you regard as the most important and most significant. Give reason for your answers. (20)
6. Makana, "The Prophet", deserves special place in the South African history. Give two reasons why he should be so respected.
7. The War of the Axe (1846), can be regarded as the forerunner of what came to be known as "The Congress Alliance" in the early 1950s, or the united front of the oppressed people of South Africa, against their common enemy. Why? And why was it called "the War of the Axe"? (10)
8. What role did DDT Jabavu play in the awakening of African nationalism and African political consciousness? (5)
9. What role did the Church play in the awakening of African political consciousness? (5)
10. Who was the first African to enter the Cape Provincial Council? (5)
11. When were the Pass Laws first introduced, and by whom? (5)
12. When did the "Bambata Rebellion" take place and what was its cause? (10)

Section 2

1. When was the African National Congress formed and what led to its formation? (5)
2. What were its aims and objectives? (5)
3. When was the ANC (Youth League) formed, and what role did it play towards revolutionising the ANC? (10)
4. The policy of the ANC, had from its foundation till early 1961, been non-violent. Would you say this policy was "negative" or "positive"? (Argue your point) (20)
5. Who said the following words and why? "We are one people ...These divisions, these jealousies, are the cause of all our woes and of all our backwardness and ignorance today ... the demon of racism, the aberration of Xhosa-Fingo feuds, the animosity that exists between Zulus and Tongas between Basothos and every other native, must be buried and forgotten." (10)
6. "The main content of South African National Liberation struggle is the liberation of the African people." Express your views on this in no less than three pages of your own exercise book. (25)
7. The Congress Alliance was formed in 1953. Name the constituent organisations which comprised it.(5)
8. What did the founders of the ANC learn from the early defeats of our ancestors? (5)
9. "We, the people of South Africa, declare for all our country, and the world to know that South Africa belongs to all who live in it, black and white." Do you agree with this declaration? Give reasons for your answer.
10. What are the primary tasks of the National Executive Committee of the African National Congress? (5)
11. The ANC is the political organisation of the African people. Is MK also a political organisation? What are the relationships between the ANC and MK? Who takes policy decisions, either to launch an armed struggle, or to call off an armed attack? Is it the Revolutionary Council or the National Executive Committee? (20)
12. When was the Communist Party of South Africa formed? (5)
13. Who was its first African General Secretary? (5)
14. Is a trade union organisation or a Communist Party a national organisation or an international organisation? Give reasons for your answers (15)
15. The African National Congress as a national liberation organisation, does not represent any single class, or any one ideology. Comment in this statement of fact. (15)
16.The first African trade union was formed by members of the "International Socialist League". What was its name and what was its slogan? (5)
Before answering questions in these two sections, revise lectures 2, 2(b), 2(c), 3, 5 and 6. Particular attention should be paid to section 4.

Section 3

1. Briefly explain what you understand by the following:
(a) Trade Union   (b) Bourgeoisie
(c) Proletariat   (d) Guild

(e) Combination Act   (f) Self-conscious discipline
(g) Brothering   (h) Journeymen.

2. Give your reasons why the study of trade unions is absolutely necessary.

3. In an attempt to ensure the security and loyalty of its members, the Friendly Society a secret organisation of the British coal-miners laid down three conditions aimed at protecting their members against police informers; what were these conditions?

4. Why were the British coal-miners forced to create secret societies? Compare this with the conditions in South Africa.

5. In your opinion, would you say that "The Combination Acts" in Britain are similar to the "Suppression of Communism Act", and the "Suppression of Terrorism Act?" Give reasons for your answers.

6. Who christened the British working class "The first-born sons of modern industry" and why? Is the statement true?

7. Give the name of the organisation which is called the "direct forerunner of "The First International", or "The International Workingmen's Association".

8. Who were the two great figures who led it?

9. What are "Guilds", and how many kinds of Guilds are there?

10. Compare the forced labour system with contract labour in South Africa.

11. Compare the peonage system with the labour tenant system in South Africa.

12. "Strikes are the military schools of the workingmen, in which they prepare themselves for the great struggle which cannot be avoided."

(a) What kind of struggle is this, which cannot be avoided?

(b) Do workers learn anything from their conduct of strikes, and if so, what are these lessons?

(c) What gives the unions and the strikes arising from them their real importance?

13. What is the difference between "private property" and "personal property"?

14. "People always have been the foolish victims of deceptions and self-deception in politics, and they always will be until they have learnt to seek out the interests of some class or other behind all morals, religious, political and social phases, declarations and promises." (VI Lenin)
What do you understand by this quotation? Give your critical comments on it.

15. What do you understand by the phrase "national intelligentsia"?

(a) Can intellectuals constitute a class of their own? That is, do they form a class?

(b) What is your understanding of the word "class", when used politically?

16. What do you understand by "Comprador Bourgeoisie"?

17. What does life involve before everything else?

18. "Consciousness can never be anything else than conscious existence, and the existence of men is their actual life process." (Marx & Engels). What is the first premise of all human existence?

19. In any interpretation of history there is a fundamental fact which one has first of all to observe. Which is that fundamental fact?

20. Which revolution broke the power of the Roman Catholic Church? And which other revolution followed it?

21. What do you understand by "emulation"?

22. Politically, what do you understand by "organisation", and where does organisation begin?

23. What is the difference between "military discipline" and "self-conscious discipline"?

24. "Communism deprives no man of the power to appropriate the products of society; all that it does is to deprive him of the power to subjugate the labour of others by means of such appropriation." Discuss critically what you understand by this statement.

25. "One element of success (workers) have number; but numbers weigh only in balance when united by combination and led by knowledge." (Marx) What does Marx mean by this statement? Give your answer in 35 words.

26. "The Communist organisation of social labour rests on the free and conscious discipline of hunger of the working people themselves who have thrown off the yoke both the landowners and capitalists." (Lenin)
(a) What do you understand by "discipline of hunger"?
Do you agree with this statement? Explain why you agree.
(b) How does "Communist organisation of social labour" come about? Is it easy to achieve it?

27. Can you differentiate between "insurrection" and "revolution"?
Would you say that the Soweto events of 1976 which are continuing now in 1977, are an "insurrection or a "revolution"? Give a critical political analysis of the events in 100 words.

28. "The question that now confronts a militant political party is: Shall we be able to make use of the correctness of our Social Democratic doctrine, of our bond with the only thoroughly revolutionary class, the proletariat, to put a proletarian imprint on the victory of revolution, to carry the revolution to a real and decisive victory, not in word but in deed, and to paralyse the instability, half-heartedness and treachery of the democratic bourgeoisie?" (Lenin)
Explain what you understand by this, taking into consideration the events in South Africa today.

29. "Undoubtedly, we still have a great deal to do in educating and organising the working class; but now the gist of the matter is: where should we place the main political emphasis in this work of education and organisation? Both serve to educate and organise the working class. Both are, of course, necessary. But in the present revolution the problem amounts to this; which is to be emphasised in the work of educating and organising the working class, the former or the latter?" (Lenin) Comment.

30. Can a revolution succeed without the working class playing a vanguard role? Give reasons for your answers.

31. The Paris Commune is regarded as "The world's first proletarian state", which taught the European proletariat to pose concretely the tasks of the socialist revolution." Comment.

(Copy of exam paper in possession of Comrade Jack Simons)

Interview with Jack Simons, 18 April 1986

Lynette Simons, Comrade Jack's niece, recorded this interview in 1986

I went to Pretoria in 1927 to join the civil service after having done a year or more as a lawyer's clerk in my birthplace, Riversdale in the Cape. You know the civil servants at that time were very badly paid. My net income was eleven pounds, twelve shillings a month out of which I spent seven pounds ten shillings on board and lodging. That left me with practically nothing for entertainment.

I spent most of the money on books because I felt that I would have to improve my qualifications if I was to get out of this mess. So I studied for a legal BA following on the work which I had done as a lawyer's clerk and passed the attorney's examinations. For about a year I did nothing but the job and spent my spare time reading for a degree because we were given inducement in the form of a year's increment if one passed a university examination for a full year which I did at the end of 1927. I went on in 1928/29 and I finished the degree taking majors in Roman Law and Political Science which interested me .

During this period my horizons widened and I became more interested in the South African situation, particularly the relationship between black and white which in the Transvaal was far more severe, violent, than in my hometown. Well there were violences amongst blacks themselves. I used to go out on Saturdays and Sundays and watch crowds of Africans beat one another up on a hillside outside the built-up area which was set aside by the authorities for so-called games, but the games consisted of physical assaults with two teams of Africans engaged in this destruction.

Later on, when I read more widely, I discovered this was a phenomenon which had appeared also among workers in Britain during the 18th century, described by the Hammonds in their Village Labourer and Town Labourer. In the absence of organised games such as football, working class people created their own entertainment and almost always this consisted of violence, kicking not only a ball but also bodies. So that was one aspect of life.

Did you get involved in politics then?
Only as an observer. When I went into the civil service I was appointed to the Department of the Auditor General and I was attached to the Police Department as an auditor, not as a member of the Police Department. I was employed in the Department of Controller and Auditor General, but it was my duty to go through applications for funds and payments made, among others to informers.

I became very interested in this business of paying informers because I noticed large numbers of blacks were selling their own political people for trivial sums like half a crown, five bob, 10 shillings. They were bought and they gave information. This attracted my attention. Now another dimension of my interest, a growing interest, in the white-black dichotomy was as an auditor I used to go around to prisons in the Pretoria area and audit the books and I came to know something about the way in which black prisoners were treated. They were stripped when they came in from work outside and the warders would examine their bodies. They were standing naked in the square and probed in their orifices to see whether they were smuggling in prohibited stuff like dagga — and all this created a consciousness.

Then I would go to meetings conducted by African National Congress speakers in this region or in Johannesburg which isn't far off and also by what was called joint councils of whites and natives run by liberals. The ANC was slowly emerging from a period of unease. It was confronted by a government headed by Hertzog and Cresswell, the so-called Nationalist labour-backed government which was pushing through a white civilised labour policy giving preference to whites — even though they were unskilled and poorly educated — at the expense of blacks and this of course created a great deal of resentment, not that the Africans could do much about it.

What happened was that their leaders, people with some education, would interview the government, put forward protests. All this is described in general terms in books that were written much later about the rise of African nationalism and especially the ANC. There was not very much literature at the time, nor did the lectures which I attended for the first year deal much with the relationship between black and white. Whites accepted that this was the normal pattern — white supremacy, black subordination and blacks for the most part were still feeling their way in new society succumbed to this impact. They were learning their way — how to cope with the new civilisation.

At that stage did you also accept the idea of white supremacy?
Oh no, I never did. I had a deep-seated repugnance to the assertion that whites had the right, the innate right to be the top dog. This I developed at home when I was still

at school and I was the only one in my family, which consisted of brothers and sisters, there were six of us. Others were conformists, I was a rebel. Why I was a rebel, well I'm not sure whether I can tell myself. All I know is I never accepted the system. I was always the odd man out. But what influenced me then greatly was the outbreak of the depression, the Hungry Thirties which began in 1929 and went on throughout the Thirties, but not so much in South Africa.

You went to London about then?
Well I went to London in 1932 but not before I had seen the beginnings of a joint struggle between black and white. Unemployed people demonstrating, marching to Pretoria to present grievances and making contact with some of the rebels and radicals, including the communists. That was my first contact with them so that when I went to London in 1932 I had this kind of background of interest in politics, political philosophy, awareness of the tension and conflict between black and white. I chose as my thesis for my PhD crime and its treatment in South Africa with comparative notes on other African states, Kenya, I remember and Rhodesia as it then was.

Where did you study?
I went to the London School of Economics.

Why did you choose the LSE?
Well it had a reputation as a radical centre. I couldn't stomach the idea of going to the old universities of Oxford and Cambridge with their ritual and conformism and LSE — which had students form all over the world, including large numbers of Asians and some Africans — gave me the kind of insights I was looking for.

What was the political atmosphere like at LSE?
Oh, that was very interesting you know. There was then taking shape a Communist Party inside the universities and I linked up with them and we ran a club which was supposed to be social but we intended mainly to get to know people so that we could recruit them to the Party. Well I played rugby being South African and I played for the college and my circle widened.

How many years were you at the LSE?
I got there in 1932 and in 1934 I was expelled.

Why?
I was expelled for leading a campaign against a professor at the university by the name of Coatman who was formerly an Indian civil servant and he was accused by Indians at the school of being a spy for the Indian office spying on Indian students. We were producing a student paper and an article appeared in which this accusation was made against him. That sparked off a big row and a ban was imposed upon the paper. The little group to which I belonged sold the paper in spite of the ban and I accepted responsibility being the oldest chap, so they chucked me out.

What did you do then?

What happened was that the rugby club came to my rescue. They told the Principal that I was a very good lock forward and I was important for their team. It was Beveridge who was the Principal, the chap who introduced the British Social Service Welfare State, and after six months or so he lifted the ban and I went back. I was very pleased that this happened because it gave me the opportunity to finish my thesis. Otherwise I would never have done it.

Then after that I was active in the Communist Party in Britain. I worked as a research assistant for Lord Hailey who was writing a monumental work, *African Survey*. Hailey was a former civil servant from India with a great reputation for manipulation and manoeuvering and I was with him when the Simon Constitution was being adopted in India.

So I stayed there until I was appointed as a lecturer at the University of Cape Town and I took up that post in 1937. I taught African Studies with a speciality in law and colonial administration. It was called Native Administration in South Africa and tied up nicely with my experience in the Prisons and Justice Department to which I was transferred to at one stage. I remained in Cape Town until I was chucked out, not by the University but by the Minister of Justice, Vorster, in 1965.

When you went back in 1937 were your attitudes very different?

I suppose by that time I had developed a critical socialist outlook. I understood much more about the nature of imperialism and the way in which the South African system had developed under British rule. The writings I did at that stage were all connected with the spread of white man's rule and the history of the struggle. You see, I came to an association with the national liberation movement out of this background of radical socialism, the study of the greater writers, Marx, Engels, Lenin and Stalin, those were the people from whom I drew my stock of ideas.

I wasn't ever a Marxist in the sense that I took over the whole corpus of ideas and made them my own. I was impatient of people who would spout texts. That was one of the things that put me off the Trotskyists because they would always recite scripture on any argument — this was the conclusive thing — and I preferred to come to my own conclusions which were often at variance with those arrived at by the Marxist leaders, although within the general framework of their theories.

Did you meet up with other communists in South Africa?

From 1932 to 1937, five years, there were very few at the time because the Communist Party in South Africa was undergoing a great upheaval. It ran into lots of difficulties and it wasn't making a contribution to a theoretical position. It was engaged in active struggle.

By the time I came back the wounds that had been left by a long period of internal dissent accompanied by dismissal with which I wasn't involved because I was absent, or because it happened before I joined the Communists, had started to heal. It was possible to build a new kind of structure and I became involved in that from the outset

What did those activities involve, did you have newspaper, a publication?

Well, one thing which occupied our attention was a campaign against fascism and war. Remember this is now two or three years before the war begins and there were Nazi and fascist groups inside South Africa, black shirts, grey shirts, who attacked the Left at public meetings, resulting in physical conflicts. There were problems connected with this. Were Africans, who had their own kind of fascism in an indigenous form, to be involved in these conflicts with whites? The tendency developed to separate them, blacks who deal with their own problems arising from oppression and racial discrimination, while the offensive against the set movements would be undertaken by the white radicals, members of the Communist Party and those associated with them. So there was a clear distinction. Now it seemed to me, and those with whom I worked, that that was a dangerous kind of dichotomy. We should bring them together. And this is what was done, first of all in Cape Town and then in other parts of South Africa. The Party was being refashioned.

Was holding a wide range of people together within the Party one of your recurrent themes?

The great emphasis was upon the absence of any form of discrimination, no racial inequality and coupled with that, in my own case, a determination that blacks should take the lead, recognising that this was a society in which the great majority of people were black and they were the oppressed majority. It seemed to me necessary that wherever possible blacks should take responsibility as chairmen, secretaries and so on and get accustomed to providing leadership. This was going on in the Party. It was the only non-racial political movement — I wouldn't have belonged to it if this were not so — that turned from being a purely white party as it was formerly to being a Party dominated by Africans in the main. This had begun 10 years before — 1928 to be precise.

How did your politics reflect your relationship with people outside the Party?

Well, I was very largely isolated. At the university there were two or three of the staff, one was a Britisher who afterwards went to Sudan, Khartoum and another an Australian.

Who was he?

I can't recall him now. They were on the staff and I think they were the only two, apart from myself. But we had a growing number of students. We conducted classes and carried on debates as students were moving into that orbit. This was a period of intense political rivalry and dispute, not only internally because of the policies pursued by the reactionary government, but also on the world front with the threat of war and actually the outbreak of war in the last resort. So that politicised a great many people and I think this is a convenient time to stop.

Recording resumes: The biggest influence on my life has been the close, and, on the whole harmonious relationship between Ray and myself. One thing she brought me into was the stream of tactical working-class organisation, which I wouldn't have gone into on my own. I had other commitments working in townships, carrying on fieldwork among Africans, and this took up a lot of my time. But her preoccupation with the practical work of organising trade unions led me to take a hand, if only drafting leaflets, talking to workers, writing a few articles about the conditions of the workers.

Can you remember how you first met her?
My recollection is that I was living in a flat in the Mowbray area and I got to know her sister. Her sister came to see me at the flat and through her sister I came to know Ray. But that was on a purely personal basis. The working relationship which afterwards deepened into a tie, marital tie, developed over the years, between 1937 when I came back and 1941 when we married.

Didn't you have a letter of recommendation for her?
Not to her, no. I had a letter addressed to chap called Schnitzer, Advocate Schnitzer, who was then prominent in the Party, introducing myself and there wasn't a very big circle. I gravitated imperceptibly to the small group of communists who were active in Cape Town and I was asked to join their committee. They were concerned mainly with trade unions and Ray was one of them, so I think that would be correct. There was no special reason why the letters should be addressed to her by people in London.

Ray told me that you brought her the letter and she was at the meeting, that was a letter of introduction, and she took it and read it and then said to you, "I'll contact you later. I'm busy now."
(Laughs.) Maybe.

What was the political situation like in South Africa in the Forties?
I told you about the campaigns we ran against war. There was a peace committee set up on which I was active and our attempts to work up resistance to the spread of fascist ideology.

Were there any conscientious objectors and were any of them thrown into jail?
When the war broke out the position in South Africa was somewhat obscure because there was a great deal of opposition to the war from the Afrikaner National Party which was in opposition to the government. In South Africa it was not like elsewhere because there was a split among the whites, some of whom, at least Afrikaners, were opposed to the policy of the government supporting the war effort while the majority of whites were for it. Africans, coloureds, Indians, were generally in support.

The Communist Party, I was then at the time on the Central Committee, took up the attitude that this was an imperialist war and that sparked off a long debate and aroused much opposition. But we stuck to it and some of our members went to prison for opposing the war and issuing leaflets condemning it. They weren't conscientious objectors because there was no conscription. One of the features of the South African scene was that the government couldn't force people to go to war, there was too much opposition spread around, but they could be punished for calling on people to oppose the war effort.

Now that the changed in 1941, June, when Hitler invaded the Soviet Union. The Communist Party then switched, it turned right round and declared this was a peoples' war, that the war was being fought by the Access Powers to crush the socialist fatherland and to smash the Soviet Union — and it was the duty of Communists everywhere to rally to the defence of the Soviet Union. From 1941 to the end of the war in 1945, four years, the Party was very active in mobilising support, while at the same time carrying on a political campaign for the removal of disabilities imposed upon blacks. That became in fact our central cry, rather than out-and-out support for the war. We demanded that in order to mobilise people in South Africa for a war effort people should be free and we got engaged in constant struggle for workers' rights.

There must have been some hope after the war?
No, this wasn't so. In 1945, as a consequence of the efforts of Communists, a trade union came to the fore — the trade union of African miners. They pulled off a strike in 1946, a big strike. The strike was broken because the army and police were summoned and they drove the men back underground, into the slopes, into the mines. As a result of this upheaval, because it created a great deal of uproar, the Central Committee of the Communist Party, of which I was a member, was charged with sedition. We went through a whole series of trials in the courts, from 1946, it dragged on through 1948 to 1950.

When the new Nationalist government came into office in 1948, it put a ban on the Communist Party and drove us into a state of illegality. So towards the end of the war we realised that there would be a marked swing to reaction and the Party actually issued a statement in 1945 warning people that they must expect a strong reaction, resumption of the struggle as was continued in the period before the war.

So the Communist Party lost many of its supporters when it went underground?
Ja, it shrunk a great deal. You can't take a party which had existed legally into an underground situation without making sacrifices. Moreover the government prepared lists of communists drawn from the files of the party which they had seized during these raids and they placed us on a banned list. All of us were banned and were exposed to penalties such as expulsion from trade unions. Ray was expelled, together with other trade union organisers. It was mainly illegal for them to carry on organising. If they did so, they had to do it underground.

How many were listed?
How many communists and trade union organisers? I'd say the numbers must have been about 60, which was a considerable part of the total experienced and skilled trade union organisers because the communists had been in the field for many years

organising blacks and coloured workers as Ray was doing and building up quite a significant body of organised trade unionists. The government was determined to smash this and unfortunately they bullied the rest of the trade union movement to follow suit.

That is how the split occurred in the formation of SACTU — the South African Congress of Trade Unions — which refused to go along with the main body of white workers who rejected black trade unions on the grounds that they were not eligible for registration under the industrial reconciliation act. Of course, all these things became very complicated. For instance, the history of SACTU, the history of the workers' struggle for trade union recognition, goes back decades before that to the introduction in 1924 of an industrial conciliation act which excluded Africans from the collective bargaining system. This consisted of industrial councils where workers and employers sat together and negotiated deals. Now Africans were not allowed to be there, either directly or by proxy.

White workers took advantage of this situation and made agreements with bosses at the expense of the African worker. They would get wage increases for themselves by denying increases to the Africans so the effect was to widen the gap between white and black workers. This exemplifies the principle which I have explained before that in a society where only a section of the population has political rights, or if you like power, it will use these rights to prejudice the position of the others who are not voters.

I think this is universally the case. Elections were fought in South Africa ever since the coming into being of the Act of Union of 1910, this is a British Act, between parties who would make a political football of the black worker, trying to improve the conditions.

What other political parties have taken up the struggle to end apartheid?
There were many non-white groups, some organising what was called the non-European Unity Movement led largely by coloureds and nowadays by Africans who tried to establish a leading position using Africans as a base but rejecting the communist-dominant position as they saw it in an ideological field.

How one can explain it is in terms of the ascendancy of sections of the population who previously were deprived of opportunities and facilities for leadership, and they compete now with the communists who include members of all racial groups and actually developed leadership among Africans, Indians and coloureds as well as whites. Now that position is challenged by coloureds, later on challenged by Indians, and challenged by some Africans who don't want to have a mixed non-racial party under communist domination.

For one thing it is dangerous. People who belong to the Communist Party are liable to be persecuted, jailed, driven out of their jobs, so there is a natural tendency for other radicals who also want change to steer clear of Marxism and maybe they don't believe in the communist approach and its philosophy. So there are different elements and groups that compete and still do.

The present situation is that the ANC heads a de facto alliance of trade unions like SACTU which I mentioned before, the Communist Party, Indians, coloureds, who formerly had separate organisations of their own but now have all merged in what is the ANC, a liberation movement, a broad one which encompasses all kinds of races. But then there is a black consciousness movement, a forum, so-called platform.

The PAC?
The PAC which isn't now very much in evidence. Are you interested in the PAC? Why?

In Australia a lot of people don't know the difference between the PAC and the ANC. Would you like to explain their ideological differences?
The Pan African Movement, PAC, came into existence round about 1958 after a dissident group resented the presence of the communists. Although the communists were illegal in the ANC only because their presence there endangered others, people found cohabiting or associating with communists were liable to police persecution.

And there were other influences at work, for instance from the United States, trying to split the liberation movement from the communists who were gradually spreading their influence, not by any devious conspiratorial methods, but because of the kind of leadership that they provided, and they were active in the ANC. Men like (Moses) Kotane, (Edwin) Mofetjenyana, JB Marks, a whole host of them were communists who were working in the mass organisation.

Now this breakaway group, which came into existence under the leadership of a chap called Sobukwe, a lecturer at the University of the Witwatersrand, attended a meeting of the Pan African Congress in Ghana. It was sponsored by Nkrumah at the time. Oh, this is a very interesting, a long history of the Pan African Movement throughout the continent. This meeting influenced people who came back to set up the Pan African Congress in opposition to the ANC. They objected to the ANC on the grounds that it was dominated by Moscow, Peking and Delhi, that it had whites who were communists, Indians who were subordinate to India and the Peking influence was supposed to be spread by adherence to Maoism.

So the PAC then launched on its own. It wasn't much in numbers or influence but in 1960 an event occurred that gave them a big boost. The ANC had called for an anti-pass law campaign and the burning of passes, a chronic issue. It cropped up periodically and it still is in the forefront of political agitation. The PAC anticipated this event and cashed in on the campaign that the ANC had been organising and called for a banning of the passes. This led to an incident at Sharpeville in the Transvaal where a whole crowd of people, Africans, came along to demonstrate.

Do you object to the PAC on the grounds of its being too militant or because it is a black consciousness movement?
Originally the communists objected to the PAC because it split the united front and it had this racialism built into it. It isn't so markedly racial now, it works with coloureds and it has had whites prominent in its ranks, but still preaches a kind of nationalism which is exclusive and therefore does not contemplate the kind of South

Africa that the ANC and the communists together think of — one in which there is unity without any racial discrimination and where people can build a common society. Now that isn't the PAC emphasis. The PAC emphasis is on Africans and we don't think that this is correct in principle or in the circumstances of the South African society.

How real do you think the changes are that are taking place in South Africa today?
I suppose you're now thinking of the government's reforms. Of course there have been changes, you might say in social relations. Barriers which were imposed in previous years have been lifted, such as the removal of a ban on interracial marriages and sex, that's gone. It's now possible for blacks to go into hotels which were exclusively set aside for whites and some beaches have been desegregated and are thrown open to people of different races.

One can go on elaborating, but the essential elements of the apartheid system and of the segregation policies that existed prior to the coming into being of apartheid, still persist. One, on the division of land which I mentioned before, no change has happened to that. In fact in the past 20 years, right down to present time as in that little booklet I showed you, blacks are still being ousted from their traditional homes where they have existed, sometimes for centuries, before the white man came and hounded into the Bantustans. The land partitioning has not been altered and no additional land has been given to blacks. The 87% set aside for white occupation remains intact.

Once apartheid is abolished and there is black majority rule, what will happen to the Bantustans? Is there going to be a problem?
Yes, the movement has not been able to grapple with it because the Bantustans are governed by men with the background of tribal authority. They are descendants of chiefs, or claim to be that, so they wear the mantle of kinship like this chap Sabata. You saw how much veneration he received from the ANC because he is a rare exception, a *rara avis*. He is a bird who has flown over into our nest and we treasure him. He's like a prodigal son who has come home and we shower praise upon him. But there are not many like that.

Most of the chiefs find it more expedient, more profitable to themselves, to operate within the framework of the apartheid system and to get benefits from the racist government. Now what are we to do about them? They created power systems. This can easily be explained. Prior to the setting up of the apartheid system, the government in Pretoria would set aside funds for the payment of teachers, agricultural demonstrators, health workers, people who are employed by the state in the rural areas called reserves.

Now, with the establishment of Bantustans, the money which was paid for their services as wages was handed over to the treasuries of these different states. It therefore became possible for the government of these states to hand out concessions, appoint and promote. They had all the power accruing to a government and they created dependencies. It is not at all clear whether the beneficiaries — the clerks, the professional people, even the teachers — will welcome a new South Africa without colour bars in which the barriers which have been created will be removed.

Now I think that the great bulk of people will follow the ANC if it does away with the restrictions on land. Because land hunger is one constant cry, as in New Zealand, as in all areas where a minority group has lost control of its ancestral lands.

So how will land be distributed under an ANC government?
The Freedom Charter, which sets out the bare elements of a democratic programme, has got a formula which says land shall belong to those who work it, but this is very unsatisfactory. Those who work it are labourers, or peasants. How are they going to work the land? On small plots with hand tools? There will have to be a radical revision because most of the productive land is in the hands of whites, many of whom are large-scale producers. They contribute agro businesses, they have farms of 20 000 hectares, huge estates growing mielies, maize, wheat, in some cases oranges and sugar plantations.

Now what's going to be done about this? If it were physically possible for land to be taken away from these groups and carved up and distributed in small plots, it is quite likely that the output would fall and there would be an acute shortage of foodstuffs. You can't afford that, so some kind of new system of agriculture on a big scale will have to be developed, like state farms where the land belongs to the state and people are employed for a wage or cooperatives.

But these are long-term solutions, you can't make the transition from private ownership to state farms or collective ownership overnight. There have to be managers, trained and prepared for this job and the cooperation of the people has to be obtained. So all this needs to be worked out and it's very difficult to do so on paper. They have to grapple with it in practice.

Can you see the white minority eventually accommodating itself to black rule?
I think some will, yes, an increasing number. We noticed this in other parts of Africa. One example of this is Zimbabwe. Most of the whites remain, a large number left. I suppose, I can't say offhand, 50% of the whites cleared off but many of them are coming back.

You ask Johan about this and you will see that that phenomenon is now giving rise to a great shortage of housing because when the whites pulled out, houses were taken over, sometimes by immigrants, sometimes by blacks. When the whites who went to South African from Zimbabwe wanted to return — and many of them do now because South Africa is even less stable than Zimbabwe was when they left — they find that there are no houses and that's an indication of the fact that whites can live under black man's rule.

But of course there is a solid core of reactionaries who will put up a stubborn resistance and it is conceivable, as in that paper that I was jotting down some ideas of a blacklash as is often talked about and white vigilantes using arms against blacks who are not attacking them.
There my tape ends

New tape (no date). Sounds of dinner time

I think you must bear in mind the numerical predominance of blacks is crucial and the source of great anxiety to whites. I told you before that the situation in Africa is greatly different from the situation in Australia or in New Zealand or Canada. Here the oppressed people are a majority. They are very vocal and visible and active. Also, they are important in the economy. The economy couldn't work without them whereas Aborigines and Indians are marginal to the economy and could be dispensed with. That is the guarantee that the South African revolution will succeed ultimately.

Do you think there will always be pockets of resistance from the Boer?
No. When blacks overcome their fear of death which is decisive then the whites will have lost the battle. That happened in Iran when the civil population stood before the soldiers. The soldiers fired into the mob and killed them and this was repeated until eventually some of the soldiers refused and I think that will happen too. The black and coloured soldiers will refuse to fight and then the whites are not able to do it in their own.

They don't have the numbers then?
They can't afford to open a race war like that. It is not acceptable, anywhere. You can be sure that Afrikaners are discussing this dilemma even more easily and assiduously than we are.

Which section of the white population would be opposing democracy most — the ones with money or the white workers?
At the moment the white workers are opposing the change. They are the hard core of the Weerstandsbeweging and other neo-Fascist groups.

Because they've got the most to lose?
They are close to the blacks on the ground and the whites' properties are protected, insulated. They are concerned with protecting their property.
Ray: South Africans would like to bring about change peacefully so that all their capital interests with multinational companies should remain intact and against revolutionary change.
Jack: I insist they don't compete. The black worker who gets education and skills may take the job from the white worker or live in the same area, but he's not going to live in Parktown or Kenilworth. There isn't unity between white workers and black workers at the moment. I think it will come slowly. If this business were to carry on for another 20 years, maybe at the end of that period the white worker will enter into a period of solidarity with blacks. In this case, the system would topple.

The other option is that the blacks won't put up with it that long which is the thing that the liberation movement envisages. They believe it will come about like that. How could it be speeded up? We have different patterns. Our major obstacle isn't South Africa — it comes from the West. There is increasing evidence that

America, which speaks for the West, is out to suppress what they call centres of communism. They'll leave the Soviet Union alone to be dealt with later. Their immediate strategy is to uproot and destroy all outposts of communist influence. Now South Africa is so regarded. They won't accept the ANC because of its communist orientations with its links to the socialist countries.

Hasn't the Ford Motor Company moved out of Port Elizabeth?
Jack: They are going to Pretoria.
Ray: Their explanation was that there was too much unrest in the Eastern Province.
Jack: That's just like the removal of American firms from the United States itself to outer space. One reason is that they get into a country without unions. You forget Witsand in Bophuthatswana. What happened last week where an estimated 30 blacks were killed by Bophuthatswana police. Any industrialisation will take place in the Bantustans. You see this area is an enclave to the white-dominated region of Pretoria. Blacks have always stayed there. They transferred this region to Bophuthatswana with the townships and slums and some industrial base and that can be expanded and this is what the Ford Company plans to do. But they do this even in America on a big scale.
Ray: Bophuthatswana also has platinum mines. The Bophuthatswana government has not given the National Union of Mineworkers the right to organise the Bophuthatswana miners but has given the right to the white miners' unions so they exposed themselves.
Tape ends

Name: Harold Jack Simons
Birth: 1st February 1907
Place: Riversdale, Cape Province
School: Riversdale

Education

BA in Political Science, Transvaal University College, Pretoria 1928;
MA Transvaal University College, Pretoria, 1931. Title: *Crime and Punishment with reference to the native population of South Africa;*
PhD London School of Economics 1936. Title: *A Study of Crime Law and Its Administration in South Africa Southern Rhodesia and Kenya.*

Employment

Employed temporarily by Department of Justice while working for MA;
UCT 1937-1967 (lecturer 1937-1954: senior lecturer 1954-1959; associate professor 1959-1967; (April 1965-December 1967 overseas on leave) Department of Native Law and Administration (CAGAL);
1969-1975 Department of Sociology (later Social Development Studies), University of Zambia, first as Reader, then as Professor and Head of Department.

Awards

Porter Scholarship awarded by UNISA to attend LSE 1931
Fellow: Simon Senior Research Fellow 1965-67 (re-awarded 1966-67), Manchester University, England.
Other: Executive Committee, SAIRR 1942-1948
Advisory Board of African Social Research. Journal of Institute for African Studies, University of Zambia 1974-1976 Joint Editor, African Social Research 1976-1980
Editorial Consultant, *Africa Social Research* 1981-1983 one of the initiators, if not the initiator of African (Scholars) Bursary Fund

Publications

Simons HJ & Ballinger, ML. "Memorandum on the need for penal reform in South Africa" prepared for SAIRR 1943.
Simons HJ & RE *Job reservation and the trade unions.* Woodstock CT Enterprise 1959
Simon HJ. *African Women: Their legal status in South Africa.* London. Hurst 1968
Simons HJ & RE. *Class and Colour in South Africa 1850-1950.* Harmondsworth.

Penguin 1969. Republished: London: International Defence and Aid Fund,1983
Simons HJ (et al) "Slums or self-reliance? Urban growth in Zambia". Lusaka:
University of Zambia, Institute for African Studies, 1976.

Contributions to books
See chapter in Lord Hailey's *Africa Survey.*
"Trade Unionism in South Africa", in *Handbook on Race Relations*, edited by E
Hellman. Cape Town. OUP for SAIRR, 1949.
"The Law and Its Administration" in *Handbook on Race Relations*, edited by
E Hellman. Cape Town. OUP for SAIRR. 1949
"Race Relations and policies in Southern and Eastern Africa" in *Most of the
World: The Peoples of Africa, Latin America and the East today*, edited by
Ralph Linton. New York: Columbia University Press, 1949.
"What are the National Groups in South Africa?" Cape Town: Forum Club, 1954.
Paper presented at the Symposium on the National Question.
Perspectives in Civilization in *The Western Tradition.* NUSAS, 1958.
The Status of Africa Women in *Africa in Transition*, edited by Prudence Smith.
London: Rheinhard, 1958
"A Statistical Comment on the Position of Women" in *Women's Rights in Zambia:
Report of a Consultation.* Kitwe. 1970.
Preface to *Passing for white: A study of racial assimilation in a South African
School*, by Graham Watson London: Tavistock, 1970.
The Urban Situation in Zambia, in *Human Settlements in Zambia.* Lusaka:
National Housing Authority, 1975.
Zambia's Urban Situation in *Development in Zambia: A reader*, edited by Ben
Turok. London: Zed, 1979.

Periodical articles
"European Civilization and African Crime", *African Observer* (Bulawayo), 2, 1934.
"The Study of Native Law in South Africa", *Bantu Studies.* 12. 1938.
"Disabilities of the Native in the Union of South Africa", *Race Relations Journal.* 6.
1939.
"Some Aspects of Urban Native Administration", *Race Relations*, 7, 1940.
"The Coloured Worker and Trade Unionism", *Race Relations*, 9, 1942.
"Claims of the African in Municipal Government", *Race Relations*, 13, 1946.
"Passes and Police", *South African*,1, 1956.
"African Women and the Law" in *South African Listener*, 55, 1956.
"Tribal Medicine: Diviners and Herbalists" in *African Studies*,16, 1957.
"Tribal Worship", *Africa South*,1, 1957.
"Mental Disease in Africans: Racial determinism", *Journal of Mental Science*, 104,
1958 also in *Race Relations Journal*, 25, 1958.
"Customary Unions in a Changing Society", *Acta Juridica*, 1958.
"No Revolution Around the Corner: An Addendum", *Africa South*, 3, 1958.
"What is Apartheid", *Liberation*, 35,1959.

"Marriage and Succession Among Africans", *Acta Juridica*, 1960.
"The Status of Customary Unions", *Acta Juridica*, 1961.
"Death in South African Mines", *Africa South in Exile*, 5, 1961.
"Prologue", *Africa Social Research*, 24, 1977, pp 259-273

Review article
"Chief, Council and Commissioner", *African Social Research*, 11, 1971.

Book reviews
Administrative Reform by GE Caiden, *African Social Research*, 11, 1971.
The Oxford History of SA, Vol. 11 1870-1966 by Thompson & M Wilson.
    African Social Research, 13, 1972.
From Protest to Challenge: A Documentary History of African Politics in SA
    1882-1964 Vol 11 *Hope and Challenge 1935-1952*, edited by T Karis,
    G Carter, *African Social Research*, 1975.
People of the Valley: Life in an Isolated Afrikaner Community in SA by Brian du
    Toit, *African Social Research*, 19,1975.
Democratie und Nationale Integration in Nigeria: Eine multivariable Analyse der
    Spaltungs — und Spannungsstrukturen des Nationbuilding-Prozesses in einen
    Afrikanischen Staat (1960 bis 1965) by Patrick Eze Ollawa, *African Social*
    Research, 20, 1975.
Class Struggles in Tanzania by Issa G Shivji, African Social Research, 23, 1977
Politics of the Tanzania-Zambia Railproject: A Study of Tanzania-China-Zambia
    Relations by Kasuka S Mutukwa, *African Social Research*, 26, 1978.
South Africa: War, Revolution or Peace? by LH Gann & P Duignan, African Social
    Research, 28,1979.

Addendum
"The Gold Coast Constitution". Discussion, Vol. 1, No 3, Forum Club,
    Landsdowne, June, 1951:52-60
"Our Party", 1981. A talk to CP members in Tanzania to commemorate the 60th
    anniversary of the SACP: 18 typed pp.
"The meaning of Race", Read at seminar at UCT: racist concepts and the scientific
    approach. 16 typed pages, moth-eaten but legible.
"From Colonial Capital to Industrial Capitalism in South Africa, A Case Study in
    Development Theory!" A paper read at a seminar arranged by the Department
    of Development Administration, University of South Africa, Pretoria, on
    Thursday, 20th September, 1990 on the theme: Development Administration,
    Now and in Future. 19 pp with biographical introduction. Unpublished.
"South Africa's Family and Marriage Law Reformed. Towards One System for all
South Africans". A paper read at a seminar held in the Centre for African Studies
    University of Cape Town, 26 June 1991, 25pp.
"South Africa's Common Society" Presented at the seminar of the African Studies
    Institute, University of the Witwatersrand, Johannesburg, February 1991.

Handed to Andries Odendaal of UWC, together with copy of paper on "South Africa's Civil War",1990.

"The Great French Revolution: An enduring heritage", *The African Communist*, no. 118, 1989: 16-30.

"The 73rd Anniversary of the Russian Social Revolution of October 1917", Read at Workers Library, Johannesburg, on 27 October 1990. with illustrations. 9pp. in press.

"African Marriage Under Apartheid", introduced at Conference on Social Change and Legal Reform in Southern Africa, Jan 13-16, Harare Zimbabwe. 35pp with bibliography.

List of interviews conducted and biographical details

Robert Mandita
MK name: Uncle, Meshengu, Raymond
Date of interview: August 19 1991
Responsibilities in Seventies: Left South Africa for military training in 1977.
Military instructor to June 16 Detachment in Novo Catengue.
Based in Military Headquarters, Johannesburg on return from exile.

January Masilela
MK name: Ché Ogara
Date of interview: August 15 1991
Responsibilities in Seventies: Member of June 16th Detachment. Trained by
Comrade Jack as political instructor. Served as regional commissar in
Angola.Served on SACP Central Committee.
On return served as MEC in Mpumalanga. Currently Secretary for Defence,
Department of Defence.

Reggie Mhlongo
MK name: Reggie Mpongo
Date of interview: August 19 1991
Responsibilities in Seventies: Member of June 16 Detachment. Trained as political
instructor under Comrade Jack.
Served in ANC Youth League Office in Johannesburg on return from exile.

Magdalena Mokoena
MK name: Comrade Precious
Date of interview: August 20 1991
Responsibilities in Seventies: Member of June 16 Detachment.
Based in Special Projects, Military Headquarters, Johannesburg on return from
exile.

Joel Netshitenzhe
MK name: Peter Mayibuye
Date of interview: August 20 1991
Responsibilities in Seventies: Member of June 16 Detachment. Famously known as
Mayibuye because of his work with Radio Freedom and the DIP publications.
Based in Shell House as Editor of *Mayibuye* on return from exile.
Serves on ANC NEC. Serves as Head of Policy Coordination Advisory Services in the
Presidency. Currently CEO of the Government Communication Information System.

Raymond Suttner
Studied under Comrade Jack at UCT in 1960s. Jailed for SACP propaganda work in 1977. Active in UDF leadership. Head of ANC Department of Political Education (DPE) since unbanning. Elected to ANC NEC July 1991.Served as MP in National Assembly and as Chairperson of Foreign Affairs Portfolio Committee. Ambassador to Sweden

Chris Thembisile Hani
MK name: Comrade Chris
Date of interview: August 16 1991
Left South Africa in 1963 as member of ANC, MK and SACP. Served as MK Commissar and then as MK Chief of Staff. Member of SACP Central Committee. Member of ANC NEC. General Secretary, SACP.
Assassinated 10 April 1993.

SP Makwetla
MK name: Thabang
Date of interview: August 21 1991
Member of June 16 Detachment.Went into exile in 1977. Trained in Quibaxe Camp, Angola 1978. Wounded in 1986/7 attack on Botswana.Jailed in Botswana for almost 10 years.
Served in ANC Youth League office, Johannesburg on return from exile. Served as MP in National Assembly. Chairperson of ANC Caucus. Redeployed to North-West Province.

Mark Shope
Date of interview: August 13 1991
Veteran trade unionist and ANC member. Treason trialist; Detained under Emergency 1960. Went into exile early 1960s. Was Chief Political Instructor under Commissar Francis Meli, then took over as Commissar in Novo Catengue 1978. Served as Chief Rep in Nigeria from 1978. Member of ANC NEC in exile.
Passed away 2000.

Ronnie Kasrils
MK name: ANC Khumalo
Date of interview: August 19 1991
Veteran of ANC, MK and SACP. Political instructor in Quibaxe camp, Angola 1977.
Regional Political Commissar in Angola. Head of Military Intelligence. Member of ANC NEC from Kabwe Conference 1985. Sought by police during Vula detentions. Indemnified in 1991. Serves on ANC NEC and SACP Central Committee. Served as Deputy Minister of Defence.
Currently Minister of Water Affairs and Forestry.

Christian Pepani
MK name: Ntokozo Phefo
Date of interview: August 14 1991
Member of June 16 Detachment. Trained by Comrade Jack as political instructor.
Head of Political Department in Novo Catengue in 1978/9. Served as ANC Chief
Rep in Libya
Brigadier General in SANDF

Mzwai Piliso
Date of interview: August 15 1991
In 1977 was Head of Personnel and Training in MK. Left for refresher training in
1979. Returned in 1981 no longer directly involved in MK structures. Served as
Head of Department of Manpower Development, ANC.
MP in National Assembly until he passed away in 1996.

Wolfie Kodesh
Veteran of SACP, Congress of Democrats and ANC. Head of Logistics Department,
MK. Currently lives in the Western Cape and has been involved in recording oral
history for the University of the Western Cape.

Thami Ngwevela
MK name: Olga Pauline
Member of June16 Detachment.
Worked at UCT, Cape Town on return from exile.
Ambassador to Ethiopia.

Albie Sachs
Left South Africa whilst still an advocate in the Supreme Court, CT. Read PhD at
Sussex University, later senior lecturer of law at University of Southampton. From
1977 to 1983, Professor of Law at Eduardo Mondlane University in Maputo,
thereafter became Director of Research at Mozambique Ministry of Justice. In 1988
survived car-bomb attack on his life. Elected to ANC NEC in 1991 until his
appointment as (current) Constitutional Court Judge.

Further Reading

A Science & social change
Scientific methodologies
Thomas S Kuhn, *The Structure of Scientific Revolutions*, Chicago: University of Chicago Press 1970
Roy Bhaskar, *A Realist Theory of Science*, Brighton: Harvester Press 1978

B Scientific & industrial revolutions
Eric J Hobsbawm, *The Age of Revolution; The Age of Capital*, London: Abacus 1998
Harry Braverman, *Labour and Monopoly Capital*, New York: Monthly Review Press 1974

C African Science
Martin Bernal, *Black Athena*, London: Vintage 1991
Cheik Anta Diop, *The Cultural Unity of Black Africa*
George M Foster, *Traditional Cultures and the Impact of Technological Change*

D Dialectics of change
Dialectics
Bertell Ollman, *Dialectical Investigations*, New York: Routledge 1993
Louis Althusser, *For Marx*, London: Verso 1996
Idealism & Materialism
Marx & Engels, *The German Ideology*, New York: International Publishers 1995
Historical Materialism
Forces & Relations of Production, *Capital*, Marx
GA Cohen, *Karl Marx's Theory of History*, Princeton NJ: Princeton University Press 1978
Bober MM, *Karl Marx's Interpretation of History*, 1962
Base & Superstructure
Marx, *A Contribution to the Critique of Political Economy*
Ellen Meiksins Wood, *Democracy against Capitalism*, Cambridge: Cambridge University Press 1995
Schumpeter Joseph, A, *Capitalism, Socialism and Democracy*, 1943
JA Banks, *Marxist Sociology in Action*, Faber and Faber 1970

E The Communist Manifesto (best translations in English)
Marx & Engels, *The Communist Manifesto*, London: Verso 1998
Marx, *Later Political Writings*, Terrell Carver (ed), Cambridge: Cambridge University Press 1996
David McLellan, *The Thought of Karl Marx*, Macmillan, 1971

David McLellan, *Marx before Marxism*, 1970
Mabhida Moses, *The impact of Marx and Marxism on the developing world in Political Affairs*

F Social Formations

Class
Marx, *1844 Manuscripts in Early Writings*, New York: Vintage 1975
Nicos Poulantzas, *Classes in Contemporary Capitalism*, London: Verso 1978
EP Thompson, *The Making of the English Working Class*
Mao Tse-Tung, *Analysis of the Classes in Chinese Society*
Jack Simons & Ray Alexander, *Class and Colour in South Africa 1850-1950*
Historical types of society
Marx, *Pre-capitalist Economic Formations*, London: Lawrence & Wishart 1975
Goran Hyden, *Beyond Ujamaa in Tanzania*, Berkeley: University of California Press 1980

G Proletarian revolutions

General
Lenin *The Tasks of the Proletariat in our Revolutions*, 1917
Lenin *What is to be Done* 1902
Sweezy Paul M, *The Transition to Socialism* May 1971
European revolutions
Eric J Hobsbawm, *The Age of Revolution*, London: Abacus 1998
George C Comninel, *Rethinking the French Revolution*, London: Verso 1987
Marx Karl and Engels Friedrich, *Writings on the Paris Commune*, Ed Hal Draper Monthly Review Press 1971
Engels, *Germany: Revolution and counter revolution*, 1851
Russia
John Reed, *Ten Days that Shook the World*, New York: Penguin Books 1986
VI Lenin, *What Is To Be Done?*, New York: International Publishers 1988
Germany
FL Carsten, *Revolution in Central Europe*, Berkeley: University of California Press 1972
Rosa Luxemburg, *Rosa Luxemburg Speaks*, New York: Pathfinder Press 1970
Europe
Antonio Gramsci, *Selections from the Prison Notebooks*, New York: International Publishers 1989
Perry Anderson, *Considerations on Western Marxism*, London: Verso 1979
Africa
Charles C McCollester, *The African Revolution: theory and practice.* 1973
Moses Mabhida, *The Impact of Marx and Marxism on the developing world*, in Political Affairs
John Saul, *Frelimo and the Mozambique revolution*, 1973
Mary Benson (ed), *The Sun Will Rise: Statements from the dock by*

Southern African political prisoners, 1981. London. International Defence and Aid Fund for Southern Africa

H Social democracy

Karl Kautsky, *The Class Struggle*, New York: Norton 1971
Michael Harrington, *Socialism*, New York: Saturday Review Press 1972

I National Liberation

Bourgeois revolutions
Marx, *The 18th Brumaire of Louis Bonaparte in Later Political Writings*, Terrell Carver (ed.), Cambridge: Cambridge University Press 1996
George C Comninel, *Rethinking the French Revolution*, London: Verso 1987
National liberation
VI Lenin, *The National Liberation Movement in the East*
J Stalin, *The Working Class and the National Question* and *Theses on the National Question*
Lenin, *The Socialist Revolution and the Right of Nations to self-determination*
Eric Mtshali, *Trade Unions, the Party and the struggle for liberation*, (SACP)
Lucy Mair, *New Nations*, Weidenfeld and Nicolson. 1963
Colonial capitalism
Colin Leys, *Underdevelopment in Kenya*, Berkeley: University of California Press 1975
Walter Rodney, *How Europe Underdeveloped Africa*
National consciousness
VI Lenin, *The National Liberation Movement in the East*, Moscow: Progress Publishers 1952

J Theory of Revolution

Permanent revolution
Leon Trotsky, *The Permanent Revolution*, London: New Park Press 1962
VI Lenin, *Two Tactics of Social Democracy*
"*Long live the October Socialist Revolution, Build our struggle Behind the Lessons of the October Revolution*", SACP pamphlet
Cornforth Maurice, *The open philosophy and the open society*. 1968, Lawrence and Wishart
Karl Marx and Friedrich Engels, *Writings on the Paris Commune*. Ed Hal Draper. Monthly Review Press 1971
The History of the CPSU(B)
Vanguard party
VI Lenin, *What Is To Be Done?*, New York: International Publishers 1988
Objective & subjective conditions; class consciousness
Georg Lukacs, *History and Class Consciousness*, Cambridge MA: MIT Press 1983
Trade unions
Michael Burawoy, *The Politics of Production*, London: Verso 1985

Jeremy Baskin, *Striking Back*, London: Verso 1991

Mike Davis, *Prisoners of the American Dream*, London: Verso 1986

K Elements of Socialist Construction

Emergent socialism

Alec Nove, *Socialism, Economics, and Development*, London: Boston, Allen & Unwin 1986

JP Nettl, *The Soviet Achievement*, New York: Harcourt Brace 1967

II Yegrov, *State Capitalism and the Reproductive Process in the Newly Liberated Countries of the East*, USSAR Academy of Sciences. Institute of Oriental Studies. Central Department of Oriental Literature. Moscow 1979

Dictatorship of the proletariat

VI Lenin, *State and Revolution*, New York: International Publishers 1983

John Ehrenberg, *The Dictatorship of the Proletariat*, New York: Routledge 1992

L Socialism & Nationalism

Class & nation

Eric J Hobsbawm, *Nations and Nationalism since 1780*, Cambridge: Cambridge University Press

The Discussion on National Self-determination Summed Up, (pamphlet,1916)

VS Shevstov, *National Sovereignty and the Soviet Union*, 1974

Engels, *The Condition of the Working Class in England*. Blackwell. Oxford. 1958

Nation & state

Nicos Poulantzas, *State, Power, Socialism*, London: Verso 1978

Martin Carnoy, *The State & Political Theory*, Princeton NJ: Princeton University Press 1984

Proletarian Internationalism

Marcel Liebman, *Leninism under Lenin*, London: Merlin Press 1975

John Riddell, (ed. — documentary history), *Lenin's Struggle for a Revolutionary International*, New York: Monad Press 1986

Peter N Carroll, *The Odyssey of the Abraham Lincoln Brigade*, Stanford: Stanford University Press 1994

Working class & black struggles in the USA

Mike Davis, *Prisoners of the American Dream*, London: Verso 1986

Howard Zinn, *A People's History of the United States*, New York: Harper Perennial 1995

Manning Marable, *How Capitalism Underdeveloped Black America*, Boston: South End Press 1983

Mark Naison, *Communists in Harlem During the Depression*, New, York: Grove Press 1985

WEB DuBois, *The Souls of Black Folks*

George Jackson, *Soul on Ice* and *Prison Letters* (Penguin)

M World Socialism
General
Lenin, *Collected Works*, volume 18. 1913
Lenin, *State and Revolution*. 1916
J Stalin, *Problems of Leninism*
Agdas Burganov, *Perestroika and the Concept of Socialism*,
Moscow: Novosti Press 1990
Self-determination
John Riddell, (ed. — documentary history), *Lenin's Struggle for a Revolutionary International*, New York: Monad Press 1986
Civil war & armed intervention
William Minter, Apartheid's Contras, London: Zed Books 1994
William I Robinson & Kent Norsworthy, *David and Goliath: Washington's War against Nicaragua*, London: Zed Books 1987
Collapse of the Soviet Union
Joe Slovo, *Is Socialism Dead?*, (SACP)
Robin Blackburn (ed) *After The Fall* London Verso 1991
Simon Clarke, Peter Fairbrother, Michael Burawoy & Pavel Krotov, *What About the Workers?* London: Verso 1993

N Imperialism & Colonialism
Imperialist state; crisis of capitalism
VI Lenin, *Imperialism: The Highest Stage of Capitalism*
Bill Warren, *Imperialism: Pioneer of Capitalism*, London: Verso 1980
JA Hobson, *Imperialism*, 1938
Neocolonialism
Colin Leys, *Underdevelopment in Kenya*, Berkeley: University of California Press 1975
Franz Fanon *Black Skins, White Masks*
Globalisation/Multinational companies
Saskia Sassen, *Globalisation and its discontents New York*, New Press 1999
Harry Shutt, *The Trouble With Capitalism*, London: Zed Books 1998
Samir Amin, *Capitalism in the Age of Globalisation*, New York: St Martin's Press 1996

O Post-modernism
David Harvey, *The Condition of Post-modernity*, Oxford: Blackwell 1990
Frederic Jameson Postmodernism, *The Cultural Logic of Late Capitalism*, Durham NC Duke University Press 1992

P Gender
Engels, Origins of the Family, *Private Property and the State*
Simone de Beauvoir, *The Second Sex,* New York: Bantam 1968
Sheila Rowbotham, *Woman's Consciousness, Man's World* New York: Penguin 1973

Carol Pateman, *The Disorder of Women,* Cambridge: Polity Press 1989

Q Environment
Robert Garner, *Environmental Politics,* London: Prentice Hall 1996
Andre Gorz, *Ecology as Politics* Boston: South End Press 1980

R South and southern Africa
Carter M Gwendolen, Ed. *Southern Africa in Crisis,* Indiana University Press, 1977
Eric Mtshali, *Trade Unions, the Party and the struggle for liberation,* (SACP)
Mzala, *Armed Struggle in South Africa*
Simons Jack and Ray, *Class and Colour in South Africa* 1850-1950 IDAF 1983 (*This has an extensive historical bibliography of its own*)
Joe Slovo, *No Middle Road,* (SACP)
Currie and Carter (Eds), *From Protest to Challenge,* (*collected documents*) Indiana University Press
NR Mandela, *No Easy Walk to Freedom*
Hilda Bernstein, Steve Biko *1978 and 1987,* International Defence and Aid Fund for Southern Africa
Biko Steve, *I Write What I Like,* Heinemann African Writers Series 1978
Jean Branford, Allan Brooks and Jeremy Brickhill (eds), *Whirlwind before the Storm, The Origins and Development of The Uprising in Soweto and the Rest of South Africa,* June–December 1976. London. International Defence and Aid fund for Southern Africa.
Jacklyn Cock, *Women in the Struggle for Peace,* Harare April. 1989
Baruch Hirson, *Year of Fire, Year of Ash, The Soweto Revolt: Roots of Revolution?,* London: ZED Press 1979
T Karis and JM Custer (ed), *From Protest to Challenge.* A documentary history of African Politics in South Africa 1882—1964 Stanford University. Hoover Institute Press 1977.
ZK Matthews *Freedom for my People Cape Town.* David Philip, 1983
Francis Meli, *A History of the ANC: South Africa Belongs to Us,* Harare, Zimbabwe Publishing House. 1988
N Barney Pityana, et al. (ed) *Bounds of Possibility, The Legacy of Steve Biko and Black Consciousness.* Cape Town: David Philip, 1991
NoSizwe, *One Azania, One Nation, The National Question in South Africa.* London: ZED Press 1979
John Pampallis, *Foundations of the New South Africa.* London: ZED Books 1991
JB Peires *The House of Phalo, A history of the Xhosa People in the days of their Independence.* Johannesburg: Ravan Press 1981
HJ Simons, *African women: their legal status in South Africa.* London: Christopher Hurst and Co 1968
B Bozzoli, ed. *Class, Community and Conflict.* Johannesburg: Ravan, 1987
B Bunting, *Moses Kotane.* London: Inkululeko Publications 1975

RH Davies, *Capital, State and White Labour in South Africa*, 1900-1960
Brighton: Havester 1979.
D O'Meara, *Volkskapitalisme: Class, Capital and Ideology in the Development of Afrikaner Nationalism*, 1934-1948. Johannesburg: Ravan 1983
E Roux, *Time Longer Than Rope*, Madison: University of Wisconson 1964
E Webster, ed. *Essays on Southern African Labour History*. Johannesburg: Ravan 1978

ANC Publications
A Short History of the ANC
The ANC Speaks
Violent and Revolutionary seizure of Power April 1986
Tasks of the Coloured People in the National Democratic Revolution 1983
Forward to Freedom
The Road to South African Freedom
The Sun Will Rise
The Struggle is My Life

Glossary

ANC — African National Congress

SACP — South African Communist Party

MK — Umkhonto weSizwe; set up in 1961 to conduct the armed struggle in South Africa by the liberation movement; MK became the armed wing of the ANC at a later stage.

SACTU — South African Trade Union Congress

Red Army Day — February 23; Anniversary of the Soviet Army; it is the celebration of the Red Army success in stopping the advance of German troops against Petrograd in 1918.

Benguela/B — name of camp used by June 16 Detachment prior to moving to Novo Catengue.

Benguela residence — ANC house in Benguela, used for comrades in transit.

Dar/Dar es Salaam — capital of Tanzania.

Novo/Novo Catengue/NC/Novo Katanga — camp used for training of June 16 Detachment in Southern Angola, which was bombed by SA Airforce and evacuated in April 1979.

Luanda — capital of Angola.

Luanda residence — ANC house in Luanda used for comrades in transit.

Young Pioneers — youth brigade of Angolan MPLA.

NEC/National Executive Committee — ANC highest body

RC/Revolutionary Council — ANC structure set up after Morogoro Conference to pursue the policy laid down by ANC Morogoro Conference to integrate external and internal political and military work.

Oath taking ceremony — ceremony through which MK members and ANC members committed themselves to loyalty to ANC and MK.

GDR — German Democratic Republic, Eastern Germany.

USSR/SU/Soviet Union — Union of Soviet Socialist Republics.

Commander — the first in command of any military structure, whose task is to see to the military orders of the structure.

Commissar — the second in command of military structure, with political function.

Chief of Staff — third in command in military structure, with responsibilities for deployment of military personnel.

Chief logistics officer — person responsible in military structure for seeing to provision of all necessary equipment and requirements.

HQ/Headquarters — based in Lusaka while the ANC and MK were in exile.

HO/Head Office — based in Lusaka while the ANC was in exile.

Director — Head of Cuban delegation in Novo Catengue.

SWAPO — South West African People's Organisation.

FAPLA — Angolan army.

MPLA — Popular Movement for Liberation of Angola.

NLF — Vietnamese Liberation movement.

PAC — Pan African Congress.

ZAPU — Zimbabwe African People's Union.

ZANU — Zimbabwe African National Union.

Patriotic Front — front of ZAPU and ZANU formed in Zimbabwean struggle.

SASO — South African Students Organisation.

SASM — South African Students Movement.

BPC — Black Peoples Convention.

LP — Labour Party.

UNIP — United National Independence Party; Zambian ruling party.

CUB — Cuban.

Makiwane Group — a group of eight tribalists expelled from the ANC in 1978/9 for contradicting ANC policy on non-racialism.

Maluti/Ulundi — names for a future South Africa that came up in a debate around whether the liberation movement should rename the country in a symbolic way to represent the future it would build.

Protocol — a term used to refer to the department concerned with security of ANC leadership.

Kwanzo — Zambian or Angolan currency

Departments in Novo Catengue — Editorial; Printing; Women's Section; Art; Library; Ordnance; Records and Administration Secretariat.

MG — Monthly Guardian.

FC/Freedom Charter — Charter of People's Rights adopted at Kliptown, June 26 1955.

COP/Congress of the People — the congress which adopted the Freedom Charter attended by over 2 000 delegates from all over South Africa.

VOW/Voice of the Women — publication of the ANC Women's Section.

Workers' Voice — SACTU publication.

Personnel Leader — Head of Personnel Department of MK.

MDC — Manpower Development Commission of ANC.

General Economic Commission — Commission in ANC set up to consider economic policy.

PCT — President's Training College, Kabwe, Zambia.

ZDN — Zambian Daily News.

Social Review — Cape Town political education magazine.

Luso — Place raided by Ian Smith's security forces.

WHO — World Health Organisation.

OMA/Organzaçao da Muhler Angolan — Angolan Women's Organisation.

UNTA — National Trade Unions of Angola.

Aeroflot — Soviet Airline.

Strala — Heat-seeking missiles.

Ack-ack — anti-aircraft guns.

Salt II Agreement — agreement between superpowers to limit arms race.

Sunday T of Z — Sunday Times of Zambia.

Morogoro/ANC School/Mazimbu — ANC School started in 1979 in Morogoro, Tanzania.

AC/African Communist — journal of the South African Communist Party.

OAU — Organisation of African Unity.

MSS — manuscript.

SAFRI states — an acronym for Southern African Frontline Revolutionary Independent States, like Mozambique, Angola, Ethiopia and Sekou Toure's Guinea.

Military Instruction Subjects — Tactics; Engineering; Logistics; Artillery; Infantry.